PACIFIC NATIONAL EXHIBITION

100 Years of Fun

PACIFIC NATIONAL EXHIBITION

100 Years of Fun

by BEVERLY CRAMP

with a foreword by
MICHAEL BUBLÉ

WRITTEN, DESIGNED AND PRODUCED BY:

Echo Memoirs Ltd.
70 East 2nd Avenue – Suite 302
Vancouver, BC V5T 1B1
CANADA

Visit our website at: www.echomemoirs.com
Writing, designing and producing distinctive company history and personal biography books since 1999.

First edition: August 2010
Printed and bound in China.

Library and Archives Canada Cataloguing in Publication Information

Cramp, Beverly, 1959–
The PNE: 100 Years of Fun / Beverly Cramp.

Includes index.
ISBN 978-0-9781811-4-7

1. PNE—History 2. Fairs—North America—History. 3. Title.

HD9999.B454K53 2010 338.7'66714097
C2010-904183-9

CREATIVE DIRECTOR John Wellwood
WRITER Beverly Cramp
DESIGNER Lindsay Simmonds
PHOTO RESEARCHERS Lindsay Simmonds, Kate Moore, Heather McLean
PRODUCTION COORDINATOR Kate Moore
COPYEDITOR Renate Preuss
PROOFREADERS Marial Shea, Lesley Cameron

With special thanks to the committed staff
over the past 100 years who have helped the PNE evolve
into the strong and vibrant organization it is today.

CONTENTS

Playland in full swing during the Fair, 2005.

F O R E W O R D

British Columbia is my heart and my home. I was born and raised in Burnaby; it helped shape my experiences and my dreams. There are so many fantastic things about this province: from the mountains and coastline, to the people and the iconic places that bring those people together. One of those icons is the PNE.

It's one of the few places where generations of people share common memories. No matter who you talk to, they have a memory of the PNE. Whether it's of a first job or first Fair ride, a concert or a hockey game ... PNE memories are part of the fabric of Vancouver and B.C.

My favourite memory of the PNE is singing my heart out at the 1995 PNE talent contest. Cheered on by my family in the crowd, I sang an old Italian song that my grandfather loved. I won the competition that summer and went on to win the National Youth Talent Competition later that fall. Since those early days my career has taken me all over the world, but I'll always remember my roots and being on stage at the PNE. In an interesting twist, I'm still involved with the PNE today — as a hockey lover. I'm part owner of the Vancouver Giants hockey team, whose home is the Pacific Coliseum.

The history of the PNE touches all of us British Columbians, and this book is filled with its memories. I'm sure you'll find a photo, a story or an event in these pages that will bring a smile to your face. I hope you enjoy the journey this book takes you on, as we celebrate 100 years of fun at the PNE.

Michael Bublé

PARADES!

FLOATS, BANDS, MAJORETTES AND CLOWNS. OPENING DAY OF THE FAIR ALWAYS DREW BIG CROWDS.

A member of the Gizeh Shrine Circus Band gets primed for the 1953 parade.

A 1949 BC Electric Kettle float celebrates living electrically.

Gymnasts in 1949 put on a show promoting recreation and fitness.

Vernon Girls Trumpet Band, 1965

"LENDING WINGS TO YOUR WORDS"

In 1949 the BC Telephone float promised to "lend wings to your words."

BSA Supplies "Hippo Oil" float, 1947

And clowns, there have to be clowns, 1953.

11 DAYS OF Fun AT THE FAIR

PACIFIC NATIONAL EXHIBI

For kids, the magic of a PNE parade was irresistible, 1949.

Hastings Street is packed for the 1953 parade.

VANCOUVER
LOTS
SALE
HORNE
ESTATE

No parade is complete without baton-twirling majorettes, 1949.

Eaton's 1949 PNE Parade float emblazoned with "Hi-ho come to the Fair."

INTRODUCTION

1900–1909

GETTING UNDERWAY

'00–'09

After the great fire of 1886, real estate offices flourished in unlikely places.

A BRASH YOUNG METROPOLIS

At the end of the 19th century, Vancouver was an exuberant place. Everything about the city was getting bigger, fast. The small, rough-hewn mill town that had burned to the ground in 1886 was transformed in the next two decades into a budding metropolis. Downtown boasted modern highrise office buildings and apartment blocks that gave way to stately homes in the city's West End.

MOTORCARS AND ELECTRIC streetcars proliferated on city streets. The waterfront bristled with new docks and rail yards that moved the British Empire's London-bound Royal Mail from sleek Empress steamships onto waiting Canadian Pacific trains. Vancouver was the final, vital link that completed Britain's worldwide imperial network.

Between 1901 and 1911, explosive growth swelled the population from 26,133 to 100,401. Land prices ballooned (at times they were the highest in North America) and Vancouver swarmed with real estate agents, from fewer than 50 at the beginning of the century to 650 in 1910.

Boosterism reigned. Newspaper headlines bragged about Vancouver's skyscrapers, industry that was the most innovative and lifestyles the most progressive. The Hudson's Bay Company opened a four-storey emporium at the corner of Granville and Georgia in 1893, and Charles Woodward launched his famous department store venture in 1902. The striking 13-storey Dominion Trust Building at Hastings and Cambie streets, built in 1909, was touted as the tallest building in the British Empire.

Lumber and fish fuelled the early boom. The Fraser River fishery attained global status as B.C. canned salmon showed up on store shelves around the world. On Burrard Inlet, Benjamin T. Rogers established a sprawling sugar refinery in 1890 — the first major industry in the city not connected to forestry or fishing. Mining companies became big employers. Coal was the number one mineral — fuelling manufacturing plants and heating homes — followed closely by copper and gold. In the hinterland, immigration and the demand for fresh local fruit transformed the Okanagan Valley, driving up the price of land from $1 an acre to $1,000 between 1900 and 1910.

The rest of the world took note. Famous performers put the brash young city on their itineraries. Sarah Bernhardt graced a Vancouver stage in 1891. Caruso sang for fans. And in 1910, celebrated ballerina Anna Pavlova danced for an adoring audience.

FROM TOP: View of downtown from the old Hotel Vancouver, 1908. Granville and Georgia streets around 1900. A map of early Vancouver, ca. 1898.

Times were good. The future looked bright and people were optimistic. Civic leaders wanted to celebrate their new-found success and power. Talk soon started about creating a showcase for the city and its larger-than-life accomplishments. And at the beginning of the 20th century there was one sure-fire way to bring the world to your doorstep — stage a grand exhibition.

Since medieval times, towns that held big fairs or markets prospered. The monthly or annual events offered agricultural produce, prize livestock, food, textiles and exotic imported goods. There were usually religious or secular celebrations, and lots of entertainment. Market centres became intersections of commerce and their citizens prospered.

As Britain launched the Industrial Revolution in the early 19th century, these quaint local fairs were being replaced by more spectacular exhibitions that trumpeted the nation's achievements. Citizens flocked to see displays of their country's industrial and commercial might, its pre-eminence in scientific innovation and the latest advances in social well-being. During the Great Exhibition of 1851, nearly a quarter of everyone living in Great Britain made their way to London. They viewed 13,000–15,000 exhibits and were proud to know they were part of the Empire's rise.

The concept caught on. For the rest of the century, countries and cities vied with each other to produce increasingly impressive displays of national wealth and power. Exhibitions became magnets, drawing a wide cross-section of visitors from across Europe. Special trains were even commissioned to haul tourists to the fairs. The *Exposition Universelle* of 1889 in Paris, which featured the Eiffel Tower, even had its own three-kilometre railway to shuttle visitors around the sprawling site. In 1893, Chicago upped the ante with an even larger exposition that promised to secure the city's position as a leader in America.

On a more modest level, the local country fairs continued to prosper and took root in North America with new colonists. They offered samplings of more modest rural enjoyments that harkened back to simpler times in Europe. Farmers displayed their prize-winning produce and livestock, experts explained the latest advances in agricultural science and techniques, local businesses flaunted their wares and proud wives and daughters put forth their finest domestic crafts.

By 1900, Vancouver's leading citizens were convinced that their town, too, needed something that offered a bit of both — some elements of the time-honoured country fair and some of the dazzle of a great exhibition. There was bounty in the province's newly cleared land that called for attention. There was growing industrial power that fuelled breakneck growth. There was unheard-of prosperity. And there was pride about being a vital part of Britain's globe-spanning enterprise. Word had to get out.

FROM TOP: Sons of the British Empire float on Hastings Street, 1900. Taking it in at the Nelson Fair, ca. 1900. Automobile fanciers at Armstrong's Fair, 1908.

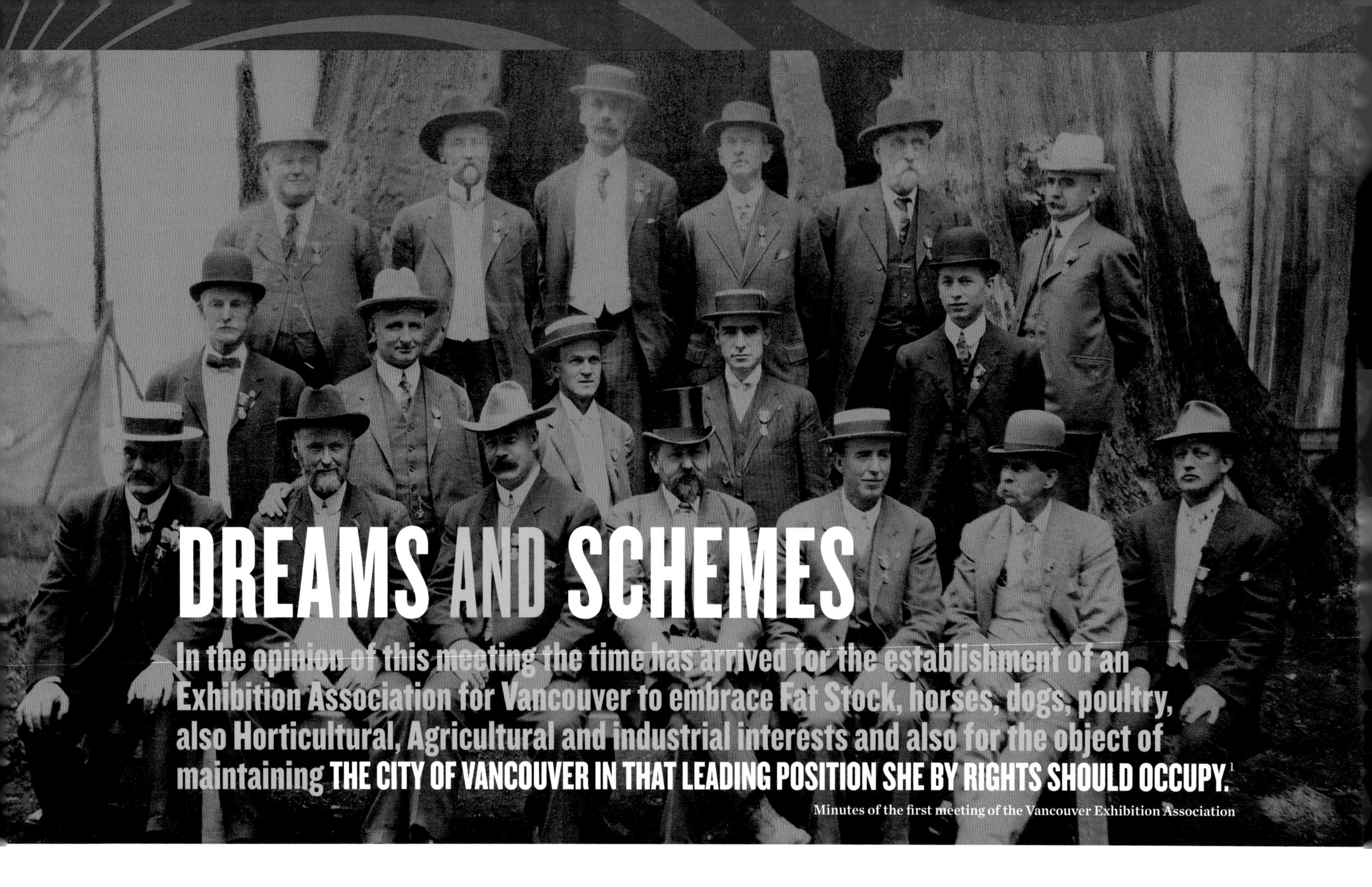

DREAMS AND SCHEMES

In the opinion of this meeting the time has arrived for the establishment of an Exhibition Association for Vancouver to embrace Fat Stock, horses, dogs, poultry, also Horticultural, Agricultural and industrial interests and also for the object of maintaining **THE CITY OF VANCOUVER IN THAT LEADING POSITION SHE BY RIGHTS SHOULD OCCUPY.**[1]

Minutes of the first meeting of the Vancouver Exhibition Association

IN THE MIDST of Vancouver's boom-fuelled optimism in the early 1900s, two major groups began to lobby for the city to have its own fair and exhibition to celebrate its accomplishments: real estate agents and land developers who saw the Fair as a promotional vehicle, and small livestock and pet associations who wanted a local fair that catered to their needs. Together, they founded the Vancouver Exhibition Association (V.E.A.).

Vancouver might have opened a fair earlier than 1910 if it hadn't been for the Royal Agricultural Show in New Westminster, a city that had earlier been more prominent than Vancouver. Once the V.E.A. got started though, they planned a grand exhibition that would go beyond being an agricultural fair: they wanted to focus on industry as well. From the start, they had big ambitions.

FROM TOP: The V.E.A. had some interesting places to hold meetings — this one was in the Hollow Tree in Stanley Park, 1909. Crowds at that rival up the river, the New Westminster Fair, 1904.

THE V.E.A.'S FIRST constitution shows the broad aims of the group. They embraced industrial exhibitions, science, innovations, the arts and business.

THE OBJECTS OF THE ASSOCIATION ARE FOR THE GOOD OF OUR COUNTRY AND OUR PEOPLE TO ORGANIZE AND CONDUCT EXHIBITIONS FOR:[2]

- The promotion of practical and scientific husbandry in all its branches.
- The improvement of the breed of horses, cattle, sheep, pigs, dogs, poultry, and other barn and domestic animals.
- The development of the industrial resources of the country.
- The dissemination of mechanical and scientific knowledge.
- The encouragement of the cultivation of the beautiful in nature and art.
- The stimulation of healthy rivalry for supremacy and excellence in the minds of the rising generation.
- The promotion of trade and commerce.
- The development of the rich mineral, fishing and lumbering resources of the country.

IF THE MEN constituting the first board of the Vancouver Exhibition had anything in common, it was the attachment of their financial interests to the growth and prosperity of Vancouver. The larger businessmen ... were involved in urban-based activities which depended for their development on the expansion of the city ... Mayor Alexander Bethune and three aldermen held similar attachments to the urban centre and undoubtedly saw the V.E.A. as a means of increasing the importance of Vancouver ... boosterism was at least as important to the early association as was the development of agriculture.[3]

Vancouver's Fair

THE EVOLUTION OF Vancouver's exhibition can be seen as an attempt to reconcile the disparate aims and ambitions of its founders, to select the appropriate level of integration between agriculture and industry, booster and country fair, local development and regional expansion.[4]

Vancouver's Fair

AS THE FAIR drew nearer to its inaugural date, both the City of Vancouver and the V.E.A. began to publicize the event to draw people from near and far. They got a boost from glowing editorials in the local newspapers.

There must be a determined effort on the part of all and sundry to make this initiation of new enterprise AN OVERWHELMING SUCCESS.[5]

The *Vancouver Daily Province*

ABOVE: Livestock show at Hastings Park in the 1890s.

THE RIVAL UP THE RIVER

Vancouverites supported the development for a major exhibition on the site, AND AS THE DATE OF THE FIRST EXHIBITION APPROACHED THAT SUPPORT INTENSIFIED.

HAVING A HEAD START on Vancouver, New Westminster's Royal Agricultural Fair (which started in 1869) received the lion's share of funding from the provincial and dominion governments. It offered the biggest prize money for contests and attracted agricultural exhibitors not only from B.C. but from the Pacific Northwest and the prairies. Most local agricultural and pet societies were committed to working with it. Further, the needs of Vancouver groups were often thwarted by New Westminster's fair directors.

HENRY ROLSTON [president of the Vancouver Poultry Association] ... claimed that he decided to join the Vancouver fair organization when the New Westminster Exhibition refused to meet the demands of the Vancouver Poultry and Pet Stock Association, the Vancouver Kennel Club, and several other similar groups. The dissatisfaction of these people with the treatment they received ... seems to have provided the spark required to launch an organizational drive to form an exhibition association in Vancouver ... It was the amalgamation of the city boosters and those who wanted to show small animals and pets which led to the formation of the V.E.A.[6]

Vancouver's Fair

IT WASN'T JUST agricultural groups that were becoming dissatisfied with the New Westminster fair. So too were fair goers from Vancouver. Alderman J.J. Miller, first president of the V.E.A., noted the great hardship people encountered getting to New Westminster.

THE B.C. ELECTRIC RAILWAY had but a single track connecting the two cities with a very limited number of interurban cars. The Canadian Pacific Railway on Exhibition days ran a special train made up of all kinds of rolling stock, passenger and freight, via Westminster Junction [now Port Coquitlam]. There was no highway, no automobiles, no buses.

With all the available means of transportation, not one half of the population could be handled ... The cost to a family was excessive. The idea of an Exhibition located within the reach of a five-cent car fare to the population of the big City of Vancouver gained ground, and in 1908 definite steps were taken ...[7]

Early History of the Vancouver Exhibition Association

ABOVE: New Westminster-bound streetcar, 1908.
NEXT PAGE: Horse racing at Hastings Park, 1905.

CHOOSING A SITE, SETTING A DATE

THE V.E.A. SETTLED on Hastings Park as the best location for Vancouver's new fair. Land near the park was virtually undeveloped, with only a few homes in the forest. The majority of the East End taxpayers wanted the fair because it would bring much-needed public utilities. Eventually the roads, public trolley lines and other civic services that were provided to serve the exhibition gave the area those amenities.

The ambitious vision of the first fair reflected the V.E.A.'s plans to be more than an agricultural fair and to include elements found only in larger world fairs — industrial displays and lifestyle exhibitions.

... THIS MEETING IS of the opinion that the time has arrived when public opinion should be awakened to the interests they possess in that splendid property — the Hastings Park — which for twenty years has been totally neglected and abandoned by the Park Authorities and has been monopolized by and for racing purposes — that a public meeting should be held in the near future to lay all the facts before people in order that their rights may be asserted and that the progress of the city may not be arrested.[8]

Minutes of the Executive Council

... STRONG SUPPORT WAS given for an exhibition by the Ratepayer's Central Executive and the East End Ratepayer's Association, both of whom criticized council not for leasing the land to the V.E.A., but for not doing so quickly enough ...
For the most part, Vancouverites supported the development of a major exhibition on the site, and as the date of the first exhibition approached that support intensified.[9]

Vancouver's Fair

IN ALL, THERE were 11 fairs held west of Hope in 1910, the first year of the Vancouver Exhibition, although most were only one or two days long. Vancouver and New Westminster held the biggest events.

Purely agricultural shows were logically held in late summer and early autumn, when produce was available for display. Vancouver chose to have its fair in the middle of August. Such a date was also more likely to have good weather. A list of fairs held in the Lower Mainland in 1910 clearly shows that Vancouver had set itself apart.

1910 FAIR CIRCUIT[10]

VANCOUVER	AUGUST 15–20
NORTH VANCOUVER	SEPTEMBER 9–10
CENTRAL PARK	SEPTEMBER 21–22
DELTA (LADNER)	SEPTEMBER 23–24
SURREY	SEPTEMBER 27
LANGLEY	SEPTEMBER 28
NEW WESTMINSTER	OCTOBER 4–8
RICHMOND (EBURNE)	OCTOBER 11–12

OUTSIZED VISION

THE V.E.A. HAD a difficult time getting the money to fuel its dreams. Early fundraising began in 1908, generating support from enthusiastic Vancouver taxpayers and individuals.

Much work needed to be done to get the Fair underway. In addition to building exhibition halls, grandstands, stables, animal pens and other structures, major costs were incurred just to clear the site. Attempts to have a fair in 1909 were frustrated by a lack of funding, but work got underway at the Hastings Park site.

One of the first actions of the V.E.A. executive was to approach City Council to ask for permission to submit a by-law to the ratepayers, initially asking for $50,000 to INITIATE THE DEVELOPMENT OF EXHIBITION FACILITIES.[11]

Vancouver's Fair

PERHAPS SWAYED BY newspaper editorials, the ratepayers turned down the request.

THREE-FIFTHS OF THE total vote was required for a money by-law to pass. Much to the dismay of the V.E.A., the association lost by a mere 43 votes ... support for the by-law was strongest in the wards closest to the proposed Hastings Park exhibition.[12] *Vancouver's Fair*

When the Vancouver Exhibition opened in 1910, the site was rough and ready. Only a few permanent buildings were in place.

In October of 1909, the V.E.A. asked council for $125,000 for the CONSTRUCTION OF A GRANDSTAND WITH EXHIBITION HALLS underneath, clearing of land, fencing, drainage and sewage and sundry other developments ... they did allow a by-law request for $85,000.[13] *Vancouver's Fair*

THE ASSOCIATION'S LUCK with the provincial government was not much better. Knowing that Victoria was accustomed to providing financial support for British Columbia fairs and exhibitions, the V.E.A. set out to ask for an initial grant of $25,000, a request later raised to $50,000. The directors were ... more than a little perturbed when the provincial government turned down their request, arguing that the Lower Mainland was being well served by the New Westminster exhibition.[14]

Vancouver's Fair

FINALLY ENOUGH WORK was done on the site for a 1910 fair. The early founders understood clearly that the Exhibition grounds and buildings would be useful for more than a late summer fair.

THE PARK WILL not be merely an exhibition grounds but will be open to the use and enjoyment of the people for the entire year. The gates will be ever open and it will be kept as a beautiful park, such as will be greatly appreciated by the people, particularly those in the Eastern side of the city. These already visit it in great numbers. The Industrial Hall will be used for conventions, exhibitions of different kinds, such as poultry, dog or flower shows. Also for balls and parties and big gatherings and meetings.

Besides the value which the association and the exhibition will be from a commercial standpoint as an advertising medium of the resources of British Columbia to the whole world and its value as a means of encouraging individual enterprises, it will be an excellent avenue for the desires of the people for recreation, pleasure and social intercourse. It will also be a means for the interchange of ideas upon all kinds of subjects and will serve as a great public school in which all may derive some education in the advancement of the world in industrial, commercial, agricultural and scientific matters.[15] Speech by V.E.A. president J.J. Miller

FROM TOP: Hastings Park race track, ca. 1905. By 1908, the Interurban had reached Hastings Park. The V.E.A.'s logo.

MABEL
10

CHAPTER 1

1910–1919

STARTING A TRADITION

'10–'19

A busy day at the Midway, 1914.

UPS, DOWNS AND THE GREAT WAR

From 1910 to 1912, the wave of confidence spreading throughout Vancouver found a ready outlet at the new Vancouver Exhibition. The city's dreams for Hastings Park were expansive. New buildings went up and displays of the latest innovations in science, industry and agriculture proliferated.

POPULAR CULTURE IN the first years of the 20th century had seized the public imagination, and everyone was keen to peer into the future. A day at the Fair promised a dazzling taste of the latest in moving pictures, electric appliances, fashion, design, music and dance. Dance crazes and the "shocking" new music sweeping the city could be found at Hastings Park. Ragtime mingled with the more staid martial airs of regimental bands, and then there was jazz.

For those with an eye to the well-being of future generations, the Exhibition founded the hugely popular Better Baby Contest in 1913. Parents flocked to the Fair with infants and toddlers, keen to have the latest advice on health care, nutrition and child-rearing. More mature diversions in the Industrial Building offered the best of modern science and manufacturing.

Car culture exploded in Vancouver during the decade. A forward-looking auto show, started in 1911 and later housed in the purpose-built Transportation Building, quickly became the jewel of the Exhibition. New-fangled models sported exotic brand names like Dodge, Chalmers and Hudson. In 1912, the first car to cross the country arrived in Vancouver. Not long after, the term, jitney, entered the city's lexicon. These privately owned automobiles darted boldly in and out of traffic, scooping up passengers waiting for streetcars. By 1916, nearly 200 of them crowded city streets.

The public was fired up about airplanes, too, after the Wright brothers' celebrated flight in 1903. Proving that the city was no slouch when it came to technology, a Vancouver-built airplane took to the air in 1911. And on May 24, 1912, a crowd at Hastings Park witnessed Canada's first parachute drop from a plane. A local newspaper reported:

TOP: Harry Hooper waits for customers in his jitney on Hastings Street, 1910.

"Several thousand people watched 'Professor' Charles Saunders rise to about 1,000 feet in a biplane piloted by Phil O. Parmalee. Without harness, success required that Saunders grasp the guy strings and hold on. He landed safely on the mudflats at Second Narrows."

In 1913, the economic boom went bust. Construction ground to a halt, real estate values plummeted and soup kitchens for the unemployed seemed to spring up overnight. But people continued to flock to the Exhibition. Attendance hit 92,000 that year. For most citizens times were tough, but the 50-cent cost of a ticket (25 cents for children) was one of the best deals in town. Besides, what better way to rally flagging spirits than spending a day at the Fair?

It took the outbreak of World War I to seriously dampen fair attendance, which dropped to 46,000 in 1914. But the Exhibition played a big role in the city's and province's war efforts: it was a major recruiting centre and training ground for enlisted soldiers, and the scene of big rallies to boost citizen morale. By the end of the war in 1918, fair numbers were back to normal. And in 1919, attendance hit 121,000.

FROM TOP: The Vancouver Exhibition, 1914. Drivers Signal Corps at YMCA Building, Hastings Park, 1919.

MAYHEM ON THE FIRST DAY

A BURST OF BUILDING ACTIVITY took place four months before the Vancouver Fair was ready for its opening on August 15, 1910. The most imposing structure, the Industrial Building, with towers and verandas, had been completed that year. Hammers and saws were still heard at another Exhibition building, the Machinery Hall, late into the night of August 14. Vancouver newspapers hyped the attractions and fun to be found.

VANCOUVER'S
FIRST
EXHIBITION
HASTINGS PARK
AUGUST 15, 16, 17,
18, 19 and 20

FREE VAUDEVILLE
in front of the grandstand
Three big bands every afternoon and evening – the Vancouver City Band, Vancouver Pipers' Band, and Clan MacLean Band

– THE HEROS FAMILY –
unequalled European acrobats

Frank & True Rice, and other comedy acts

HORSE RACING WITH BIG PURSES

A man diving 75 feet into a tank of flames
Industrial and agricultural exhibits, horse competitions and a session of the United Farmers of Alberta

And of course CARNIVAL RIDES AND FOOD.

AT 12 O'CLOCK noon today the gates of the first annual Vancouver Exhibition swung open to admit the public. A large crowd had already gathered for the occasion and when ticket windows opened, there was a rush for change as aside from the season tickets, all admittances are paid in cash.[1]

Vancouver Daily World

AN ESTIMATED 4,000 people crowded to the Fair on the first day. The organizers hadn't been expecting anything like that number. Admission was 50 cents. A founding director and later manager of the Exhibition, Henry Rolston, recalled what that opening day was like.

THE ARRANGEMENTS FOR the first fair were very inadequate, particularly the handling of the crowds. Many of the directors tried to handle the crowds at the gates. The fence was knocked down; we collected cash and let the people in, put the cash in our pockets and emptied our pockets at the office. Everything was in turmoil ...[2]

Early History of the Vancouver Exhibition Association

THE HIGHLIGHT OF the first day of the Exhibition was a visit to the Fair site by Sir Robert Baden-Powell, founder of the Scout Movement and one of the most famous men in the Empire. Vancouver newspapers gave considerable coverage to this distinguished gentleman. While at the Fair he had a chance to inspect some of Scouting's finest who were mustered there for the occasion.

ORGANIZER OF BOY SCOUTS IN CITY

THE MAN WHO has done, and is perhaps doing more today, for the youth of England and Canada in training them to lead lives of morality, build themselves up mentally, attaining confidence in themselves and removing for all time the snobbery that has so long been a prominent feature of the younger manhood to both the amusement and disgust of those with whom they came in contact, is in Vancouver today in the person of Lieutenant-General Baden-Powell.[3]

Vancouver Daily World

DAILY PROGRAM AT THE FAIR[4]

– MONDAY AUGUST 15 –

OPENING DAY

REVIEW *of* BOY SCOUTS
BY SIR BADEN-POWELL

– TUESDAY AUGUST 16 –

CANADA DAY
FORMAL OPENING *by*
SIR WILFRID LAURIER

– WEDNESDAY AUGUST 17 –

SCHOOL CHILDREN *and* LADIES DAY
UNITED FARMERS'
of ALBERTA MEETING
SONS *of* SCOTLAND MEET
PIPERS BAND IN ATTENDANCE
CHILDREN UNDER 12
ADMITTED FREE

– THURSDAY AUGUST 18 –

MERCHANT'S DAY.
MEETING *of* B.C. POULTRY MEN
RETAIL B.C. GROCERS' CONVENTION
OPENING *of* DOG SHOW.

– FRIDAY AUGUST 19 –

AMERICAN DAY

– SATURDAY AUGUST 20 –

LABOR DAY
ATHLETIC SPORTS
CLOSE *of* EXHIBITION

PREVIOUS PAGE, FROM TOP: Crowds strain to see the PM on opening day, 1910. The Industrial Building was later renamed the Womens Building, 1918.
LEFT: Sir Baden-Powell inspects a troupe of Boy Scouts at Hastings Park, 1910.

A ROUGH GEM

SOME HAILED THE Vancouver Exhibition's Industrial Building as one of the most beautiful in the city. Many other structures put up for the opening were temporary. There had been little time to properly landscape the site and the grounds had large expanses of dirt littered with tree stumps. Boardwalks connected some areas but dust and mud were to be part of the first fair. Still, people turned out in droves.

YESTERDAY WAS PREPARATION day and opening day combined at the exhibition. All the exhibitors were hurrying on the finishing touches in anticipation of the crowd which arrived shortly after 12 o'clock. The rain of Saturday night and Sunday morning was just sufficient to settle the dust properly though in some places it was a trifle muddy, but this soon became firm during the afternoon when the sun got a strong play on it, and by the end of the day the ground was as good as could be desired.[5]

Vancouver Daily World

ONE EXHIBIT HAS a very attractive four-room scene portrayed. It shows the most up-to-date arrangement of a kitchen, living room, library and bedroom. The kitchen is neat and clean, the living room furnished in rosewood throughout, the library in oak and the bedroom is papered in the most appropriate style.[6]

Vancouver Daily World

THE FIRST MAIN entrance was at Powell Street ... We therefore constructed a three-plank sidewalk from Hastings down the west side of Renfrew Street as far as the entrance at Miller Drive. It was up hill and down dale, owing to the logs and timber on the ground; sometimes the plank walk was as much as eight feet above the earth beneath, so that we had to put a rail down one side of the three planks. The next year the City Council graded the street, and put in a broad plank walk.[7]

V.E.A. Manager-Secretary Henry Rolston

IN THE MACHINERY hall, firms exhibited gasoline and electric motors, the most improved farming machinery, marine engines, gas plants, and horse vehicles of every description.[8]

Vancouver Daily World

ABOVE: Fairgoers jammed the Powell Street trams on opening day.
NEXT PAGE: A mounted contingent adds some pomp to the opening day parade, on Granville Street, 1910.

THIS FAIR EXCEEDED the wildest expectations of the promoters, and gave them renewed vigor, hope, and encouragement. If this can be done in a crude way, amongst the forest trees and knee-deep in dust and loose earth, what can be done on a properly completed exhibition ground?[9]

Early History of the Vancouver Exhibition Association

WHEN ALL THE BUILDINGS are erected and the grounds complete, which will be in about three years, we estimate that the people will possess a public asset in the value of upwards of one million dollars and such as we will all feel proud of.[10]

J.J. Miller, addressing a Fair crowd

THE AMUSEMENT AND food area was called the "Skid Road" — probably because it had been staked out on the dirt ground with an avenue made from logs (this kind of construction used in the forest industry was nicknamed a skid road) along with boardwalks. The *Vancouver Daily News-Advertiser* described its special attractions:

To do the Skid Road properly would take at least half a day. To witness each show, see all the dancing attractions, ride the merry-go-rounds, eat a sandwich, drink lemonade, and smoke cigars would require more than $5 …

Starting at the south end of the Road, the first concessionary is a rotund gentleman, who proclaims in stentorian tones the fact that he has in his show a petrified woman. Proceeding north, the 'educated horse' is the next show. The promoters promise a number of things from this animal, calling him Independence, the horse with the human brain. Passing several cigar and concessionary stands the visitor comes to the Spanish theatre, a place where Oriental dances, a burlesque show and singing and dancing performances are given. On the east side of the Road, one can find a knife rack, the Egyptian queen, a palmist and candy booths galore …[11]

WELCOMING MR. LAURIER

ON AUGUST 16, 1910, after days spent travelling from Ottawa on a Canadian Pacific train tour of the west, Sir Wilfrid Laurier, the prime minister of Canada, was greeted in Vancouver by a mob of well-wishers. He was there to officially open the city's new Exhibition, which he did on the second day of the Fair.

IT WAS ALL hail to the chief when Sir Wilfrid Laurier arrived in Vancouver yesterday morning. He was greeted by both the old and the new. While he was being driven around in automobiles an Indian street parade was given in his honour, the chiefs and their followers from across the Inlet turning out in the panoply of state. Bear skin caps, feathers, blankets and rainbow colours in their attire imparted a picturesqueness to be seen nowhere but in the west, while the skirl of the piper's band recalled the wild and war-like spirit that swept over the highlands in the days of Rob Roy.[12]

Vancouver Daily News-Advertiser

MAYOR LOUIS TAYLOR welcomed Sir Wilfrid Laurier, who famously predicted that the 20th century belonged to Canada. Mayor Taylor made it clear that Vancouver was part of that vision.

YOU HAVE DOUBTLESS witnessed many evidences of growth and development, and been enabled to form a lively conception of western aims and western needs. Our city reflects more fully perhaps than any other centre of population in British Columbia the results of the period of expansion and development ... it must be the cause of legitimate pride to one whose endeavour has been towards making Canada a great nation within the great British Empire.[13]

Vancouver Daily News-Advertiser

I wish you success in your efforts and assure that I think you have a place which THE PEOPLE MAY WELL BE PROUD OF.

Sir Wilfrid Laurier

THEN IT WAS off to the Exhibition ...

THE PARTY ARRIVED at the Exposition grounds promptly at 2:30 p.m. in the afternoon, in the large B.C. Electric Company's observation car. The car was well decorated with bunting and flags, making a pretty sight as it rounded the curve leading to the grounds. Outside the large gate was gathered part of the Exhibition reception committees, with their wives, while just inside the fence the Sixth Regiment band and the rest of the committee were gathered ... As the party proceeded to the stand, the crowd ahead and behind the prime minister and his party grew deeper every foot, and the members of the party who brought up the rear of the delegation walked in a dense cloud of dust.[14] *Vancouver Daily News-Advertiser*

ABOVE: PM Laurier, in the bowler hat, behind the driver, gets the red carpet treatment at the CPR station, 1910.

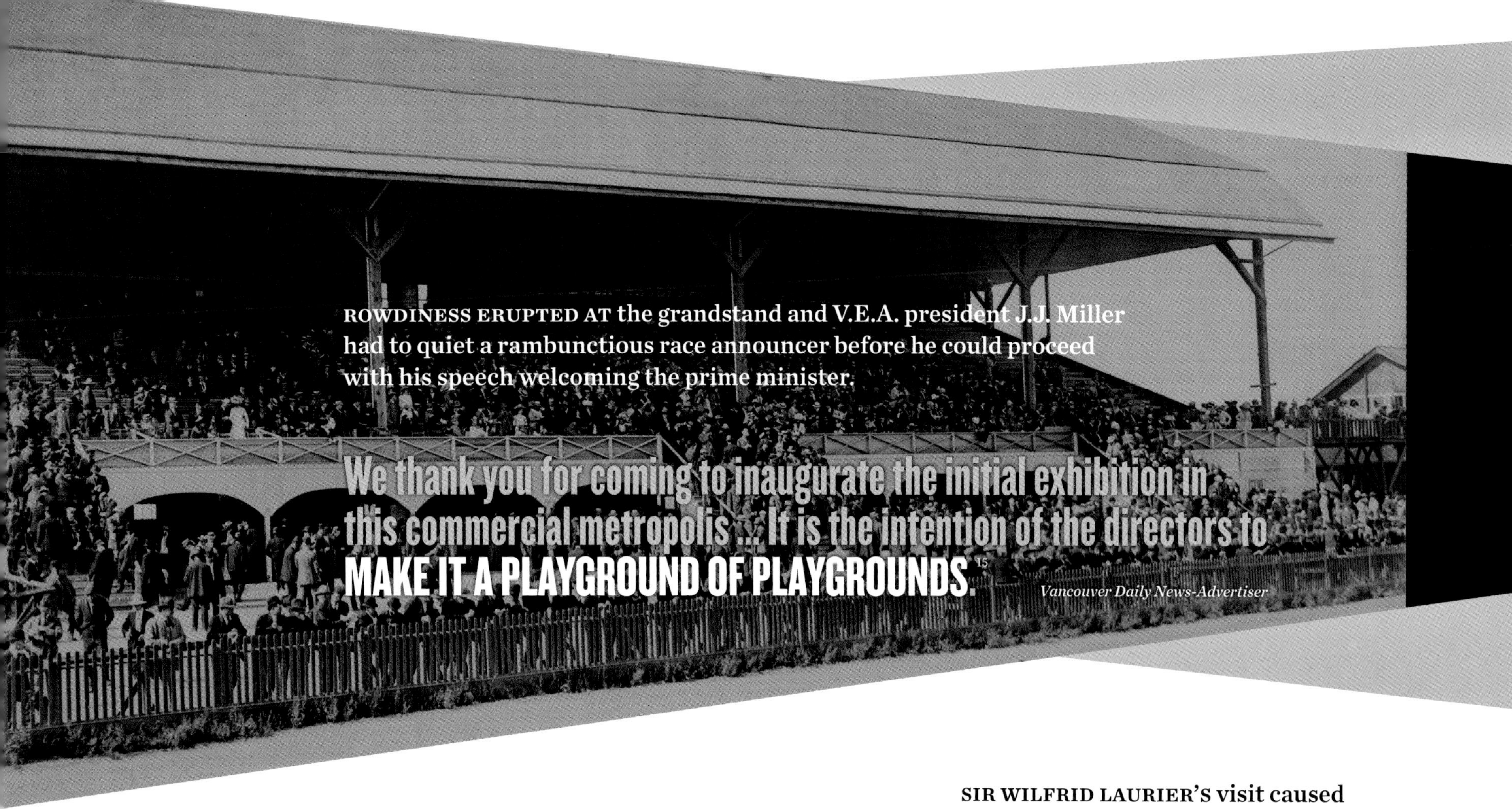

ROWDINESS ERUPTED AT the grandstand and V.E.A. president J.J. Miller had to quiet a rambunctious race announcer before he could proceed with his speech welcoming the prime minister.

We thank you for coming to inaugurate the initial exhibition in this commercial metropolis ... It is the intention of the directors to **MAKE IT A PLAYGROUND OF PLAYGROUNDS.**[15]

Vancouver Daily News-Advertiser

SIR WILFRID DID not disappoint, offering in his speech high praise of what he saw before him.

I CAN APPRECIATE the immense value which this exhibition association will be to British Columbia, and I will say further, to the whole of Canada ... I appreciate very highly the honor which you have done me in asking me to open this splendid exhibition today for I appreciate anything that contributes to making this country greater and more prosperous ... I understand that you intend to make this beautiful park the meeting place of the people. I wish you every success in your efforts and assure that I think you have a place which the people may well be proud of.[16]

Sir Wilfrid Laurier

THE PREMIER, AFTER a few minutes rest, was taken from the stand by Mrs. Miller and escorted to the Church of England tea tent, where refreshments were served him by the ladies in charge ... Just before the luncheon, an incident, portraying the great character of the man, took place. Little six-year-old Estelle Buttrum, daughter of Rev. Mr. Buttrum, pastor of St. Saviour's church, had expressed a desire to her father for some time past to see the prime minister, and when he was led into the tent, the father taking the child by his hand, led her up to the table at which the party was sitting. The father presented the little girl to the prime minister, and Sir Wilfrid, taking the child in his arms, kissed her. It is safe to say that no happier little girl could be found on the exhibition grounds yesterday.[17]

Vancouver Daily News-Advertiser

SIR WILFRID LAURIER'S visit caused such acclaim for Vancouver's new Exhibition that the leader of the provincial government, Premier McBride, hastily reversed his original decision not to provide the V.E.A. with financial support.

LAURIER'S SUPPORTERS AND admirers joined in the welcome to their chief and leader, and the whole public were awake to the great import of the occasion. At this point the Government of British Columbia began to view the movement in a different light for on the morning of the opening day, Mr. McBride sent a letter to the President, regretting his inability to be present at the opening, tendering the Association his best wishes for the success of the Exhibition, and enclosing his Government's cheque for $10,000.[18]

Early History of the Vancouver Exhibition Association

ABOVE: The grandstand at Hastings Park was a favourite weekend destination for horse-racing fans and those seeking the thrill of a modest bet, 1911.

TEN THE DAILY NEWS-ADVERTISER, VANCOUVER, BRITISH COLUMBIA, WEDNESDAY, AUGUST 17, 1910

ON THE NORTH AISLE

IN THE

MAIN EXPOSITION BUILDING

YOU WILL FIND A BOOTH THAT CONTAINS MANY ITEMS OF INTEREST

MARRIOTT & FELLOWS

REAL ESTATE AND

FINANCIAL BROKERS

Get a Copy of "IN THE SHADE OF THE OLD APPLE TREE."

Evans & Hastings

PRINTERS TO THE FINE TRADE

Ask the Attendant to Show You Samples of the Strikingly Different Work Done by this Firm

MERRITT & WORSNOP

Specialists in Port Mann Properties

Five-Acre Tracts, Immediately Adjoining the Townsite of Port Mann at the Right Price and Terms

"Ads" Ltd., *Advertising Managers and Publicity Agents*

Exclusive British Columbia Representatives of the... PACIFIC MONTHLY *Circulation 120,000*

Ask for a Copy of "WINNING THE PUBLIC" by "Ads" Ltd. *City Address 1210 Dominion Trust Building*

ABOVE: Realtors, financial experts and manufacturers saw the first Exhibition as a prime place to do a bit of business.

A BIT OF BUSINESS ...

THE FIRST FAIR provided opportunities aplenty for commercially minded people to advance their ventures. It was also a place of fun for everyone, especially children.

TODAY IS MERCHANTS' DAY out at the fair, and it is estimated that there are at least 17,000 business men and women present.[19]

Vancouver Daily World

THE PROMINENT EVENT of the day, however, is the meeting of the poultry men of the province, who are here for the purpose of forming a provincial association. The object of the association is to enable all who breed poultry to get together annually and discuss the best means of helping the expansion and improvement of the industry in the province.[20]

Vancouver Daily World

... A BIT OF PLEASURE

A MAJOR ATTRACTION for Vancouverites was the daily entertainment staged on the grounds. Bands were a particularly popular feature, with the V.E.A. bringing in a series of groups to play for the assembled crowds. Indian bands from Sechelt and Squamish, the Kilties Band, and a Regimental Band were among the acts providing free shows throughout the park. A series of vaudeville presentations, including a gymnastic troupe ... also drew spectators ... These various entertainments, bands, and acts proved to be extremely popular and were responsible for attracting many people to the exhibition.[21]

Vancouver's Fair

YESTERDAY, FOR THE whole day, there were well over 5,000 children and 12,000 adults ... The children and their mothers and fathers presented a pretty sight. All the young ones appeared to be enjoying themselves to the utmost. In this respect the venders of toy balloons reaped a harvest.[22]

Vancouver Daily World

LADIES' & CHILDREN'S DAY

Children Under the Age of 12 Years Will Be Admitted

FREE – FREE – FREE

BIG FEATURE TODAY

Sensational Dive of 75 feet into Tank of Flames

THE HAYRICK RUBES

You owe yourself a laugh and FRANK and TRUE RICE will hand you one hurricane of hilarity and breezy nonsense

RAVE REVIEWS

> **More and more this great annual fair of British Columbia's is going to serve as a medium for the bringing together of the east and west of this wide Dominion. WE NEED TO BE MORE ACQUAINTED WITH EACH OTHER, and this is one of the best means for accomplishing that end.**[25]
>
> Rev. G. F. Dawson of Chatham, New Brunswick

AT THE END OF THE FAIR the public was hooked on the idea of a Vancouver-based fair. The V.E.A. had proved it could attract large crowds, run a profitable event and provide invaluable promotion for the city.

VANCOUVER'S FIRST EXHIBITION, which came to a close last night, was in almost every way a marked success. With an attendance roughly estimated at 75,000 for the week, the treasurer hopes to show a balance of $12,000 on the right side of the sheet.

Today the stables will be empty, the poultry pens and dog kennels silent, the Industrial hall dismantled and the denizens of the joyous 'Skid Road' will have folded their tents like the Arabs and silently stolen away; but while the first exhibition will have passed into history, its effect will remain in the incentive it will give to reach out for bigger things in the years to come.[23]

Vancouver Daily News-Advertiser

THE SHOW FROM every point of view was an unqualified success; being far in excess of our most sanguine expectations ... From our past experience and conversation with exhibitors, both in and out of town, we have no hesitation in saying that with proper facilities ... your show will in a couple of years be the banner show on the Coast, and in five years, will excel even the Canadian National Exhibition.[24]

Letter to the V.E.A. from the Vancouver Kennel Club

CRITICISM OF THE first Fair was muted by the resounding commendations and the V.E.A. chose to make light of the disapprovals.

Even church people had CROWDED THE GRANDSTAND TO SEE THE HORSE RACES, while some were overheard talking about buying horses.[26]

ABOVE: By 1917, the dust had settled and the fairgrounds had a more established feel.

BETTER BABIES

FOR A FIFTY-CENT registration fee, a mother could bring her family to the exhibition grounds, have the children examined by a team of physicians and nurses, have them rated according to a standardized scoring system, and depending upon the health of the baby either receive medical advice and treatment or win prizes and recognition ... The show was consistently successful, attracting 600 entrants in 1914, a high of 1,100 two years later and 800 in 1918. It was credited with many achievements in the amelioration of child health problems, including improving maternal awareness of medical problems, selecting sick or diseased children and directing them to a hospital, and even creating such a demand for better medical facilities for children that 20 beds for youths were added to the Vancouver General Hospital.[27]

Vancouver's Fair

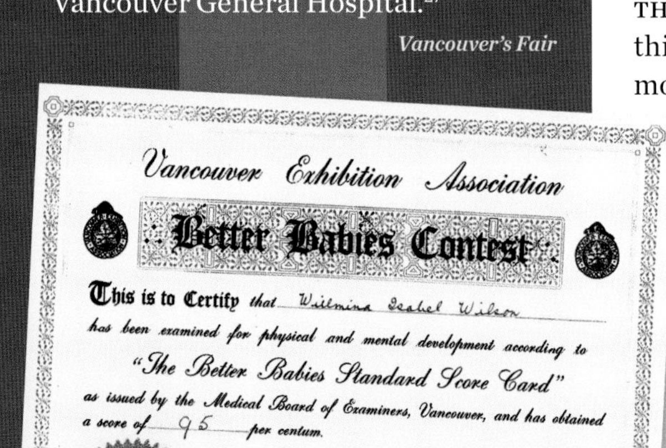

Vancouver Exhibition Association

Better Babies Contest

This is to Certify that Willmina Isabel Wilson has been examined for physical and mental development according to "The Better Babies Standard Score Card" as issued by the Medical Board of Examiners, Vancouver, and has obtained a score of 95 per centum.

In testimony whereof the following signatures have been affixed:

Emma W. Scott, Convenor of Contest

Margaret P. Hogg, Managing Director of Contest

John J. Banfield, Director of Vancouver Exhibition Association

W. J. MacEachern, M.D., Consulting Director of Contest

Dated at Vancouver, B.C. Aug. 24 1918

FROM SUCCESS TO SUCCESS

FIRED UP BY the success of the first exhibition, the V.E.A. forged ahead in the next four years with improvements to the Hastings Park site and new programming. They laid the foundation for what the exhibition was to be in the future — one of the biggest fairs in North America.

THE PHYSICAL DEVELOPMENT of the Hastings Park grounds, hampered somewhat by the ever-present funding difficulties, continued apace. A Stock Judging Pavilion was erected in time for the 1911 exhibition, although other buildings planned for that year were deferred owing to lack of funds. 1913 saw a flurry of construction activity as a 300-foot long Transportation Building, slated to serve as an exhibition hall for machinery and automobiles, was completed and work commenced on a major Forestry Building, to be constructed entirely from local timber and to serve as a showcase for that important industry ... 1911–1914 saw a marked change in the exhibition programme, with ever-increasing importance being placed on agricultural contests and the province's natural resources. A mineral exhibit was added in 1911, as was an international egg-laying contest. Further developments included a small forestry display, a Fisheries Building designed to house an aquarium and an exhibit of the ocean resources of British Columbia, and the beginnings of a small zoological collection.[28]

Vancouver's Fair

Through the Exhibition, Vancouver has been advertised not only throughout the Dominion, but in many of the states to the south, and the VANCOUVER EXHIBITION IS A HOUSEHOLD WORD.[29] J.J. Miller

THE V.E.A., STILL referring to horse racing as its 'Speed Department', attempted to cloak this major attraction under its agricultural programme, but it was obviously serving more as entertainment than as a display of horse breeding or training expertise. An important addition to the amusement package after 1910 was the incorporation of sports, both amateur and professional, into the schedule. Lacrosse matches, athletic meets, and motorcycle races, among others served as popular attractions.[30]

Vancouver's Fair

ATTRACTIONS SUCH AS the Wild West Shows, the North-West Mounted Police, and Olympic games have been introduced to the public here on the grounds, and recreation and sport have been fostered and encouraged ... every man, woman and child in the community can find some individual interest, no matter whether it be agricultural, industrial, commercial, educational, inventive or sublime.[31] J.J. Miller

FROM TOP: Bigger, better and musical too — at the Better Babies Contest, 1920. The wee winners always received a certificate, 1918.

> **Then let the people realize that Hastings Park at their doorstep is slowly but steadily being accomplished and developed, a people's gigantic public school and playground** WORTHY OF A PROGRESSIVE PEOPLE, A PROGRESSIVE PROVINCE AND A PROGRESSIVE COUNTRY.[32]
>
> J.J. Miller

CLOCKWISE FROM TOP LEFT: There was lots to see at the Fair — a fleet of electric trucks (1913); livestock on parade (1919); proud displays of heifers; cars galore; our Mounties on parade; a satisfied group of Jersey breeders (1921); and the live action of lacrosse.

CLOCKWISE FROM TOP: In the first decade of the Fair, Vancouver Police went man-to-man in tug-of-wars, donkeys raced at the track, and the Vancouver General Hospital Tent tended to the bruised and broken.

The Directors wore the colours. THE LADIES WORE THE COLOURS. The stores downtown, for weeks before the Exhibition, wore the colours. It was good advertising, and prompted people to take pride in their Exhibition and wear the colours.[33]

FLY YOUR COLOURS

THE NEW EXHIBITION'S colours were green and gold. Attaching colours to associations or organizations, such as military regiments, racing horses, schools, clans and whole nations, helped to galvanize the public. To keep the momentum going, a local newspaperman named Felix Penne composed a poem celebrating the Exhibition's colours.

Hurrah for the Green and Gold then.
In our Exhibition Week
You can find no colours fairer
no matter where you seek,
Than the green of ocean wavelets —
the green of forest tree,
And the gold that gilds the cloudlets
when the sun sinks down at sea

For one week in burning August,
let no fair one here be seen
Without a pretty favor of
Vancouver's Gold and Green,
Yes, one and all, the short and tall,
the timid and the bold,
And kiddies, too, of every hue,
must sport the Green and Gold.[34]

Excerpt from "The Green and Gold,"
Early History of the Vancouver Exhibition Association

FROM TOP: At Hastings Park, you might catch some circus elephants or head for the roller coaster.

WHEN BRITAIN DECLARED war on August 4, 1914, Canadians were automatically drawn into the conflict. Most exhibitions across the country announced that they would postpone their activities, some holding the view that during wartime it was inappropriate to engage in the frivolous and amusing activities of a fair. The V.E.A. had other ideas.

ALTHOUGH WARLIKE TALK fills the air, it is not intended that this will interfere in any way with the Vancouver exhibition, which is to be held September 3 to 12 ...[35]

The Vancouver Sun

PARTS OF THE Exhibition grounds were given over to a military training facility and the Fair did its part in raising the morale of the citizens.

IT WAS FOUND that Hastings Park with the numerous Exhibition buildings was the only logical place for assembling and training of troops, and for four years, the exhibition grounds did its share in defense of the Empire ... Here on the grounds families said "Good-bye" to their men, thousands of whom never returned. Here men received their first lessons in warfare and were sent overseas, efficient and well-equipped soldiers. And during those four years of warfare, the Exhibition never closed its doors. The Exhibition opened, year in and year out, to encourage the people to carry on, produce more and better ... It was a good thing for the Allies that there was such a splendid depot for the reception and training of soldiers.[36]

Early History of the Vancouver Exhibition Association

FIVE TIMES SINCE the outbreak of war we have carried out an exhibition. A false idea at one time took possession of many minds that exhibitions should be closed during war time. This view was not taken by the Imperial and Dominion governments, who saw in them an influential means of educating and inspiring the people to devote their best energies to greater and better production, besides being an important factor in maintaining the commercial and social equilibrium of communities in times of danger and unrest.[37]

V.E.A. Bulletin

ABOVE: Canada's fighting men take a break from the regimental grind, at Hastings Park, 1917.

CLOCKWISE FROM TOP LEFT: Women in the military, assembled here at the race track, added to Canada's war effort, 1915. A 1914 poster rouses patriotic fairgoers. The 231st Battalion Pipe Band on the steps of the Womens Building, 1916. Some soldiers trotted to war in style, 1918.

WELCOME
CANADIAN WOOD PIPE
& TANKS LTD.

C H A P T E R 2

1920–1929

THE BEST IN THE WEST

Entrance to the Fair, on Renfrew, 1927.

AN EYE ON THE FUTURE

In the 1920s, the Vancouver Exhibition vaulted to the top spot among provincial and Western Canadian fairs. This was achieved while Vancouver's economy stagnated after the end of World War I in 1918. Unemployment shot to 22 percent and it wasn't until 1924 that the city regained some of its earlier swagger.

EXHIBITION ORGANIZERS WERE undaunted by this slow start to the decade; they had their eye on the future. From their vantage point, things were looking good. While the economy languished, Fair attendance dipped a bit for two years but rebounded by 1921. For people on a tight budget, a day at the Fair was still unbeatable entertainment value.

Construction of a modern Dance Pavilion (completed in 1920), an auto court and golf course meant jobs for more than 2,000 returning war veterans. Later in the decade more buildings went up to house the new Winter Fair, which promised another round of attractions and commercial opportunities at Hastings Park. In 1926, the popular but rough Skid Road was replaced by a bright, boisterous new entertainment facility called Happyland, which was to draw fairgoers for more than 50 years.

Slowely but surely, prosperity made a comeback. Construction boomed downtown and crowds flocked to the Fair to see astonishing new consumer goods.

ABOVE: Spectators take in the game from the comfort of their beloved automobile, 1929.

Sleeker, more affordable “wireless” radios, which could beam entertainment right into Vancouver living rooms, were a hit, along with other new electrical marvels such as toasters, irons and vacuum cleaners.

To the dismay of some, and the joy of many, Vancouver was in the grip of fads — vaudeville, flapper girls, jazz and the Charleston were just a few. Billed as Canada’s largest entertainment venue, the lavish 3,000-seat Orpheum Theatre opened in 1927. And at the Exhibition, big bands started making appearances.

In 1922, Vancouver’s first radio station (CJCE) hit the airwaves, soon joined by more than 100 other stations. Bands performing year round at the Dance Pavilion were broadcast live. Those who couldn’t make it to Hastings Park crowded round their radios, rolled up the carpets and foxtrotted into the night.

Business representatives for the province mounted impressive exhibits in the Manufacturer’s Building, touting the potential of B.C.’s forestry resources to overseas investors. British journalists reported that the utilization of the total annual forest growth in B.C. would bring in at least $150,000,000 — a huge sum for the times.

The Exhibition’s Auto Show attracted ever bigger crowds as Vancouverites took to the roads. City streets were proof that the new car culture was taking hold — numbers shot from 6,500 car owners in 1920 to 36,500 in 1929. To combat the new gridlock, city hall made a decision to install Vancouver’s first traffic light, at Main and Hastings.

At the start of the 1920s, the combined population of Vancouver, Point Grey and South Vancouver was 175,000. The numbers swelled to more than 246,000 in 1931 after the three municipalities amalgamated under one civic government, making Vancouver the third-largest city in Canada.

By the end of the 1920s, the Vancouver Exhibition had a new name — Canada’s Pacific Exhibition. It was B.C.’s premier fair and one of the most significant in Western Canada and the Pacific Northwest. With a growing list of exhibitors eager to show their best, the volume of applications became overwhelming and some had to be turned down. But the renamed fair kept growing; it was where everyone wanted to be.

In 1929, 280,000 visitors graced Vancouver’s fairgrounds — triple the attendance in 1921.

FROM TOP: Dignitaries, bands and cheering fairgoers at the Exhibition’s opening day, 1928. The Orpheum was at the centre of Vancouver’s vaudeville culture — its marquee trumpets the charms of “exotic” dancer, Vanessi, 1929. Long before the official launch of annual parades, the Fair’s opening day offered floats and music, 1925.

BIG PLANS

OPTIMISTIC AND BRIMMING with enthusiasm, Vancouver Exhibition organizers were thinking big. It wasn't easy raising money for their ambitious fairground plans during an economic slump. Many changes came in programming rather than the more expensive new infrastructure. But the V.E.A.'s grand schemes continued apace.

IN THE STEADILY improving international prestige of the fair ... The organization was placing increasing attention on its role as a British Columbian and Western Canadian Association.[1] *Vancouver's Fair*

IMPROVEMENT OF HASTINGS Street and the development of a street-car line along that route made it essential that the association not only erect a new archway facing onto the corner of Hastings and Renfrew, but also that all future development of the grounds be oriented towards Hastings Street.[2] *Vancouver's Fair*

Vancouver is the city above all others in Canada that has the punch, and it is making good ... THE EXHIBITION IS CARRYING ON VALUABLE WORK AND ACCOMPLISHING A GREAT DEAL not only for the agricultural life of the country, but for industries in general.[3]

Hon. S.F. Tolmie, minister of Agriculture (later premier of B.C.)

IT IS CLAIMED by the directors that this year's exhibition will be one of the most representative in every detail that has ever been held in the Pacific Northwest. From the Canadian prairies a whole trainload of exhibits has reached the grounds, and among them are some of the big prize winners of this year's exhibitions east of the Rockies. The prize stock of Alberta's ranches, of the farms of Manitoba, and even the blue ribbon holders from many of the leading fairs of Ontario, are included in today's arrivals at the grounds. In competition with these will be the kings and queens of B.C. dairy and stock farms, practically every well-known breeder of the province having entered in the different sections.[4] *Vancouver Daily World*

Beauties and the beast: Young ladies display the latest in swimsuit fashions atop a bovine contender in the Fair's Agricultural Show, 1927.

SOLE DISTRIBUTORS FOR THE
SUPER
ROYAL
ELECTRIC
B.C.Electric
THE NEW SUPER ROYAL
IS THE BEST CLEANER MADE
We Sell It Exclusively
B.C.Electric
HEDLUND'S
Delicatessen
DISHES
REG. TRADE MARK
"Just heat it
and eat it"
"OUR OWN BRAND" BUTTER
HAND CARVED...
THE LANDING OF
COLUMBUS

I HAVE A very distinct recollection of the time when the exhibition association was started. That it should have attained its present importance is most noteworthy.[5]

W.C. Nichol, lieutenant-governor of B.C

COME — BRING THE family and have the time of your life — inspiring, educating, entertaining — an occasion you'll never forget! Growing year by year with our great province, the Exhibition grows better and better.[6]

Vancouver Exhibition ad in *The Vancouver Sun*

See the 'Show Window' of British Columbia. INTERESTING AND EDUCATING EXHIBITS OF WIDELY VARIED PRODUCTS. Do you know that in this rich province — greater in productive area than the states of Washington, Oregon, and California combined — there are more than 3,566 industries — an increase of 300 per cent in the past seven years?[7]

Vancouver Exhibition ad in *The Vancouver Sun*

AN ALL ROUND increase in the number of exhibits of 28% is reported by Mr. H.S. Rolston, manager, who stated yesterday that every available foot of space had been taken by exhibitors.[8] *The Vancouver Sun*

FROM EVERY PART of the province visitors are already reaching the city for the big Exhibition which opens tomorrow. From places farther afield the same story is being told, and it is expected that many thousands of people will pass through the gates of Hastings Park during the ten days on which the Exhibition holds sway.[9]

The Vancouver Sun

PREVIOUS PAGE, CLOCKWISE FROM TOP LEFT: The Fair was the place to catch a glimpse of B.C.'s wealth and bounty — a grand champ Ayrshire cow, the latest in household gadgets, roosters that strut their stuff, butter carvings of Christopher Columbus arriving in the New World, a prize Shropshire ram and the latest in deli delights. **THIS PAGE, FROM TOP:** A giant ham on the hoof and Dainty Dates.

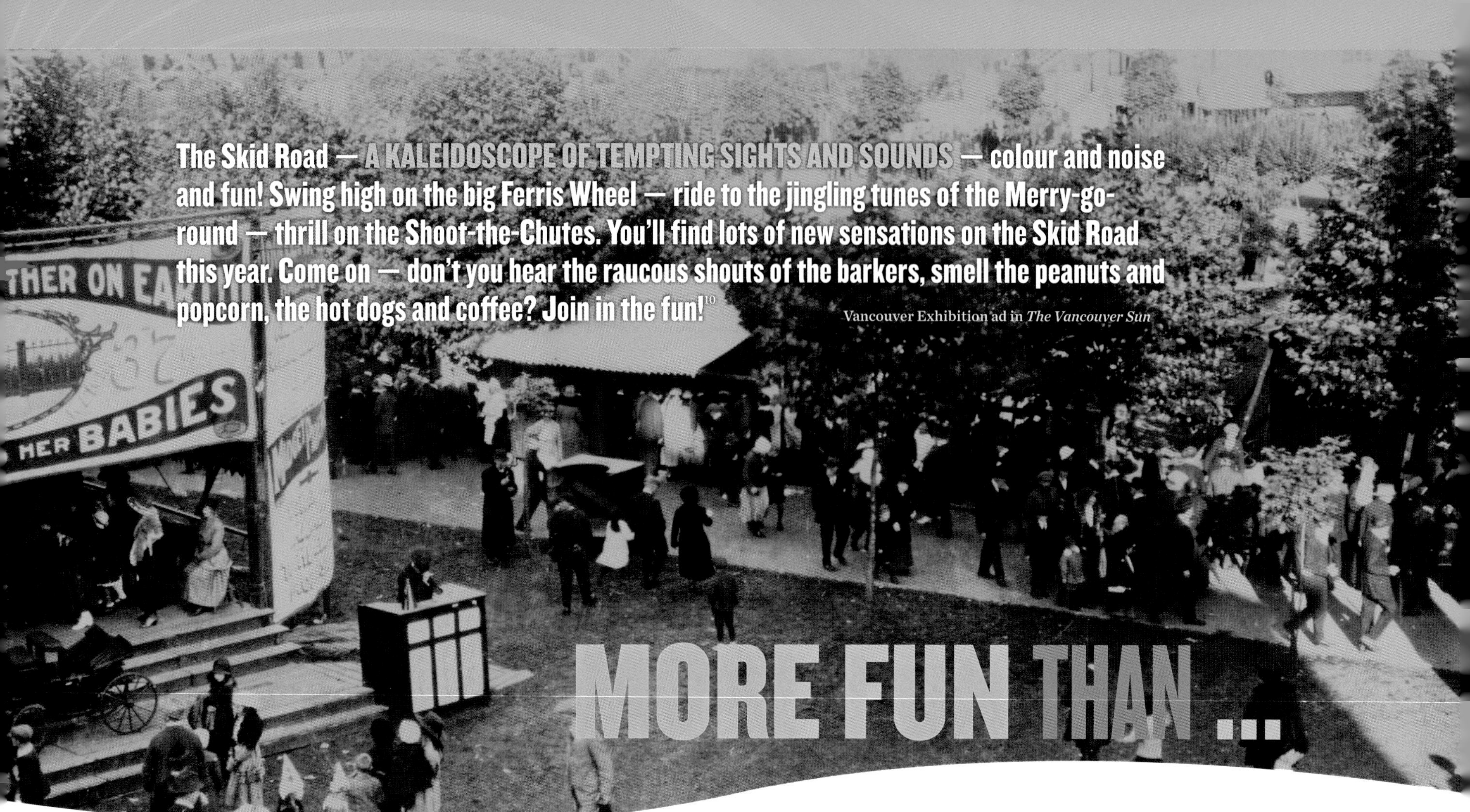

The Skid Road — A KALEIDOSCOPE OF TEMPTING SIGHTS AND SOUNDS — colour and noise and fun! Swing high on the big Ferris Wheel — ride to the jingling tunes of the Merry-go-round — thrill on the Shoot-the-Chutes. You'll find lots of new sensations on the Skid Road this year. Come on — don't you hear the raucous shouts of the barkers, smell the peanuts and popcorn, the hot dogs and coffee? Join in the fun![10]

Vancouver Exhibition ad in *The Vancouver Sun*

MORE FUN THAN ...

AFTER THE GRIM years of the Great War, people craved the lighter side of life. The 1920s were synonymous with innovation and change — in dance, music, amusements for the whole family and popular entertainment on a mass scale. Hemlines shot up, everyone shimmied and inhibitions were dropped. It was all about fun.

WILD WEST RIDING and various other stunts on horseback, in addition to a display by a troop of Royal Canadian Mounted Police, who will give an exhibition of fancy riding, musical rides, will help to make a big grandstand programme full of good things. Dancing in the handsome new ball room, during the afternoon and evening, and the roundabouts, leap-the-dips, and various and ingenious methods of taking a speedy and hair-raising ride will claim many devotees.[11]

The Vancouver Sun

ANOTHER SPLENDID FEATURE will be the band contests and musical competitions in vocal solos and duets. This has gone over in splendid fashion and the directors consider this as important an exhibition development as anything which is being worked.[12]

The Vancouver Sun

Whoop-ee! Let's Go to the
BIG STAMPEDE
Greater Vancouver Exhibition

FROM TOP: By the 1920s the Gayway and Wild West shows drew bigger and bigger crowds.

THE MOST SIGNIFICANT development of the fairgrounds in the 1920s was the addition of a permanent amusement complex ... While several permanent devices, including a 'Scenic Railway', the dancing pavilion, and merry-go-round, were in operation on the grounds, the association still had to contract with a travelling carnival to provide additional rides and games.[13] *Vancouver's Fair*

THE VANCOUVER EXHIBITION ASSOCIATION named its permanent amusement area Happyland. Fairgoers endured long line-ups to enjoy the thrills.

HAPPYLAND OPENED IN 1926. It was built as a means to provide employment to the youth living on the east end of Hastings Park and to help bring more entertainment to a growing rural area. New permanent rides were added. The Giant Dipper replaced Hastings Park's 1915 Coaster, Dip-the-Dips, in 1925. The Dipper was designed by Fred Church who was a coaster designer in southern California. Soon all the other rides filled up the east side of the Exhibition grounds. The Shoot-the-Chutes was said to have been one of the most popular rides which usually consisted of long lines of thrill seekers.

Rollercoastersofthepacificnw.com

ONE OF THE new buildings erected on the fairgrounds was a dance pavilion, a much ballyhooed venue that attracted hundreds of dance fanatics.

PRESIDENT J.J. MILLER and the directors of the Vancouver Exhibition Association were hosts on Friday evening at a very enjoyable dance at Hastings Park, the occasion being the formal opening of the new $12,000 dancing pavilion. The pavilion is located at the northwest entrance to the park and is said to possess one of the finest dancing floors in the city. The building has cloakrooms for both ladies and gentlemen, quarters for preparing and serving lunch and has been designed so that only those taking part in a dance need step on the floor. It will be used as an added attraction during exhibition week.[14] *Vancouver Daily World*

FROM TOP: A day at the Fair in the 1920s was not complete without a ride on the Giant Dipper or Shoot-the-Chutes. Crowds at the Exhibition entrance. The recently opened Dance Pavilion was the place to try out new dance steps.

BIG KIDS, LITTLE KIDS

BY THE '20S, everyone seemed to be exploring their inner child. Fun was big. And the Fair was just the place to find it.

EXHIBITION ORGANIZERS CONTINUED to find new initiatives to entice families, and especially children and mothers with babies.

ONE OF THE departures of this year's exhibition and one that will doubtless be a very welcome one to many, will be the day nursery in the big pavilion, where trained nurses will accept the care of little tots from mothers who are anxious to see the exhibition without being burdened with the care of their children. The nursery has been fitted up with cots, cradles and the other necessary paraphernalia and the interior painted in white with green shades over the windows to soften the light.[15]

Vancouver Daily World

SHRILL AND HAPPY laughter of a veritable tide of children will sweep over Hastings Park at the opening of the fair tomorrow, for the Elks lodge, following an annual custom, are inviting every boy and girl in Vancouver up to 15 years of age to enter the park free of charge as their guests and will play bounteous hosts. It is expected that 40,000 children will respond.[16]

The Vancouver Sun

ANOTHER CALLING

Vancouver's celebrated big-band leader Dal Richards' earliest memory of the PNE goes back to 1925, when he almost found another calling.

"I WAS ABOUT seven years old, walking along the midway with my father. We got separated. I must have looked confused because a barker fronting one of the shows came down off his stage, took my hand and took me onstage with him. 'Put out your hands,' he said. I did, and he pulled out a straitjacket and put it on me. Just about then my father located me and came bounding up the stairs. I wasn't distressed, but my dad certainly was."

One More Time: The Dal Richards Story

In 2009, Dal marked his 70th straight year of playing with his band at the PNE. He has every intention of continuing.

LEFT TO RIGHT: The popular merry-go-round at the Exhibition's amusement park, 1923. Dal Richards performs at the Fair in 2005.

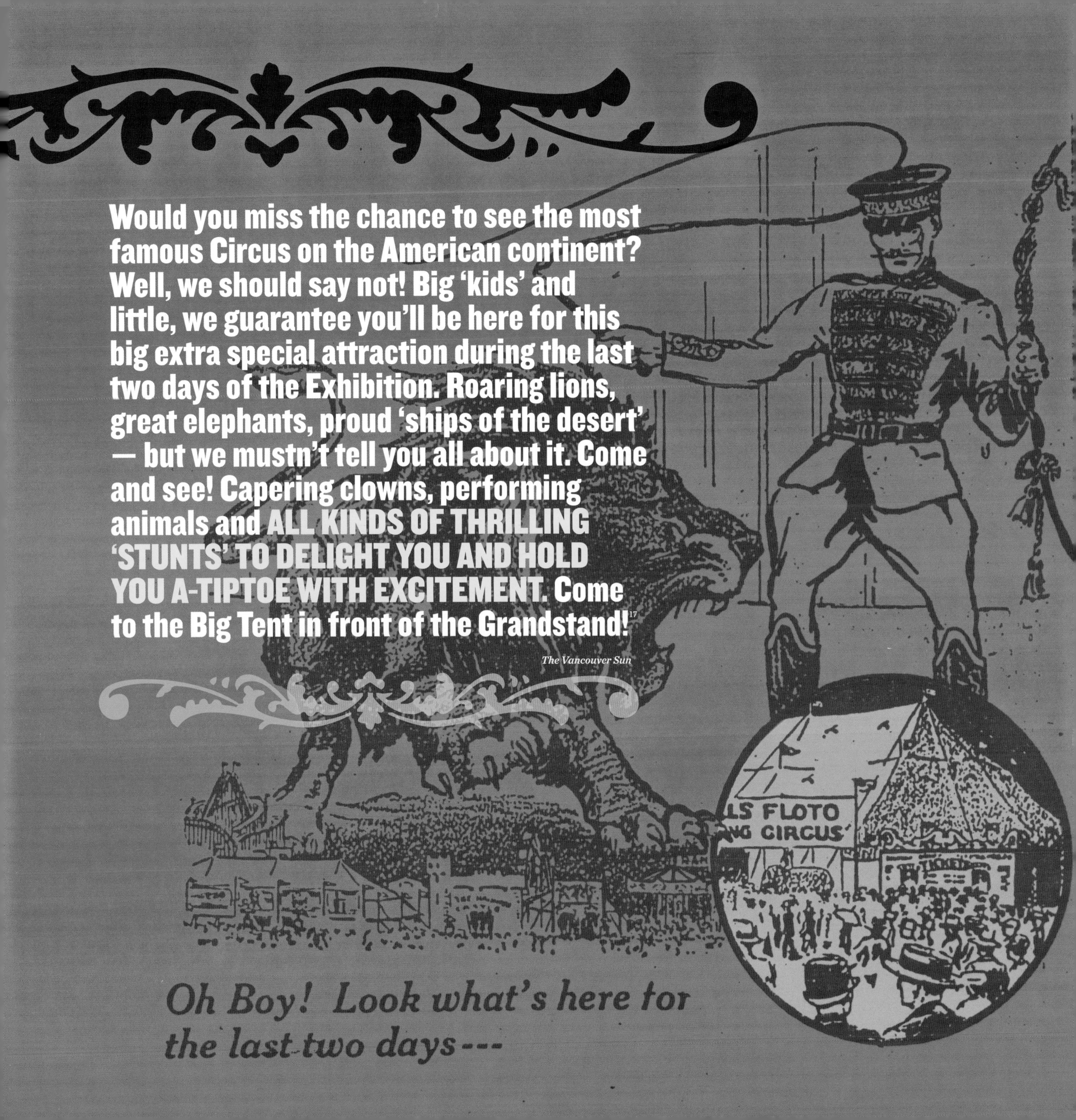

Would you miss the chance to see the most famous Circus on the American continent? Well, we should say not! Big 'kids' and little, we guarantee you'll be here for this big extra special attraction during the last two days of the Exhibition. Roaring lions, great elephants, proud 'ships of the desert' — but we mustn't tell you all about it. Come and see! Capering clowns, performing animals and ALL KINDS OF THRILLING 'STUNTS' TO DELIGHT YOU AND HOLD YOU A-TIPTOE WITH EXCITEMENT. Come to the Big Tent in front of the Grandstand![17]

The Vancouver Sun

A RUSH OF EXHIBITORS

AS THE FAIR grew, so did the ambitions of the exhibitors. The Vancouver Exhibition was the place to showcase the impressive innovations of Canadian business and industry that were flooding the market.

PROBABLY IN NO section of this year's exhibition are the evidence of growth and development so noticeable as in the big building devoted to manufacture. Only three years ago the directors went out into the highways and byways to beg exhibitors to favour the annual gathering with their presence and displays, and even up to two years ago the directors were compelled to purchase displays ... But this year a different story is told. Every foot of space is occupied and weeks before the date set for closing of entries the directors were turning would-be exhibitors away.[18] *Vancouver Daily World*

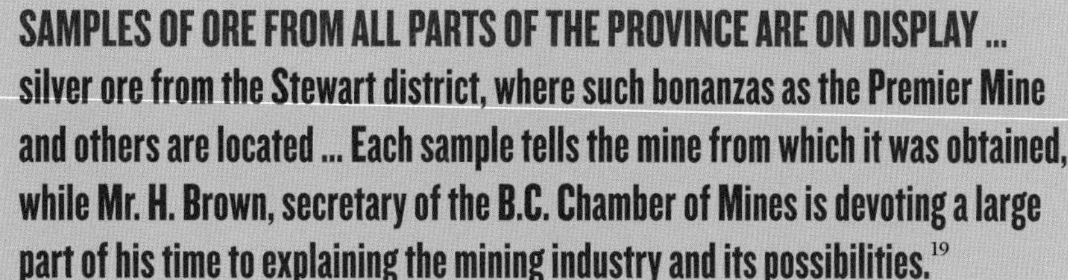

SAMPLES OF ORE FROM ALL PARTS OF THE PROVINCE ARE ON DISPLAY ... silver ore from the Stewart district, where such bonanzas as the Premier Mine and others are located ... Each sample tells the mine from which it was obtained, while Mr. H. Brown, secretary of the B.C. Chamber of Mines is devoting a large part of his time to explaining the mining industry and its possibilities.[19]

Vancouver Daily World

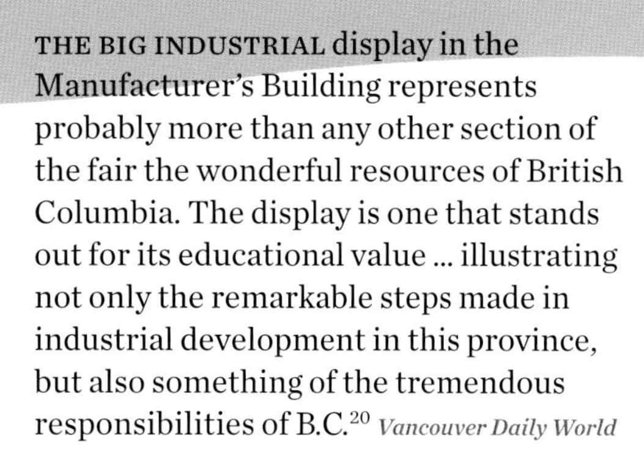

THE BIG INDUSTRIAL display in the Manufacturer's Building represents probably more than any other section of the fair the wonderful resources of British Columbia. The display is one that stands out for its educational value ... illustrating not only the remarkable steps made in industrial development in this province, but also something of the tremendous responsibilities of B.C.[20] *Vancouver Daily World*

THE FIRST POWER lawn mower to be manufactured in Canada has just been completed and is in operation on the lawns of Hastings Park. Yesterday, hundreds watched the machine at work and marveled at its speed and efficiency.[21]

Vancouver Daily World

ONE OF THE happiest exhibits in the Manufacturer's is that of the Graham Hirst Co., sole agents for British Columbia for the handy Corona Typewriter. This is the most compact machine on the market ... The machine can be bought complete with case for $65.[22] *Vancouver Daily World*

WELL TO THE fore at the Exhibition this year is the booth of the Steffens-Colner Studios in the Industrial Building. This enterprising firm has perfected a colouring process which brings out the flesh tints in portraiture to perfection.[23]

Vancouver Daily World

CLOCKWISE FROM TOP LEFT: The Manufacturer's Building was packed with exhibitors, 1920. The Forestry Building drew big crowds, ca. 1925. Former Vancouver mayor, Louis Taylor, posing in front of a mining display, 1926.

CLOCKWISE FROM TOP LEFT: A Seymour Placer Gold Mines display boasted a giant 22K nugget, 1928. Dioramas gave fairgoers a taste of logging operations, 1928. The East Kootenays showcased a mineral bonanza, 1928. Vancouver Typewriter Co. offered sleek new models.

A BOUNTY OF BOUNTY

BRITISH COLUMBIA HAD bounty from the land and the Vancouver Fair became the place to showcase the best its farms had to offer.

VANCOUVER LED THE province in the number of agricultural products last year and this fact should silence those who are pleased to state that Vancouver Fair is a carnival and race meeting only. The fact is that there will be a bigger and better carnival and more and better races and more attractions than ever, but there will also be a bigger and better agricultural fair than has been held in this province.[24]

Vancouver Daily World

THIS YEAR THE exhibit of the P. Burns Company is one of the dominating features ... Exhibits of Shamrock products, placed there by artistic hands, range from the choicest bricks of British Columbia butter to tempting hams and bacon sides, hung high against the cream background of the exhibit. Great tubs of snowy white lard at the corners of the exhibit, the cooked meats on display, the delicatessen products shown there — these combine to intrigue the thousands who pass through the building to hold their attention and impress upon them the wealth and productivity of the soil of B.C.[25]

Vancouver Daily World

FROM TOP: An ad for the 1927 Agricultural Show. Traders with Kerry Cattle, 1920.

LADIES (AND GENTLEMEN), GATHER ROUND

ALONG WITH IMPRESSIVE industrial and agricultural displays, the Fair offered a bonanza of new comforts and gadgets for the home.

LAST, BUT NOT LEAST, IS THE HOME COOKING. Dainties of every description are arranged on a prettily decorated table and look most tempting.[26] *Vancouver Daily World*

THE WOMENS BUILDING, previously called the Industrial Building, brimmed with the latest household goods and techniques for making both amusing and useful articles.

THE MAGNIFICENT DISPLAY of all kinds of needlework is an outstanding feature of the exhibits shown in the Womens Building at the exhibition ... Everything from hand knitting to hand-made lace is on exhibit, and neatly arranged on long tables and in cases. Autumn leaves and evergreens have been used in abundance, draped here and there, around the tables and over cases with striking affect.

A peep at the cushion counter would make even an energetic worker want to test the softness of the cushions. Many other articles on display are worth seeing. Two, in particular, are rather out of the ordinary: one, a fancy dancing costume made of purple and brown satin, with an overdress of paper beads, Chinese coins and other trinkets; the other a dressing gown, made from a paisley shawl, over one hundred years old.[27]

Vancouver Daily World

VISITORS TO THE Vancouver Exhibition are cordially invited to inspect our Pianos, Player Pianos, Phonographs and Radio Receiving Sets, before purchasing elsewhere.[28]

Lewis Piano House Ltd. ad in *The Vancouver Sun*

CLOCKWISE FROM TOP LEFT: In the 1920s, more shows catered to women, and prominent citizens' wives got the royal treatment, 1927. Baking contests tempted the palette. And flower shows at the Horticultural Building tempted the eye, 1920.

One of the great attractions of this year's fair will be the automobile races, which will be staged on the race track this afternoon. The American Automobile Association has brought over SOME OF THEIR FINEST RIDERS AND MANY EXCITING RACES WILL BE WITNESSED ... The one-mile race against time is being looked forward to with keen anticipation. Included in the other events are two eight-mile races for two types of machines and a 15-MILE RACE FREE-FOR-ALL.[29]

The Vancouver Sun

AUTO SENSATIONS

AUTOMOBILES MADE AN early debut at the Vancouver Exhibition. Car shows started as early as 1911, and popular races were staged at Hastings Park by the end of the first decade. In the 1920s, Henry Ford's mass-produced vehicles took the continent by storm. The Vancouver Fair was in the thick of it, with offerings for every taste.

GIVING VANCOUVER SPORTS fans their first taste of what is claimed to be the acme of recreational sports, American and Canadian athletes will line up this afternoon at the Hastings Park court for the opening auto polo game of the week's antics ... Spills and thrills galore are promised by the promoters of the new sport for the fans who have an appetite for excitement. Fences and barricades fail to halt the machines after the game gets under way. Cars are often times completely demolished as the result of head-on collisions while the opposing players repeatedly imperil their lives in their reckless attempts to score goals.[30] *The Vancouver Sun*

THIS EVENT IS proving one of the most attractive features of the daily programme at the Exhibition. The game has been perfected during the last couple of years, and the wonderful dexterity of machine and driver are real thrill-making hazards.[31]

Vancouver Daily World

WITH THE INEFFABLE satisfaction of a well-done task, the Vancouver Motor Dealers' Association has just finished the most successful automobile exhibition ever held in Western Canada ... They went beyond the mere matter of selling cars. They visualized the future of the automotive power that went far into the future.[32] *The Vancouver Sun*

FROM LEFT: Car racing at Hastings Park drew enthusiastic crowds, 1927. All the big car manufacturers made sure they had their latest models on display at the Fair, 1926.

THE NEWLY DUBBED Canada's Pacific Exhibition celebrated national events with great drama.

MONDAY EVENING BEGINS the pageant grand ... that magnificent thrilling spectacle staged in commemoration of Confederation. A clever cast, composed of 1000 actors, will move through the brilliant episodes, creating an epic scene. Dramatic pages from the history of British Columbia and the Dominion will be enacted among beautiful, realistic settings. Gorgeous costumes strike their note of artistry.[33]

Poster ad in *The Vancouver Sun*

A GRAND NAME FOR A GRAND ASPIRATION

THE VANCOUVER FAIR outstripped the competition in the '20s and the V.E.A. took stock of its growing stature. With its ties to markets and industry throughout the province and across Canada, it was now much more than a city fair. A new name seemed like a good idea.

ALTHOUGH THE NAME of the fair was not officially changed, 'Canada's Pacific Exhibition' replaced the 'Vancouver Exhibition' as the title of the annual summer show. The aspirations of the association clearly had evolved from predominantly local concerns to a desire to become the 'Toronto of the West' with the exhibition slated to serve as the showcase for all of the Canadian West.[34]

Vancouver's Fair

CANADA'S PACIFIC EXHIBITION attracted some of the biggest names in the British Empire.

WELCOMED AND CHEERED at every turn, the Prince of Wales and Prince George, clad in light summer grey flannel suits and straw hats, made the rounds of the exhibition shortly before noon, after spending some time with the patients of the Shaughnessy Military Hospital. The brothers got the thrill of their lives when they were taken on a ride of the 'Shoot-the-Chutes' as the final event of their exhibition tour.[35] *The Evening Sun*

FROM TOP: The Fair celebrated our history with re-enactments of great moments, such as the driving of the last spike on the CPR, 1927. Pageants stirred citizens' love of country, 1927. Even the royals paid visits — here HRH, Edward, Prince of Wales and his younger brother, Prince George, 1927.

THE WEATHER IS ALWAYS WITH US

RAIN IS INEVITABLE. It wouldn't be Vancouver without it. From the early days, waterlogged clouds tested the stamina of the public and frayed the nerves of V.E.A. planners. Management even tried to find a waterproof scheduling formula that flipped from August to September and back. But the planning proved fruitless. In later years, the phrase "PNE weather" came into parlance, used by legions of Fair stalwarts who cheerfully headed to Hastings Park in the face of a looming front.

THE LOW ATTENDANCE in 1920 was attributed to a return of Vancouver's wet September weather, since rain fell during all but the final two days of the exhibition. Despite President Miller's argument that a return to August dates would be at the expense of the agricultural sector it was decided to abandon the fall in favour of a late summer show. Ironically, after a summer of fine weather the clouds opened on the second day of the August 1921 fair ... [36] *Vancouver's Fair*

TOO BAD THAT we had a trifle of bad weather in mid-week, but even at that, Vancouver never saw a better crowd that ever gazed at the finest assembly of motor cars that has ever been seen in Western Canada.[37] E.H. Parker, sales manager of Begg Motor Car Co.

WILL WEATHER MAN SMILE AT FAIR OPENING?

Right. Hon. Arthur Meighen Will Declare Exhibition Open

EXHIBITS ARE MOST NUMEROUS IN YEARS

The auto races planned for this afternoon were ... OFFICIALLY POSTPONED UNTIL NEXT WEEK OWING TO ... HEAVY RAIN.[38] *Vancouver Daily World*

SOMETHING FOR THE WINTER

IN 1925, THE Vancouver Exhibition Association launched an annual Winter Fair, no doubt to match Toronto's yearly Royal Winter Fair. It was an enormous undertaking, calling for new facilities to shelter the exhibitions and the public in the cold and wet winter.

THE ONLY SIGNIFICANT structure erected in the 1920s was the new livestock building, which was not planned for the annual summer exhibition, but rather as a part of the new yearly Winter Fair. This Winter Fair was the single most important expansion of activities in this decade. It was designed exclusively as an agricultural event, with virtually no attempt made to add carnival-type activities. [39] *Vancouver's Fair*

THE WINTER FAIR served as a marketing outlet for the province's livestock breeders, providing them with a ready forum for the sale of their animals ... Local slaughterhouses and butchers would attend the show and auctions would be held to sell the cattle. The V.E.A. saw this fair as an excellent means of bringing farmer and city dweller together.[40] *Vancouver's Fair*

THE BRITISH COLUMBIA Winter Fair is destined to become a Pacific Royal to match Toronto's Royal Winter Fair and as such can do immense good work in the development of the agricultural policies of the Dominion government.[41]

The Vancouver Exhibition Association in a letter to the federal government asking for financial aid for the Winter Fair, January 1927

THE VANCOUVER EXHIBITION association maintained and expanded the show throughout the remainder of the decade, adding such features as an industry- and province-sponsored National Apple Show in 1927.[42] *Vancouver's Fair*

BY 1924, THE GOLF LINKS HAD BEEN COMPLETED at a cost of less than $18,000 ... The next golfing year saw the commencement of operations at Vancouver's first public golf course. From this point on, the shape of the course was altered regularly, as it was in 1930 when it was expanded from its original nine-hole layout to A FULL EIGHTEEN-HOLE COURSE.[43] *Vancouver's Fair*

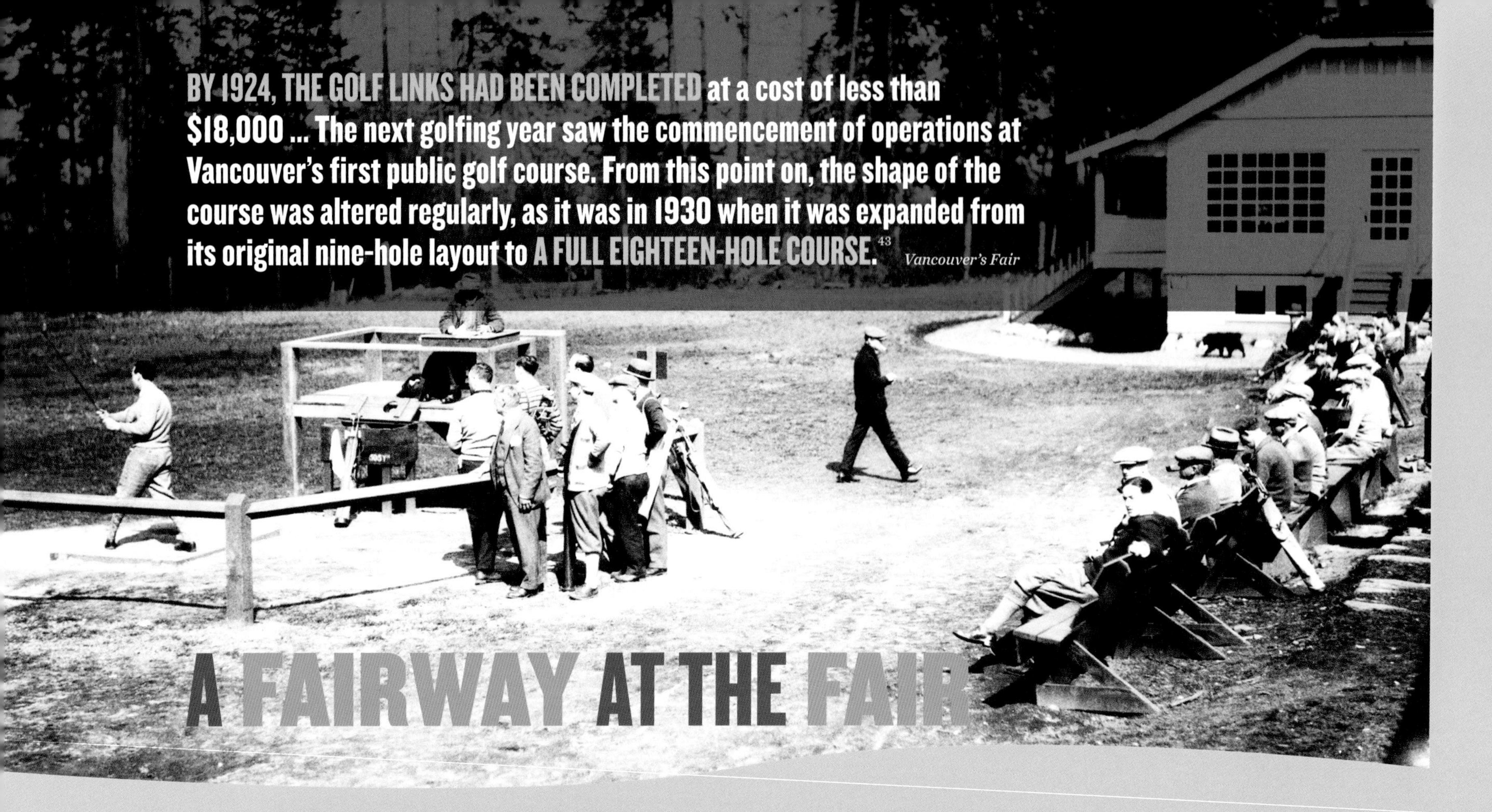

A FAIRWAY AT THE FAIR

FROM THE BEGINNING, the V.E.A.'s vision for Hastings Park included year-round public amenities. The vision started taking shape two years after the association negotiated with the city for a new lease on Hastings Park in 1921.

THE V.E.A. WAS ... required, as an ongoing condition of the lease, to erect and maintain a Tourist Auto Camp and to improve and operate a golf course on the property.[44] *Vancouver's Fair*

NEW EQUIPMENT HAS been purchased for the comfort stations at the park and a double partition will be built between the men's and the women's sides ... Two new stoves have been secured and one has been installed. An additional man has been employed to keep the stoves working and the camp clean. Further improvements are planned.[45]

The Vancouver Sun

THE HASTINGS PARK OVAL was converted from a lawn into a standard playing field, thus providing much needed athletic grounds for the east side.[46] *Vancouver's Fair*

FROM TOP: Ardent golfers wait their turn to tee up at the Hastings Park links, 1927. Other outdoor fans could opt to relax at the campground.

COMING OUT ON TOP

THE VANCOUVER EXHIBITION started in an age when fairs were plentiful; every town with ambition boasted one. The odds against success were daunting. But the sweepstakes went to Vancouver, and the V.E.A. worked hard to ensure their show stayed on top. Even so, after the 1925 Fair, talk turned to the Vancouver Fair merging with its old nemesis, the New Westminster Exhibition, and possibly even moving.

MANY SUGGESTED THAT ... Vancouver and New Westminster amalgamate their operations on one site. Indeed, as the debate progressed, it became increasingly evident that such a union was inevitable and that the sole issue was whether the new exhibition should be staged at Hastings Park, at Queen's Park in New Westminster, or at some alternative location.[47]

Vancouver's Fair

CENTRAL PARK IN Burnaby was suggested as a compromise location the following year [1926], with supporters of the site arguing not only that it was equidistant from the competing fairs, but also that it was directly in line with the way in which Greater Vancouver was expanding.

The V.E.A. harshly criticized the proposal, comparing the size of Hastings Park, buildings, financing, amusements and transportation facilities with the suggested locale and concluding that the Vancouver site was superior in every possible regard.[48]

Vancouver's Fair

AS TO AMALGAMATION itself, this is easy of accomplishment, if New Westminster will recognize Hastings Park as the logical place, which undoubtedly it is from every conceivable angle.[49]

Draft letter on the Proposed Amalgamation of New Westminster and Vancouver Exhibitions

IT IS NOT too bad that some Federal influence cannot induce Vancouver and New Westminster Shows to get together and put on one really good show with facilities for a winter fair, rather than have these two competing expensive exhibitions so close to each other ... Needless to say, we are called upon to support both of these with our exhibits and it is quite a bill of expense from our appropriation ...[50]

E.S. Archibald, federal minister of Agriculture

THE ISSUE WAS resolved unexpectedly in 1929.

New Westminster's major advantage, its fine set of agricultural exhibit facilities was wiped out by fire. The Royal Agricultural and Industrial Society [New Westminster's fair organization] was not altogether eager to, or for that matter financially capable of, rebuilding Queen's Park.[51]

Vancouver's Fair

FROM TOP: The Fair grounds in 1922 showing the Womens Building and the Giant Dipper. The rival New Westminster fair's pavilions were a major attraction until they were destroyed by fire.

FAIR ENTICEMENTS
In the early decades of the Exhibition lavish advertising offered up a host of tempting reasons for visiting Hastings Park.

Horse Show

Many of the finest horses on the continent are showing in the Horse Show Building each evening, Commencing at 8 o'clock. Come and enjoy yourself.

Grand Opening Vancouver Exhibition

HERE'S AN EXHIBITION that each year is pronounced "BIGGER AND BETTER THAN EVER." We're not going to disappoint you this year, either! The gigantic and brilliant exhibits and the splendid feature attractions will demonstrate to you what we mean by "Bigger and Better Than Ever."

Industrial Exhibits that will supersede all other previous attempts; the most wonderful exhibit of purebred cattle ever shown in the province; a splendid and comprehensive exhibition of our lumber and mining resources; agricultural, horticultural and apiarian exhibits that are superior in every way to any other prior endeavor; an incomparable poultry display that will be a treat for every poultry admirer; a horse show that will be both entertaining and educating. The household arts and needlework exhibits will delight the hearts of all women. A cat and dog show that will win the approval of all lovers of these animals.

The attractions are varied and many---dancing exhibition, novelty diving, performing bears, slack-wire and trapeze artist, community singing, brass bands, carnival shows, and on the race track there will be horse races, both harness and running events. Horse show. Come and see your Exhibition; bring the whole family. Remember, it's your show. Come and have a day of fun!

PROGRAMME

MONDAY, AUGUST 2[illegible]

Manufacturers' Day

[illegible]

SKID ROAD AND OTHER ATTRACTIONS

[illegible]

IN FRONT OF GRANDSTAND

[illegible]

ON THE RACE TRACK

[illegible]

Band Concert in Park—Afternoon and Evening

IN STOCK JUDGING PAVILION

[illegible]

NOTICE

REDUCED FARES

Fare and one-third return

Vancouver Exhibition

Today is New Westminster and Fraser Valley Day

BE sure to see the exhibits of our Natural Resources, mainstay of British Columbia's and Vancouver's prosperity. . . . The Mining Exhibit this year shows ore samples from every district, including spectacular gold quartz from Zeballos, samples of Ore of Mercury and Diatomite; also displays of coal and coke. . . . The Agricultural and Horticultural section includes fine displays of Field Crops, Fruits, Garden Vegetables, Poultry, Honey and Dairy Products. These are exhibits every citizen should study — see them and be proud of your province!

CANADA PACIFIC EXHIBITION

AUG 28 — SEPT 4

SPECIAL PRIVILEGE TICKETS for Sale Everywhere—3 for $1—Eligible for $5100 Prizes

Tickets purchased at Exhibition gates are not valid for prize participation.

AUG. 28 - SEPT. 4
AT HASTINGS PARK

THE SPORT OF KINGS . . . no other spectacle is packed with so much color and gaiety . . . thrills and excitement. The gay silks of the jockeys against the green of the infield . . . the glossy thoroughbreds prancing daintily to the post . . . make an unforgettable picture. Whether or not you are backing your judgment, you'll tense with the crowd as the barriers springs . . . and leap to your feet with them as the field flashes into the stretch. The excitement grips you.

● The Special Privilege Combination Ticket admits you to the grounds and to the races. No extra charge. Get your tickets early.

3 FOR $1 • FROM STREET SALESMEN, STORES OR LOCAL AGENTS

DON'T MISS ANY PART OF THIS GRAND EVENT CELEBRATING THE KING'S JUBILEE

FRIDAY, AUGUST 30TH (FRASER VALLEY DAY)

10:00 a.m.— All Buildings open. Splendid Exhibits. Continuation of Livestock Judging in Horse Show Building. Great Exhibit of Animals in every section. Commencement of Judging in Holstein, Guernsey and Beef cattle classes. Continuation of Cat Show.

12:00 Noon—Province Rest Room open.

2:00 p.m.— High-class Happy-Go-Lucky Hour, platform on lawn.

2:00 p.m.— Resumption of Livestock Judging, championships.

2:00 p.m.— House of Magic special performance, and at 3:30, 5:00, 7:30 and 9:00 p.m.

2:30 p.m.— Special Horse Racing at Track.

3:00 p.m.— Visit all buildings for demonstrations in 45 departments.

4:00 p.m.— Visit the Mining Exhibit.

6:30 p.m.— Band Concert in bandstand for two hours.

8:30 p.m.— Special Happy-Go-Lucky Hour and Vaudeville Program in Horse Show Building. Visit the Forestry and Indian Shows. Moving Pictures in Forestry Building.

10:00 p.m.— Buildings closed; midway in full swing, also dancing.

CANADA PACIFIC EXHIBITION

FREEZERS
HOY'S FROSTED MALTED
MALTED
BAKING POWDER BLUE RIBBON TEA COFFEE
BRITISH COLUMBIA PACKERS LIMITED
BRAND
SEA FOOD
5¢

CHAPTER 3

1930–1939

WHEN TIMES GET TOUGH

'30-'39

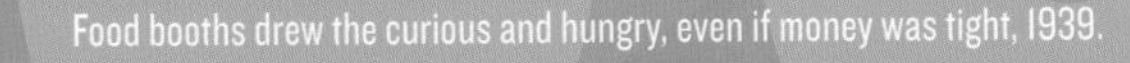
Food booths drew the curious and hungry, even if money was tight, 1939.

A BRIGHT SPOT IN DARK TIMES

People thought the party would last, so the 1929 stock market crash came as a shock. In Vancouver, factories and mills started closing and breadlines formed. Soup kitchens sprang up to help the neediest, and a reporter for *The Vancouver Sun* counted 1,250 men in one meal lineup at a local church.

AT ITS WORST, the Great Depression pushed around 34,000 Vancouverites onto relief. People were frightened and unhappy. Some even took to the streets in mass demonstrations that pitted unemployed citizens against the authorities. As the Great Depression deepened, the Roaring Twenties turned into the Dirty Thirties.

Hastings Park was one of the few places where a bit of fun and good news could be found. The Vancouver Exhibition Association's planning during the 1920s bore fruit at the right time. As the city ground to a halt, Hastings Park bustled with projects and swarms of construction workers. One of the best-known buildings to go up, the Forum (completed in 1930), was a marvel. For a while, it boasted the largest sheet of artificial ice in North America. Hockey and curling sports became popular community events and the Forum soon became a major venue for a variety of entertainments throughout the year.

Fads got zanier and put everyone in a better mood — the Fair's freckle contest was one notable hit.

FROM TOP: Advertisements trumpeted the Fair as B.C.'s show window, 1938. Despite the bleak times, people flocked to the fair, 1935.

In these tough times, everyone was on the lookout for cheap escapes from the grind. People filled movie theatres and dance halls in record numbers. Radio was enjoying its golden age, with shows like *Amos 'n' Andy* and *Fibber McGee and Molly*. Mickey Mouse became a household word, jive talk was the rage and everyone played pinball, bingo and the new jukeboxes. Fads got zanier and put everyone in a better mood — the Fair's Freckle Contest was one notable hit.

Then there were cowboys. When *The Lone Ranger* hit the airwaves, the radio show launched a decades-long love affair with the myth of the Wild West and the strong, silent hero who rides to the rescue. The Fair's playbill soon included Western shows.

Meanwhile, the Dance Pavilion tempted dreamers year-round with all-night dance marathons. They didn't cost much, you could strut your stuff until dawn and, if you were lucky — and awake — you might win the grand prize.

In 1935 the first official Exhibition parade seized the public imagination. If you couldn't afford the 25 cent admission to the Fair, you could always find a curb seat and get a taste of the fun to be found on the other side of the imposing new Hastings Street gates. Mindful of the times, the Exhibition had reduced its entrance fee two years earlier, to make it even easier for cash-strapped people to come to the Fair. And each year the Elk's Club sponsored a free day for children.

Turning conventional wisdom on its head, Fair attendance in the Great Depression grew to a high of 377,000 in 1936, when Vancouver celebrated its 50th anniversary. Hastings Park was the best place to shake off those blues. Everyone knew the lyrics to "Brother, Can You Spare a Dime." But the playful message of "Life Is Just a Bowl of Cherries" struck a happier chord — "Don't take it serious, life's so mysterious."

CANADA PACIFIC EXHIBITION

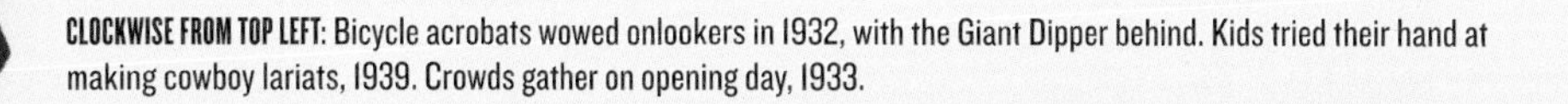
CLOCKWISE FROM TOP LEFT: Bicycle acrobats wowed onlookers in 1932, with the Giant Dipper behind. Kids tried their hand at making cowboy lariats, 1939. Crowds gather on opening day, 1933.

THAT BOWL OF CHERRIES

EXHIBITIONS ACROSS CANADA, particularly Vancouver's Canada's Pacific Exhibition, enjoyed greater popularity during the Depression. Fair organizers continued to introduce new attractions each year while refining many of the older ones. Their efforts delighted Fair visitors and helped them temporarily forget the grim reality outside the Exhibition gates.

EVERYTHING IN FULL swing with wheels spinning, rides in full tilt, avenues of games, people winning things and grinning. Ballyhoos, snake charmers, dancers, beating drums, calling voices, people buying tickets. Crowds, slow sauntering, good-naturedly looking at everything. Hot dogs sizzling! Little children laughing at a Punch and Judy show and big children smiling in reminiscence!

All day it goes on like that — hundreds of things to see and do and the carnival travels around the face of the clock until the sun goes down and a thousand lights twinkle into the fairyland which is the exhibition at night. So the happy days are here again![1]

The Vancouver Sun

PROMPTLY AT 10 o'clock when the gates swung open, the children commenced to throng through, many of them accompanied by their elders ... Boys of the Vancouver Model Aircraft Club under the direction of W. MacReady gave a display of flying models immediately following the formal opening. Others contributing to the opening program which was under the auspices of the B.P.O. Elks, were the Mary Isdale dancers, the Vancouver Ladies' Pipe Band, the Kitsilano Boys' tumbling team and the Kitsilano Girls' Pyramid team.[2]

The Vancouver Sun

In the early 1930s, when future bandleader Dal Richards was barely a teenager, he was too young to get into the Happyland dance pavilion. That didn't stop the eager young hot-footer from finding out what all the excitement was about.

I DISCOVERED THAT if you stood on tiptoe outside the window of the Happyland Ballroom you could see the Ronnie Hart orchestra and hear Ronnie sing his theme song, 'One Hour with You,' with his little speech at the finish about how he'd like to spend one hour with you — finger pointed to the audience — you. I was just a kid in love with music and willing to go anywhere to hear it.[3]

One More Time: The Dal Richards Story

LEFT: Photo montage from a 1936 *Vancouver Sun* article highlighting the fun to be found at the Fair.

ENTERTAINMENT WAS TO be had in every corner of the Fair, inside and out.

THROUGHOUT THE GROUNDS entertainment was provided for those who could not find room elsewhere by a dozen clowns whose antics and capers added to the general fun. Four bands, stationed at strategic points, gave concerts during the afternoon, while the B.C. Rangers, well-known to radio audiences contributed their share to the fun within the main building.[4]

The Vancouver Sun

ONE OF THE oldest forms of entertainment is being provided at Canada Pacific Exhibition in the machinery building by Shell Oil Company of B.C. Ltd. — puppet shows, the diversion of young and old. Continuous performances will be given daily and evenings ... and the quaint doll-like figures controlled by a hidden puppeteer promise to add considerably to the outstanding attractions arranged this year.[5]

The Vancouver Sun

GIVEN THE LEAN times, people were grateful that some attractions came with free benefits.

TWENTY GALLONS OF milk and an additional 10 cases of chocolate drink were consumed before 3 p.m. Monday by the thirsty youngsters who visited 'Dairyland', the children's playground at the Exhibition. The drinks were 'on the house'.[6]

The Vancouver Sun

Great air-gliding demonstrations will constitute a THRILLING ITEM in front of the grandstand daily.[7]

The Vancouver Sun

CLOCKWISE FROM TOP LEFT: Band music was featured in the 1936 Fair. Music at the bandstand, 1934. Fans jammed the grandstand to celebrate, 1935. Puppets at the Shell Oil display drew a big audience, 1935. Sonny Richardson and his Kampus Kings played at Happyland, 1930. Opening day felt like Christmas for the young at heart, 1933.

SOMETIMES UNSCRIPTED COMEDY got the biggest laughs.

THE SIGN ON the building said 'Cats and Dogs', which may account for the little black mongrel finding himself in the cat show at the exhibition Friday. The dog show however doesn't open till Monday and there was nothing but rows and rows of cats and kittens in the building. The little dog didn't discover his error until he was well in the building. For one horrified moment he halted in indecision. Then, with tail between his legs he made for the nearest exit, followed by the amused laughter of the spectators and utter indifference on the part of the cats.[8]

The Vancouver Sun

Occasionally a little bovine melodrama in the stock parade brought the house down.

A SMALL PRIZE calf with a straw hat cocked perkily over one eye called down a round of laughter, while an unruly bull attempting to charge the boy leading it had to be removed from the field in disgrace.[9]

The Vancouver Sun

HELPING RED

Ernie Dougherty owned and operated a number of hamburger and ice-cream stands at the PNE for 68 years, becoming the longest-running concessionaire the Fair has ever had. It all started in the summer of 1936, when Ernie was looking for work.

"I WASN'T QUITE 12 years old. I only lived a block and a half from the park, so I went to the fairgrounds to see if I could find a job. I came across this fella who was unloading a pick-up truck and a trailer. 'Mister, you got a job for me?' I asked him. 'What can you do kid?' he replied. I said anything he wanted done. 'Help me unload then.' It was a hamburger stand. He was one of those travelling carnival people and had just come from another fair. His name was Red Barry.

When I finished helping Red, I asked 'Any job for me when the fair's on?' He asked if I could peel onions. I'd never done it before but thought I could do it. So that was my job, peeling onions and slicing buns. I also had to skin the wieners — they came linked together in skins in those days.

I got to the grounds the first fair day around 9:30 a.m. and Red let me go around nine o'clock at night. When I got home my Dad asked how much I was getting paid. 'I don't know,' I said. The fair was eleven days long then. We started on a Wednesday and we were busy until Friday. On Saturday it rained really hard so Red let me go right after lunch, because there weren't too many people around. In those days we didn't work Sundays. On Monday, one of the counter girls quit. So I had to work the counter as well, and make juice from lemon, lime and orange powders. Red was at the griddle and if someone ordered a hamburger or hot dog, I was told to ask, 'And what did you want to drink?'

I worked to the end of the fair and went back after my first day of school to help Red tear down. When he was packed up and ready to go, he looked down at me. 'I guess you want to get paid now. What do you think you're worth?' I told him that I thought I did pretty good. 'Yeah, you did pretty good, getting people to buy drinks.' Red pulled out a $5 bill. Then he counted some ones until he was up to $9. I kept looking at him. 'What the hell, I guess you want another one don't ya?' he said. I got the $10 I was looking for — a $5 bill and five ones. That was a lot of money then.

I added it to the $5 I had saved; my parents each gave me $2, and I bought a CCM bicycle."

Ernie worked at the Fair for the rest of his teen years. Before he was 20 years old, he took a 10 percent stake in a company owned by Nat Bailey (founder of the White Spot Restaurants) and Les Smith. In 1956 he bought the company and eventually owned two hamburger stands, an ice cream trailer, two gambling wheels, a 50% interest in two bingo stands, plus a maltbar.

FROM TOP: By the 1930s, the 4-H Club was an important part of the Agricultural Show. Young farmers from across the province dreamed of being a winner at the Fair. Ernie Dougherty in his 1948 concession trailer.

Come out to the

CANADA PACIFIC EXHIBITION

---the Stampede is in full swing!

Every moment of this breath-taking programme is packed with thrilling action as clever cowboys match their skill with wild antics of the bucking bronchoes in the World Championship Stampede. Don't miss the thrilling Roman, chariot, chuck-wagon racing . . . the steer-decorating . . . the spectacular roping, throwing and trick riding contests. These hair-raising rodeo events start at 2:00 p.m. every day.

FREE ADMISSION

HOW THE WEST WAS WON

BY THE 1930S, the West was strewn with stampedes — those big urban rodeos that gave a taste of life on the range. Crowds flocked to the Exhibition to catch a glimpse of real-life cowboys ropin', wrastlin' 'n ridin'.

Greeted by the cheers of a **CAPACITY GRANDSTAND AUDIENCE**, Pete Knight, Calgary cowboy, was acclaimed world champion wild broncho rider. Cowboys have been competing for the honor throughout the week ... Three Vancouver kiddies, Bill Adams, Edward Chow, and Richard Collins won the children's roping contest ... The two roses, Rose Smith and Rose Wall did their **HORSEBACK STUNTS AND CARRIED OFF THE PLAUDITS OF THE SPECTATORS**.[10]

The Vancouver Sun

CLOCKWISE FROM TOP LEFT: Chuckwagon races, 1931. Some stampede bucking broncos were even mechanical, 1938. A display ad for the 1931 Stampede. A bucking bronco lets it rip at the 1931 Stampede.

Hey! Freckles?

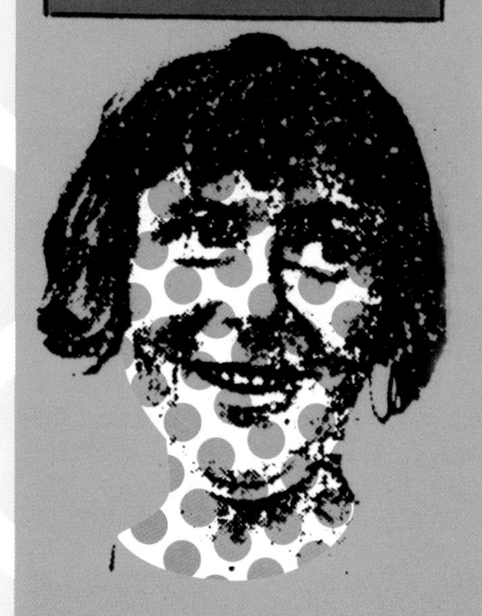

EULA FORSYTH

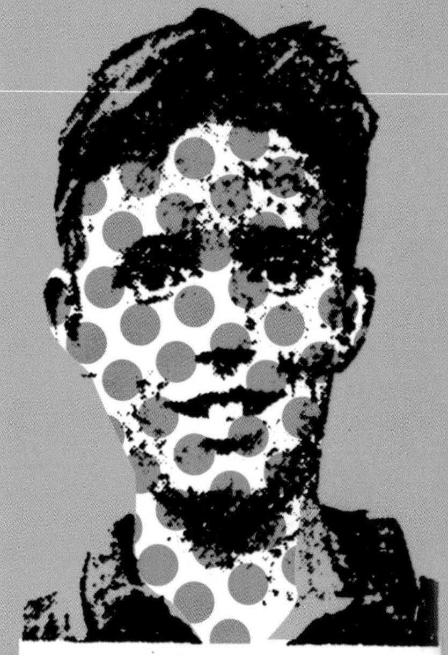

ROY COPLE

Hey! Skinnay! Betcha can't boast a bunch of freckles like these 'uns. Betcha. Aren't they beauties? Perfectly good healthy coats of freckles made these two youngsters the champeen freckle-faced kids of Vancouver at the B. P. O. Elks' twelfth annual Children's Flag Day Wednesday afternoon at the Canada Pacific Exhibition.

They are Eula Forsyth, 14, of 1956 Graveley Street, and Roy Cople, 12, of 4260 Cambridge Street.

Freckles, warts and good red heads were worth real money to the youngsters Wednesday when the Brother Bills staged novelty competitions for these unusual features.

SUN TAN WINNERS IN FINALS AT FAIR

MORE PHOTOS ON PAGE 18 AND MORE TOMORROW

IT'S GETTING A BIT ZANY

DURING THE THIRTIES novel and wacky contests ruled. They didn't cost much, if anything, and brought people together. Canada's Pacific Exhibition added to the fun with its share of shenanigans.

IN THE SHELTER of the big Horseshow Building at the exhibition grounds, out of the rain, a big crowd is expected tonight when all the Sun-Tan contestants who become eligible for the finals will be judged. While judges Funk and Devaney inspect the Sun-Tan contestants — male and female — on one big stage, vaudeville attractions will be presented on another stage ... On Thursday night the judges will complete their work, the Sun-Tan King and Queen will be proclaimed, and the runners-up named. Prizes valued at $1,000 are the awards for the successful candidates. The contest is being staged by *The Vancouver Sun* and the Famous Players' suburban theatres as a health-promotion feature.[11]

The Vancouver Sun

FOR BARNYARD AFICIONADOS, the "international" egg-laying contest, launched in 1911, was still going strong in 1930.

The hens wear anxious brows in the yard adjoining the poultry building at the exhibition. THEY HAVE REASON TO LOOK A BIT STRAINED FOR THEY ARE COMPETING FOR NOVEL HONORS. It's a question of which will lay the most eggs before the morning of August 14. From all over British Columbia, they've come to compete ... Twenty-five pens holding five hens each have averaged 89 daily ...[12] *The Vancouver Sun*

FROM LEFT: The Freckle Contest was a perennial favourite, 1933. Finalists at their bronzed best show their stuff in the suntan contest.

THAT OTHER OLYMPIAD

IN THE 1930S, Canada's Pacific Exhibition [sic] took on a high-profile role providing facilities and management for major sports events. School and community athletic competitions were held at Hastings Park's sporting venues year-round. A first for North America, and copied continent-wide, was the city's high school Olympiad.

PROMISES OF A plethora of prizes for the second annual B.C. High School Olympiad to be held at Hastings Park, August 7 and 8, are already being realized. The B.C. High School Olympiad, which was last year the first of its kind in Canada ... will be again held this year under the joint auspices of the Vancouver Exhibition Association and *The Vancouver Sun*.

Besides the medals being offered some lucky young high school champion will go home with a high-class shotgun, already equipped for the fall shooting season. This acceptable additional prize for the Olympiad has been donated by Mr. Frank D. Gross, one of the directors of the Vancouver Exhibition Association, who was so impressed with the fine young talent that took part in the inaugural Olympiad last year [that he] decided to offer something in the way of a special prize that any healthy youth would particularly appreciate.[13]

The Vancouver Sun

THE OLYMPIC PARADE — like the Olympiad itself — is modeled after the grand national parade of athletes that is such a feature of the Olympic Games ... Last year ... there were 115 high school champions representing 31 high schools throughout the province. Following the example of about a half dozen of the teams last year, it is probable that every high school team will have the name of their home town or city displayed across the front of their costume. To make this feature still more attractive it is proposed to offer five silver medals to the team adjudged to be the best in the Olympic Parade.[14]

The Vancouver Sun

Olympic Day! — the first of the two days devoted to record-breaking by High School athletes from every section of British Columbia — the B.C. Olympiad ... now being copied clean through to the Atlantic Coast as ONE OF THE FINEST CONTRIBUTIONS TO COMMUNITY LIFE AND NATIONAL WELFARE AND SPORTSMANLIKE SPIRIT.[15]

The Vancouver Sun

RIGHT: Sports champions from high schools across B.C. took part in the second "Olympiad" staged at Hastings Park, 1930.

STARS AT THE OLYMPIAD

Canada's Pacific Exhibition took on a high-profile role providing facilities and management for major sports events.

WHEN CLANS GATHER

SOME INSIST THAT the Scots built the British Empire. When the clans gathered at Hastings Park for a wee bit of sport, there was brawn enough to settle the argument.

TARTANS FEATURE AT FAIR — Scots Foregather for Caledonian Games Event

MORE THAN 200 of the 260 recognized clan Tartans were represented in the great gathering of Highlanders at Hastings Park today, which marks the forty-fourth annual Caledonian Games. Skirl of pipes started as early as 8 o'clock when enthusiastic pipers commenced practicing for their competition later. Kiddies in kilts and older kids ditto — for all Scottish lads and lasses are young again on Caledonian Day — dotted the grounds, grandstand and athletic oval ... Entries for both the piping and dancing, as well as the athletic events were more numerous than their previous years and that means another new record in a series of 'bigger and better' each year as applied to the Caledonian Games.[16] *The Vancouver Sun*

CLOCKWISE FROM TOP LEFT: Highland dancers take a bow at the Caledonian Games, 1938. Onlookers admire the shot put, 1938. A Caledonian hero and his wee fan, 1930. Another demonstration of Gaelic might, 1930. Only a hardy few could toss the caber, 1928. Highland games were not complete without the skirl of bagpipes, 1930.

VAST CROWD SEES SCOTTISH EVENTS

The huge crowd enjoyed one of the finest programs of sport ever offered anywhere. There the MCGREGORS AND MCPHERSONS, THE MCPHAILS AND THE MCDONALDS GATHERED IN FORCE ... The St. Andrews and Caledonia Society prided itself on one of the greatest meets in history.[17] *The Vancouver Sun*

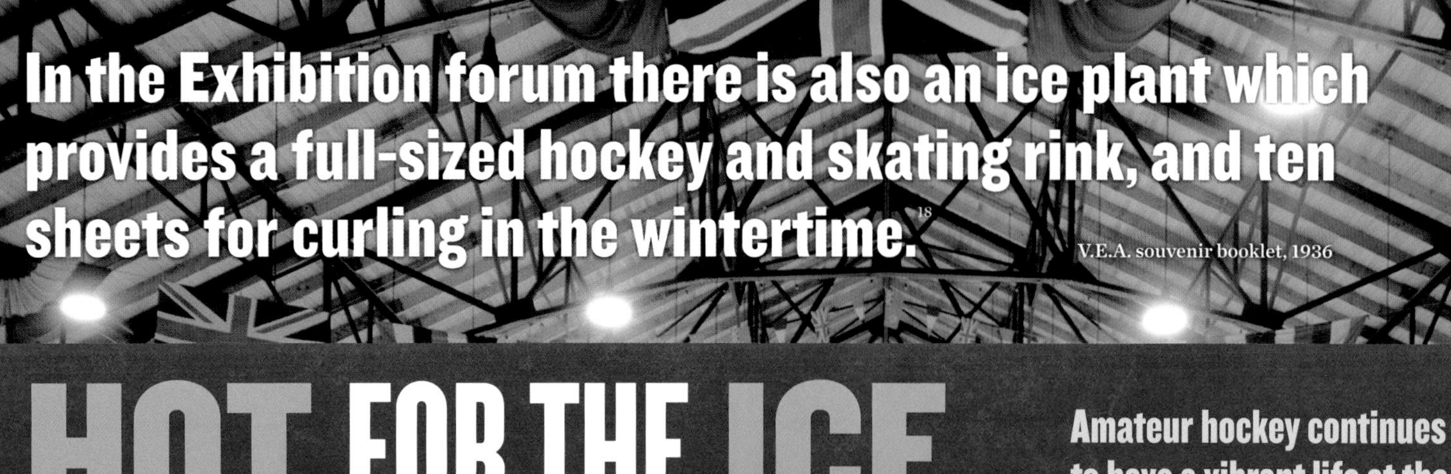

In the Exhibition forum there is also an ice plant which provides a full-sized hockey and skating rink, and ten sheets for curling in the wintertime.[18]

V.E.A. souvenir booklet, 1936

HOT FOR THE ICE

LONG BEFORE THE NHL, Hastings Park played host to high-energy community and professional hockey leagues. Tickets to a night at the Forum, with a seat at centre ice, were hot.

Amateur hockey continues to have a vibrant life at the PNE with 30 community teams competing on the ice.

IN 1939, ART Jefferd, Lyle Barr and John Clark initiated the Vancouver Minor Hockey Association at the Hastings Park Forum. That association continued under the names P.N.E. Minor Hockey Association and Hastings Minor Hockey Association until 1997–1998. With the New Westminster Pee Wee Hockey Association, formed two years earlier, the associations and their constitutions provided the mould for many new associations that have come into being over the intervening years. One of their objects was 'to encourage and foster amongst its members, and all citizens in general, sportsmanship and good citizenship.'[19]

The Pacific Coast Amateur Hockey Association

ODE TO THINGS THAT GROW

EXHIBITIONS AT THE Fair became more elaborate. They reflected modern trends and tastes, but some had more practical applications, such as demonstrations of vegetable gardens that could help cash-strapped households. Other displays trumpeted the wealth of our forests.

A COOL FRAGRANCE greets the visitor to the Horticulture Building at the Exhibition. The effect of coolness is accentuated by the rockery set up in the centre of the building by Dickson Brothers. Here a miniature stream falls into a lily pond through which fishes swim lazily ... One of the most interesting sections of the Horticulture Building is the district vegetable exhibit which shows what can be done in British Columbia gardens. From artichokes to the lowly turnip the groups indicated a wide range of produce.[20]

The Vancouver Sun

THE B.C. LUMBER and Shingle Association will show every wood produced in Canada. Under the supervision of Ralph Perry, of the U.B.C. Forest Products Laboratory, University of British Columbia, articles manufactured from wood will be displayed. Another feature will be the miniature logging scene and mill in operation ...
The entire Forestry Building will be decorated in green trees, moss and shrubs.[21]

The Vancouver Sun

THE CANADIAN FORESTRY Association has taken a unique way of stressing fire protection and showing the wealth of British Columbia forests in its exhibit ... Wild geese, Mallard ducks, fawn deer, beaver and fish have been put in their natural setting. There are scenes showing the development of lumber from logs, other scenes showing logging activities, mountain communities, fishing camps and finally the devastating forest fire.[22]

The Vancouver Sun

FACING PAGE: In its day the Forum boasted cutting-edge rink technology, 1936. Pee Wee hockey team at the Forum, 1936.
CLOCKWISE FROM TOP LEFT: An agricultural display takes you down the garden path and lays out prize vegetables for inspection, 1937. The Canadian Forestry Exhibit showcases wood products in a model of Vancouver, 1931. James Canadian Seeds' floral display, 1934. Vancouver Lumber Company's presentation of Big Chief Lumber, 1932.

THE SENSATION OF THE WORLD'S FAIR

EVERY DAY

At 2, 3.30, 5, 7.30 and 9 P.M.

AUG. 28 SEPT. 4

SILVER JUBILEE CELEBRATION of CROWN

THIS great feature occupies the whole of the Women's Building, with accommodation for 1000 people. Here you will see all the startling inventions recently developed by the world's greatest electrical scientists. You will marvel at the wonderful electric eye, you will SEE sound and actually HEAR light. There will be wonderful and awesome demonstrations of invisible electric rays, and electric arcs that climb ladders. These and a thousand other fascinating experiments will be performed before your very eyes. Don't miss this highly educational feature of this year's great Exhibition.

- ★ MAMMOTH PARADE (Wednesday)
- ★ HORSE RACING EVERY DAY . . .
- ★ GRAND EXHIBITS . . .
- ★ AUTO SHOW IN FORUM . . . .
- ★ THE GREAT MIDWAY . . .

CANADA PACIFIC EXHIBITION

LET US SHOW YOU WHAT WE CAN DO

STUDENTS, SCIENTISTS AND inventors had their day too.

A COLONIAL HOUSE, one quarter full size, is one of the many attractions in the school exhibits ... The house has been built by students of the Technical Schools of Vancouver. In its construction the students have mastered the problems of framing walls, floors, and roofs; and stair planning and simple porch construction. Other sections are devoted to the motor mechanics department and sheet metal department ... one section of the school exhibit is devoted to the home economics department, both sewing and preserving are on display. The correct method of setting a breakfast, afternoon tea, and luncheon table has also been demonstrated.[23]

The Vancouver Sun

YOU'LL SEE THE newest creations for indirect home lighting! The new 1936 radio receivers with the new metal tubes! Thrillingly modern kitchen appliances in clever settings! Automatic robots for the home-like water heaters, air-conditioning gas furnaces, food mixers and ranges! Plus wonderful prices![24]

B.C. Electric Stores ad

FROM LEFT: The House of Magic drew hundreds to see its electronic marvels, 1935. The B.C. Electric home display, 1938.

BOOMING WHEN ALL IS BUST

THE FAIR BECAME a major source of jobs during the Depression, providing temporary work in the summer and full-time construction and maintenance jobs in buildings rising on the grounds throughout the year. The Forum went up in 1930 and the Pure Foods, Showmart and Rollerland buildings were all completed before 1935. Efforts were made to finish the massive livestock building, partially completed in 1929, within the decade.

SINCE IT WAS a civic institution, the exhibition was eligible for relief grants and was allocated large gangs of relief labour to work on the grounds. The men were employed on a variety of projects, including the golf course, park extension and ground clearance, renovation of the race track oval, and sundry other chores. In return for their work, the association usually paid the men's streetcar fares and supplied the required tools and materials, while the city gave the unemployed workers meal tickets. These relief operations were often substantial affairs, involving fifty or more men working on one project at a time.[25]

Vancouver's Fair

The vast number of unemployed in the city made work at the annual fair a valued prize. In 1930, over one thousand people applied for two hundred available jobs ...[26]

Vancouver's Fair

FROM 1929 TO 1934, the fair put up several large, span-concrete buildings. They were inexpensive because you could build with unskilled labour and the material — board-form concrete — was relatively inexpensive. The original part of the livestock building was done in 1929, but the massive part, which is about three acres, was built in 1939. It was a conscious make-work program that also provided big new spaces for the Fair and the city. Many buildings were used throughout the year, particularly the Forum, which was open all year.

The Depression was quite a significant time not only for the Fair but for Vancouver. The city was turning 50, its golden jubilee, and other big projects like the Burrard Street Bridge and Lions Gate Bridge were being completed. The fairgrounds were part of that activity.

Donald Luxton, Heritage Consultant, 2009

CLOCKWISE FROM TOP LEFT: Construction of the Pure Foods Building provided jobs for Vancouver's unemployed. Work on the Lions Gate nearing completion in 1938. Construction on The Forum.

THE BIGGEST PRIZE OF ALL

IN 1934, FAIR organizers offered up an astonishing prize that would go to one lucky fairgoer — a fully furnished home that came with a free city lot. The new contest brought thousands of the curious and hopeful to the Exhibition that year. For many, the prize home was a dream; for the more practical-minded organizers it was a great way to showcase B.C.'s wealth of home-grown materials and talent.

THE FIRST PNE Dream Home was won in 1934 by Leonard Frewin, a mechanic from Vancouver who was courting Emily Leitch. Emily's father insisted that Leonard couldn't properly provide for his daughter, so he did not support the match. As fate would have it, Leonard attended the 1934 PNE on the last day of the Fair, where he purchased a Dream Home ticket for twenty-five cents. He heard his name announced as the then-called 'PNE Dream Home' winner while listening to the radio that night, went to Emily's house and proposed on the spot.

The Frewin family lived in the original Dream Home for over 60 years until both Emily and Leonard passed away within months of each other in the 1990s and their children sold the home. The 1934 Dream Home was 800 square feet, and the lot along Renfrew Street, the home and its furnishings (provided by the Eaton's company) were valued at the time at an astounding $5,000. The home was relocated from the Fairgrounds a half block away by a team of Clydesdales. The most exciting feature of that original Dream Home was the inclusion of an electric stove.

PNE news release, 2009

The 1934 Dream Home was 800 square feet, and the lot along Renfrew Street, the home and its furnishings ... were valued at the time at an astounding $5,000.

FROM TOP: The 1934 Dream Home cost only $5,000. From its start, the Dream Home (now the PNE Prize Home) has always been a favourite with crowds, like this one in the 1950s.

GONE TO THE PARADE. BACK SOON

A FAIR ISN'T a fair without a bit of hoopla and a parade. From the start, the opening day of the Exhibition was marked by a bit of public spectacle. There were gatherings and speeches, lots of ribbon cuttings and colourful and quirky processions. But it wasn't until 1935 that a fully fledged parade heralded the start of the Exhibition. It was such a hit that Fair organizers made the parade a permanent part of the program.

SPURRED ON BY Vancouver Mayor G.G. McGeer, who was looking for a suitable outlet for a demonstration of civic pride and determination, the V.E.A. agreed to stage a parade on the opening day of the fair. The project was not undertaken without considerable apprehension ... the exhibition association was able to pull it off, and on 20 August, 1935, it staged an elaborate exhibition parade complete with marching bands, floats and clowns through downtown Vancouver.[27] *Vancouver's Fair*

THOUSANDS OF MEN, women and children in holiday mood jammed sidewalks along the route taken by the Canada Pacific Exhibition procession today and testified by their expressions of admiration that it was the finest parade ever staged in the city ... crowds viewed the parade from the streets and from every vantage point as it passed through the downtown streets. It is estimated that it took an hour to pass a given point.[28] *The Vancouver Sun*

In the 1930s, a young boy moved with his parents to Vancouver to escape the harsh life on the prairies. His name was Jimmy Pattison, and he would go on to become one of British Columbia's most famous business leaders — and the province's first billionaire.

"MY MEMORIES OF the PNE are mostly of the big parade downtown. It was a *big* deal. I came downtown early with my parents, usually my mother, to get a good seat. We didn't have enough money to go to the Fair; the parade was how I experienced the PNE as a child. Later, I did have the money and went many times to the Fair."

At the first official Exhibition parade, in 1935, the B.C. Electric Company's float wowed the public.

AMONG THE MOST elaborate of the commercial floats was the B.C. Electric. Against a shimmering silver background is the coat of arms of Vancouver with the motto 'By Sea and Land We Prosper' ... The story of why tourists mean big business to British Columbia is told in the spectacular float entered in today's parade by the Vancouver Publicity Bureau. At the far end of it a golden cornucopia pours forth a harvest of tourist dollars ... A touch of old Winter was given the parade by the Rotary Club float which represented its annual ice carnival. Mrs. Verna Miles Fraser, dainty star skater for a number of years held the reins and with her were a bevy of juvenile skating stars ... Most spectacular were the B.C. Association's two floats with their realistic forest fire and firefighting machinery. Marching with the men were red-shirted members of the junior fire wardens ... Reminiscent of the olden days when the crack of whips and the sound of horses' hooves resounded along the Cariboo Trail was the old coach with its Cariboo Cowboys.[29] *The Vancouver Sun*

WINNERS ANNOUNCED IN the Canadian Pacific Exhibition parade Wednesday are: Grand prize for most effective float: B.C. Electric Co.; second, City Playgrounds section, Department of Education. Service Clubs: First: Rotary Club; second, Kiwanis Club. Most artistic float: First, City of Playgrounds section, Department of Education; second, Kerrisdale Suburb ... Most comical float: First, Association of Associated Dairies; second, Auto Wreckers.[30] *The Vancouver Sun*

Whatever their intentions, Tuesday, most small shopkeepers closed shop this morning and stuck hurriedly scrawled notices in their doors to announce: 'GONE TO THE PARADE. BACK SOON.' There were, however, few people around to read them.[31]

The Vancouver Sun

THE FOLLOWING YEAR, the Exhibition parade was even more boisterous and colourful. At the request of City Hall, it was one of the big public celebrations marking Vancouver's 50th birthday.

VANCOUVER TURNED OUT en masse today with all her thousands of Jubilee celebrants at the biggest and most spectacular parade in the city's history, the 'Parade of Progress'. The crowds jammed the sidewalks all along the route from Georgia and Bute to Hastings and Clark Drive, climbed jubilantly to grandstand seats on the roof-tops, hung perilously out of upper windows and perched on any raised projection in sight.
In carnival mood they cheered floats that pleased their fancy, joshed with each other, and laughed uproariously at the antics of the clowns and other comic entries. It was a gala start for the twenty-seventh Canada Pacific Exhibition — an opening under the most auspicious circumstances in its history.[32] *The Vancouver Sun*

FROM LEFT, ABOVE: B.C. Telephone at the inaugural parade. The Vancouver Tourist Association got in the spirit at the 1936 parade.

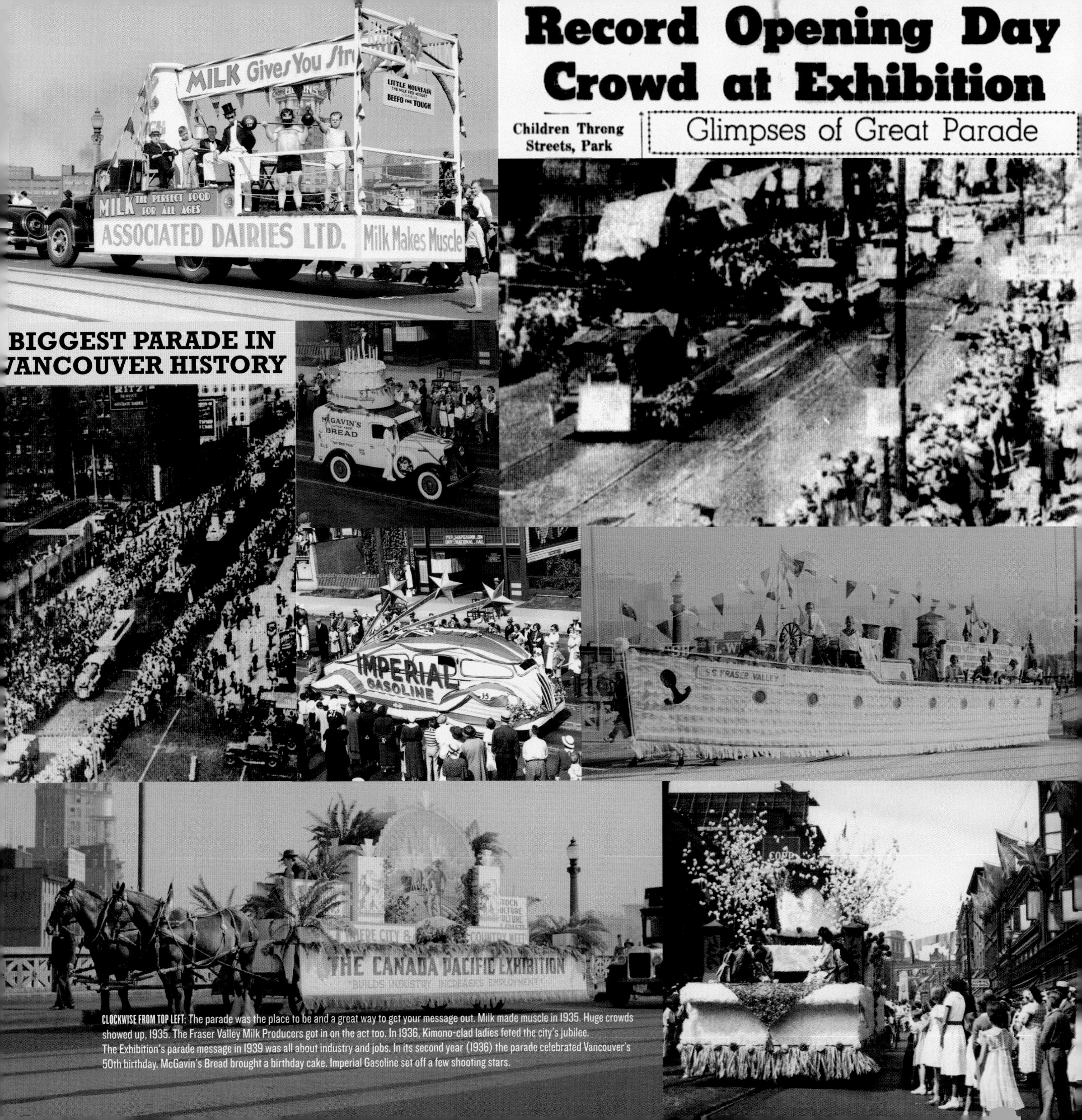

CLOCKWISE FROM TOP LEFT: The parade was the place to be and a great way to get your message out. Milk made muscle in 1935. Huge crowds showed up, 1935. The Fraser Valley Milk Producers got in on the act too. In 1936, Kimono-clad ladies feted the city's jubilee. The Exhibition's parade message in 1939 was all about industry and jobs. In its second year (1936) the parade celebrated Vancouver's 50th birthday. McGavin's Bread brought a birthday cake. Imperial Gasoline set off a few shooting stars.

GREAT DANE
112

GOING TO THE DOGS
From the Fair's opening in 1910, dogs of every size, stripe and bark have strutted their show-stopping stuff for thousands of adoring fans. One hundred years of prize-winning pooches on parade include this Great Dane in 1954 (previous page) and the 1941 winner of the Best Dog prize.

PNE
PNE
EXHIBITION PARK
PNE AUG 23 TO SEPT 4
A FAIR FOR ALL THE FAMILY
PACIFIC NATIONAL EXHIBITION
PNE PROGRAM PRIZES
OWN TICKET
IN THE BOX

CHAPTER 4

1940–1949
WAR, VICTORY AND SOMETHING NEW

'40-'49

PNE entrance gate, 1949.

OVER THERE, AGAIN

By 1940 Canada was back at war and Vancouver got over the Depression. Factories and shipyards sprang up across the Lower Mainland. Tens of thousands of workers streamed into new plants. Burrard Dry Dock shattered tradition by hiring over 1,000 women to build ships. As Rosie the Riveter became a war hero, young ladies were spotted on Granville Street wearing pants.

THE VANCOUVER EXHIBITION ASSOCIATION did its part by continuing the Fair and the parade, helping stoke morale on the home front. In the 1940 parade, to martial airs and the rousing skirl of bagpipes, phalanxes of troops mingled with armoured cars, heavy artillery and larger-than-life patriotic floats festooned with proud symbols of Canada's might.

The Exhibition grounds themselves were transformed as the bright spectacle of the Fair made room for long lines of military tents. Playing fields swarmed with young men in uniform. The accommodation worked well enough until 1942, when the military demanded full use of the site, ending the annual exhibitions for the next five years.

Uniformed men became a common sight everywhere. The military base at Jericho was enlarged, an airforce depot was built at Kitsilano Point and an armory was erected at U.B.C. Imposing gun emplacements were housed at Point Grey, Stanley Park and First Narrows. The "old" Hotel Vancouver was commandeered as a military headquarters, Hycroft Manor turned into a military hospital. Deadman's Island in Coal Harbour was refitted as a training facility, and the airport became a training school for pilots.

ABOVE: Jimmy Durante hams it up with the chorus line at his PNE Fair show, 1948.

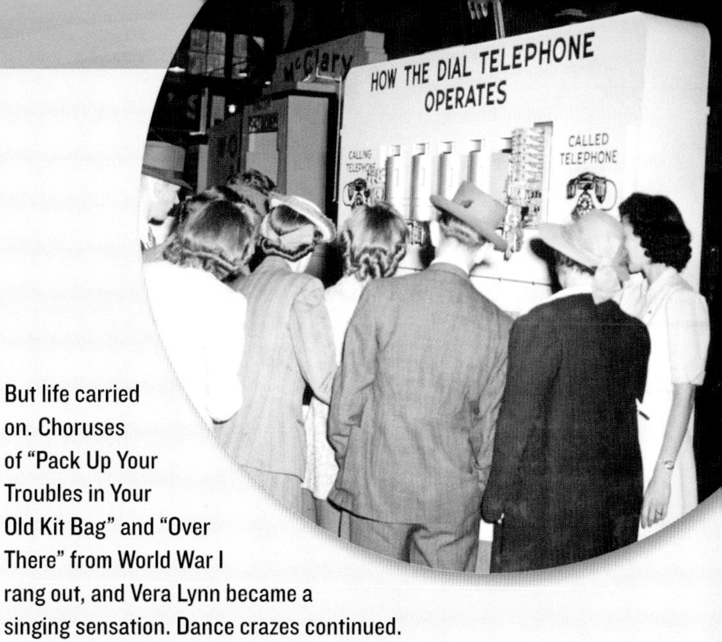

But life carried on. Choruses of "Pack Up Your Troubles in Your Old Kit Bag" and "Over There" from World War I rang out, and Vera Lynn became a singing sensation. Dance crazes continued.

On December 7, 1941, Canada declared war on Japan and Vancouver found itself on the front line. Everything changed again. With rumours of Japanese submarines entering Canadian waters, alarm ran through the city. Acting on fear and uncertainty, the government rounded up an estimated 9,000 Japanese-Canadians living in Vancouver and sent them to internment camps in the interior of the province. Exhibition buildings at Hastings Park were hastily converted into a transit camp for processing the thousands on their way.

August 14, 1945 — Victory! For a few short days the city erupted in celebration. After years of blackouts, air raid drills and shortages of household goods, people were hungry for good times.

Exhibition organizers spent five years planning for a renewed Fair after it had been moved off site in 1942; now, 1947 was the target date. Soon, Hastings Park was renamed Exhibition Park, and the Fair became the Pacific National Exhibition. It was all new, for a new era.

At the 1947 Exhibition, entertainment got top billing. People lined up to see Hollywood stars, and a year later the Shrine Circus opened. Something called television came along and, in no time, TV antennas sprouted on rooftops as viewers strained to pick up signals from Seattle. Frozen food, a phenomenon of the war, was repackaged as TV dinners. And displayed on modern kitchen tables was a dazzling new culinary concept: margarine.

The baby boom kicked in, car culture went ballistic and suburbs were the place to be. It was a different way of life. And, once again, the PNE was the place to find out about it.

FROM LEFT: A last goodbye to Dad, in the early months of the war, as troops march down Eighth Street in New Westminster. All you do is dial — curious fairgoers crowd around a PNE Fair demonstration booth to find out about the latest in phone technology, 1947.

WE MUST CARRY ON

IT WAS FAIR season when World War II broke out in September 1939. Citizens were roused and afraid; the press and politicians called for patriotic Canadians to do their part. Recalling moments of public criticism for continuing the Fair during World War I, the V.E.A. found themselves tested again. Should Canada's Pacific Exhibition continue with war raging in much of the world?

THE DOMINION GOVERNMENT supported the decision of many exhibition associations to proceed with their annual shows ... noting that it was important for public morale that life continue on as before as much as possible.[1]

Vancouver's Fair

FIVE HUNDRED GUESTS at the annual directors' banquet, marking the opening of the 31st Canada Pacific Exhibition, applauded as John Dunsmuir, president, told how the directors decided to hold the fair as usual despite wartime difficulties. 'After long consideration of the problem, we unanimously decided we must carry on,' he declared, 'and we believe now that we have made more progress during the last 12 months than in any previous year of the Association's history.'[2] *The Vancouver Sun*

Exhibition Parade Presents Downtown Military Spectacle

DON'T RAIN ON MY PARADE

MANY VANCOUVERITES AGREED with the decision to host a fair during wartime but some balked at the celebratory parade, arguing it was a frivolous waste in time of war and that the public display should at least be given over to the more serious business of featuring soldierly brawn and technical might. The naysayers were silenced by the military's highest-ranking officer in the city, Major-General R.A. Alexander.

THERE WAS ... A MINOR PROTEST BY SOME PROMINENT BUSINESSMEN, WHO OPPOSED THE CONTINUATION OF AN EXHIBITION PARADE and favoured instead a display of Canadian military might ... Major-General R.A. Alexander, Officer Commanding, Pacific Command, quickly allayed such concerns by offering his '100% SUPPORT' TO THE V.E.A.'S PLANS.[3]

Vancouver's Fair

CLOCKWISE FROM TOP LEFT: The benefits of joining Canada's military go on display at the Fair, 1941. The 1940 RCAF enlistment booth. War Bonds enjoyed brisk sales at the 1940 Fair. Crowds jam downtown streets to cheer Canada's finest, marching in the 1941 Fair parade.

HEAVY RAIN FAILS TO DIM BRILLIANCE OF ANNUAL EXHIBITION PARADE

Thousands Turn Out to Watch Great Spectacle. Military Bands, Soldiers and Airmen, Patriotic Floats Stir Enthusiasm.

headline in *The Vancouver Sun*, August 26, 1940

STOKING A MIGHTY RESOLVE

GETTING A GREEN light for the Fair and the parade didn't mean business as usual though. In step with the public mood, Exhibition organizers shifted the spotlight onto the fighting men headed overseas. And it was time to bring the home front together — there was lots to be done to keep up morale and boost productivity. What better way to strengthen Canada's resolve than with a parade avidly watched by hundreds of thousands?

CHEERS GREETED THE B.C. Electric float, too, on which was mounted a great conventionalized white lion, with representatives of the three military services bearing the colours of each. Britannia rode high over all in the Hudson's Bay Company's striking float in which various naval, military and air units were represented by pretty girls in uniform.[4]

The Vancouver Sun

IN 1941, THE parade and Exhibition took on an even greater military flavour.

KHAKI AND AIR Force Blue, and the deeper blue of the Navy, will set off the brilliant colourings of the gala floats. For the Defense Forces will form an important part of the great parade, as they will of the Exhibition itself ... Two full battalions, the Edmonton Fusiliers and the Rocky Mountain Rangers, will march later at the grounds with their mechanized equipment ... Fifty men of the Royal Canadian Navy are on their way over from Esquimalt ... Two hundred and fifty men wearing the lighter blue of the Air Force will also be there under arms.[5]

The Vancouver Sun

A CHEERING, YELLING, clapping crowd that jammed sidewalks, hung from windows, and perched on posts and on roofs, stamped its approval on today's big 'All Out for Victory' parade that preceded this afternoon's formal opening of the 1941 Canada Pacific Exhibition. Not only was the parade one of the biggest and most colourful the city has ever viewed, but it presented one of the greatest military spectacles ever seen here. Navy, army and air force were all represented in the alert, trim marching figures. With these representatives of the armed forces were military bands and mechanized equipment, strangely new to many of the spectators.[6]

The Vancouver Sun

CLOCKWISE FROM TOP LEFT: PNE floats in the 1941 parade roused Canadians' patriotism — Britannia rules the waves. Tourist dollars buy battleships. A poke at Hitler got people laughing. Birks Jewellers' float brought out the big-bang bling for the war effort.

ALL'S WELL ON THE HOME FRONT

PEOPLE WANTED REASSURANCE and hope, a sense that the world had not gone completely crazy. Patriotic exhibitions were abundant, but much of the Fair's programming remained true to its original mission: fun and celebration, education and innovation, and the lure of a bright future. Building projects added new facilities: the final expansion of the livestock building – bringing the comples to three acres – was completed in 1940, along with the Garden Auditorium.

WITH THE START of World War II, ... the fair's parades, displays and entertainment all took on a military flavour, and patriotism was the theme. Many government displays encouraged the buying of war bonds or recruitment into various armed forces branches. The midway offered a 'Nudist Village' side show and other risque presentations, along with The Freak Show which featured an alligator-skin man, a fat lady, a four-legged woman, and little people dwarves/midgets. Midway photos show a kiddie aeroplane ride (Herschell?), a carousel, the two coasters, a ferris wheel, a 'Tilt-A-Whirl' and 'Shoot-the-Chutes' ...[7]

Coaster Enthusiasts of Canada

MY BEST MEMORY was the circus! My grandmother made hot dogs wrapped in foil and put them in an empty cereal box. On the bus from New Westminster to Stanley Park and on to the Renfrew stop! In the dark out came the hot dogs. My grandmother is gone but the memories continue.

Fairgoer, *PNE Memory Book*, 1999

FROM LEFT: From the Gayway to hobbies, livestock, flowers, crafts and minerals, a display ad proclaims the 1940 Fair the greatest. The roller coaster was a perennial hit, 1940.

NEXT PAGE, CLOCKWISE FROM TOP LEFT: Fun-seekers packed the sideshows. Some caught a glimpse of the four-legged woman, or took in an acrobatic show. Many cheered a fetching chorus line, or hopped on the Loop 'O' Plane. Everyone applauded the baton twirler's skills at the Outdoor Theatre.

The Fair's programming remained true to its original mission: FUN AND CELEBRATION, EDUCATION AND INNOVATION, and the LURE OF A BRIGHT FUTURE.

FORGETTING FOR A WHILE

FAIR ORGANIZERS WORKED hard to soften the grim reality of war. A bit of silliness had lifted spirits during the Great Depression; it worked wonders for people fearful their world was about to be turned upside down, again.

BORN TO MRS. Greybrook Milley II, purebred Ayrshire cow, at the Cattle Hospital in the new, up-to-date Livestock Building of the Canada Pacific Exhibition, a daughter. Both are doing well.[8]

The Vancouver Sun

IN HIS FAMED radio feature, Hobby Lobby, which was given last evening from the New Exhibition Gardens Building at the Canada Pacific Exhibition, Dave Elman, popular director of the program, introduced on the air a number of British Columbia residents. Among those who appeared on the show was Ernest Forbes Bezanson, Vancouver cabinet maker, whose hobby is constructing cigarette-holders from toothbrushes and pipestems used by convicted murderers.[9]

The Vancouver Sun

MRS. J. E. BUERK JOAN TAYLOR

REHEARSAL ON ICE—A highlight of the winter season is the annual Rotary Ice Carnival, to be held this year in the Forum on December 10 and 11. Above: Mrs. J. E. Buerk watches Joan Taylor, talented young skating star and daughter of Cyclone Taylor, rehearsing

Second annual Hobby Show — MANY WEIRD AND NOVEL EXHIBITS — raw potato statues ... crime weapons ... collections of dolls, clocks, walking sticks, lucky charms ...[10] *The Vancouver Sun*

AND CHILDREN CONTINUED to love fun contests from the decade before.

CHILDREN ARE EVERYWHERE ... thronging the skidway, taking in all the free exhibits, eating quantities of cotton candy and consuming hot dogs by the hundreds. Their big moment comes at 6:30 p.m. when the Freckle-Faced Contest finals take place ...[11]

The Vancouver Sun

FOUR FRECKLE-FACED YOUNGSTERS are eagerly awaiting next Saturday, each hoping that on that day he will become the owner of a new bicycle ... For a moment judges were afraid they might have to spend the remainder of the evening counting spots. One irate mother asserted ... that her youngster's freckles extended well around his neck, while those of the winner ventured no further than his face. It was the second time that Shirley Pierce's freckles had netted a prize for her. Last year she took second prize at the Seaforth annual picnic. Her father, Pte. N.S. Pierce, is now overseas ...[12]

The Vancouver Sun

FROM TOP: At the 1941 Fair you could see model airplanes, catch Joan Taylor at the Forum rehearsing for the Rotary Ice Carnival, or admire the ferris wheel built from thousands of toothpicks.
NEXT PAGE: A Norris cartoon pokes fun at the Hobby Show, 1953.

"... Now don't fret my good man ... fortunately the PNE doesn't open until tomorrow."

A MUSEUM WOULD BE NICE

IN 1941, TWO members of the Vancouver Exhibition Association, Edward and Mary Lipsett, donated their collection of American Indian artifacts to the Fair. They were lifelong collectors and wanted the public to have free access to these materials. The V.E.A. jumped at the offer.

B.C. INDIAN ART ... In the Museum Building. Be sure to see the Edward and Mary Lipsett Collection — Assembled during a lifetime, donated to the people of Vancouver, now shown in public for the first time — Many beautiful examples of B.C. Native art, comprising Black Slate carvings, beadwork, baskets, blankets, masks, totem poles, etc.[13]

Poster ad in *The Vancouver Sun*

THE NEW ATTRACTION displaced the aquarium, which had been a fixture ... for almost two decades. The museum was later moved to the B.C. Building where it remained until it was transferred to Vancouver's new Centennial Museum in 1971.[14]

The Pacific National Exhibition: An Illustrated History

ABOVE: The Lipsett Museum housed a wealth of First Nations art, including (inset) baskets and pottery, 1941.

SOLUTIONS FOR SHORTAGES

WAR DISRUPTED TRADE around the world. Some products were in short supply, and many items that people took for granted vanished completely. Canadians responded by starting new ventures to fill in the gaps. At the Fair, innovative solutions took centre stage.

WITH FOREIGN SOURCES of supply largely cut off by the war, British Columbia is starting to develop a number of new industries. For instance, out at the Esperanza Lily Farm in Langley Prairie, Alwyne Buckley is growing the lily bulbs that he and other florists formerly imported from Japan. He has a fine display of bulbs in the horticultural show at the exhibition. Loss of European supplies is also developing another horticultural industry at Gillatly B.C., where J.V. Gillatly is growing nuts of many varieties. He has an exhibit of 22 varieties ...[15]

The Vancouver Sun

BEEKEEPING IS GROWING rapidly in popularity among British Columbia farmers. John W. Wood, 73, of Vancouver, beemaster, who ably demonstrates the fine art of handling these insects in the Forum Building at the Exhibition, claims that the production of honey is doubling annually in this province ... Commencing Wednesday afternoon, Mrs. R.S. Chamberlain will lecture daily on how to cook and preserve with honey.[16]

The Vancouver Sun

It was 'ALL OUT FOR VICTORY', and the exhibition was prepared to do its part to aid the national war effort.[17]

The Pacific National Exhibition: An Illustrated History

MILITARY MANEUVERS

THE VANCOUVER EXHIBITION Association knew they would have to facilitate the Canadian armed forces at Hastings Park, just as they had done in World War I. As soon as war was declared, arrangements were made for the military to use some of the V.E.A. facilities for part of the year. But the V.E.A. made sure the fairground buildings would be available for Fair use in the summer. This agreement worked for the 1940 and 1941 exhibitions. But events were about to change all that.

IN AUGUST 1941, the Air Force declared its intention of using the Industrial and Women's Buildings and of building additional structures immediately after that year's exhibition ... Once again, the V.E.A. was prepared to fulfill its patriotic duty, provided these obligations did not interfere with the normal functioning of the annual fair. Events soon conspired to ensure the V.E.A.'s immediate concerns would be altered.[18]

Vancouver's Fair

FROM LEFT: The 1941 B.C. Honey Display was the place to learn about bees. Growing bulbs became a local growth industry during the war, 1941. The Crystal and Turners Dairy display, 1940.

City On War Basis as Pacific Erupts[19]

Headline in *The Vancouver Daily Province*

INTERNMENT

AFTER PEARL HARBOR the government made a decision to move Japanese-Canadian citizens out of Vancouver. The military tone of Hastings Park changed overnight as the site was transformed by the government into an evacuation centre. The Fair closed for five years.

BRITISH COLUMBIA WENT to war against Japan Sunday a few minutes after the first bombs fell on Honolulu and the Philippines. Long before Canada's official declaration of war against Japan was announced, the Dominion's western outpost had taken three steps to meet war in the Pacific face to face: 1. MILITARY– All army, navy and air force bases were on the alert. Leaves of members of the armed forces were cancelled ... Air and sea approaches to Vancouver were carefully guarded. 2. DEFENSIVE – British Columbia's A.R.P. organizations sprang into action. Provincial and civic officials held emergency conferences. Sweeping defensive measures were forecast. Coastal black-outs became immediate possibilities. 3. SECURITY – R.C.M.P. and Provincial Police swiftly rounded up dangerous enemy aliens while spokesmen for British Columbia's 24,000 Japanese declared their unswerving allegiance to Canada.[20] *The Vancouver Daily Province*

... IN THE resulting turmoil after the Pearl Harbor attack, Hastings Park was completely taken over by the Canadian military authorities.[21] *Vancouver's Fair*

FROM TOP: In 1942, during the relocations of Japanese Canadians, the Forum doubled as a men's dormitory, and women and children ate in a separate dining room.

GENERAL ALEXANDER NOTED that: 'The situation with regard to the Japanese residents in British Columbia is assuming a serious aspect. Public feeling is becoming very insistent, especially in Vancouver, that local Japanese should be either interned or removed from the coast.' Public pressure for the removal of the Japanese grew rapidly ... Faced with thc possibility of racially inspired violence, the federal government reluctantly agreed to order the evacuation of all Japanese within certain 'protected zones' along the Pacific Coast ...[22]

Vancouver's Fair

HASTINGS PARK WAS then turned over ... for use as a transshipment point for the Japanese ... Workmen descended upon the grounds quickly turning the former livestock building into a temporary dormitory ... It quickly became evident that the temporary holding site first envisaged would not suffice and that more substantial arrangements were required. The Pure Foods, Manufacturing and Forum Buildings were brought into service, cooking facilities expanded, a small store opened, and additional sleeping arrangements provided ...[23]

Vancouver's Fair

MORE THAN EIGHT thousand persons of Japanese descent passed through the camp between March and September, 1942. For most, the days in Hastings Park were fairly short, since the camp was intended primarily as a way-station for people destined for resettlement in the interior of the province.[24]

The Pacific National Exhibition: An Illustrated History

Laura Ballance started working at the Fair doing publicity in 1992. Every year she looks forward to a special occasion that began shortly after she joined the PNE.

"I HAD BEEN working at the PNE less than two years when one Tuesday morning, before the Fair opened, I was walking through the grounds planning a tour for journalists. I saw an older Japanese gentleman standing at the corner of the old Forum building, looking around. I thought maybe he was lost. I asked him if he needed help. 'No,' he said with a smile. 'I'm just remembering. I was interned here.'

I was only about 20 years old then and didn't know what to say. 'I'm so sorry,' I managed to get out. 'Don't be sorry,' he said.

Then he and I went for a walk and he started telling me stories. 'You know the soldiers were nice to us,' he said and began to point out places that held important memories. 'This is where they kept my mom and my sister, and this is where me, my brothers and my dad were. Then my dad got sent to the Interior.'

He told me about candy being smuggled in for the kids and what a treat it was. His family lost everything but somehow this gentleman remembers the time he was interned here with a kind of fondness. So each year now, on the Tuesday before the Fair starts, at about 11:00 a.m., I come to this particular spot where we first met. He is always there. We greet each other and go for a walk. I tell him what is happening at that year's Fair and he tells me more stories.

Yet in all the years I have been doing it, I couldn't tell you his name, he doesn't know my name. We just meet there and connect every year at the same time.

Good, bad or ugly, history lives and breathes here. The Japanese internment is part of our history."

ABOVE: Some Exhibition buildings were converted into temporary classrooms so thousands of school-age children in transit would not miss out on school work.

A WHOLE NEW THING

WHEN THE WAR ended in September 1945, Vancouver went wild. Crowds swarmed the streets, people danced, strangers kissed — it was a party. Once the dust settled, the V.E.A. started planning to get back into the business of running the West's biggest and best exhibition. There was no time to get the Fair site ready for 1946, but there were big plans for '47.

... A 'NEW-LOOK' exhibition association followed from the Second World War. Different in approach and different in style from its predecessor, the 'new' association dropped its old name in 1946, choosing instead to be known as the 'Pacific National Exhibition'. At the same time, Hastings Park was renamed Exhibition Park ... Pacific National Exhibition symbolized an amalgamation of the association's provincial ambitions and new international aspirations. Vancouver's fair had matured, but in turning from local connections in favour of the greater potential of a fair of national and international standing, it still displayed the booster mentality that marked its origins.[25] *Vancouver's Fair*

WELCOME TO THE P.N.E. ... You will have in Vancouver 'By The Mountains, On The Sea' a grandstand seat looking out on the World's greatest theatre of future trade and human activity — the Pacific Ocean.[26]

Senator G.G. McGeer

CLOCKWISE FROM TOP LEFT: In 1947 a "new-look" Fair emerged — kids packed decorated cars. Floats heralded the bigger, better and newly named Pacific National Exhibition. Exhibition Park was packed with fun. Thousands lined Hastings Street to cheer the first peacetime parade.
NEXT PAGE: This trunk comes with attachments — a youngster meets the strange and wonderful at the Fair.

There will be gaiety and the contagious carnival atmosphere of the

GREATEST EXHIBITION IN THE HISTORY OF THE WEST.[27]

The background has been modernized in keeping with the general character of the pageant being enacted. **BUILDINGS HAVE BEEN REMODELED** and lighted with pastel shaded illumination. **COSTLY INNOVATIONS ARE PLANNED TO CREATE THE ATMOSPHERE OF EXCITING NOVELTY THAT IS THE MOOD OF THE FIRST POST-WAR EXHIBITION.**[28]

British Columbia Digest

MESS TO MARVEL

WHEN THE MILITARY cleared out, the PNE facilities were in a shambles. The organizers had a big job on their hands, getting the grounds and buildings ready for the grand reopening in 1947. Fortunately, there was help from the federal government.

A RECENT $375,000 settlement between the Federal Government and the Exhibition for army use of the fair grounds and buildings during the war was 'very fair' to both sides said Mackenzie Bowell, president of the Pacific National Exhibition. The Exhibition has been reborn financially as a result of the government settlement and the fair group now has close to $500,000 with which to get the first post-war exhibition underway.[29]

The Vancouver Daily Province

SPECTACULAR ACTS IN magic and illusion plus the imagination and hard work of committees, contractors, executives, craftsmen and laborers have transformed Hastings Park from a battered and deserted army depot to an exceptionally attractive postwar Pacific National Exhibition. I received something of a shock and a pleasant surprise when I went out to the grounds ... for when I visited the grounds last spring the sight was one of big, weather-scarred buildings with long lines of broken windows, smashed doors, and sagging frames set in heaps of rubble.

But the great transformation has just about been completed. The painters and electricians are putting the finishing touches on the four white and blue flood-lighted pylons, surmounted with the golden crest of the PNE. From that point, new roads and new curbing lead one toward new and renovated buildings, in pastel shades, where new sights await an estimated 500,000 persons who will enjoy their first big fair in Vancouver in six years.

Near the B.C. Products Building I ran into Ben Williams, manager of the PNE, who was taking progress pictures of the work. I said: 'Are you a member of the Magicians' Association?' 'No,' he smiled. 'But I know what you mean.'[30]

The Vancouver Daily Province

MOST OF THAT DAY WAS A BLUR

"MY FIRST PNE memory is of traveling all the way from New Westminster, without our parents, on the electric trolley car. How exciting. We were 12 and 13 years old. That was in 1949. We represented two families who just migrated from Saskatchewan after the war. There were so many people and things to see that most of that day was a blur, except for the bumper cars and Ferris Wheel."

Fairgoer, *PNE Memory Book*, 1999

FACING: The Livestock building, 1947.
FROM TOP: When the Fair reopened in 1947, Hastings Park came alive, day and night. A shot of one of the park's new outdoor areas, 1945.

SHOOT THE CHUTES

TAKING OFF
Hold on tight darlin'! A couple take a ride, Happyland, 1948. Aspiring aviators take to the air.

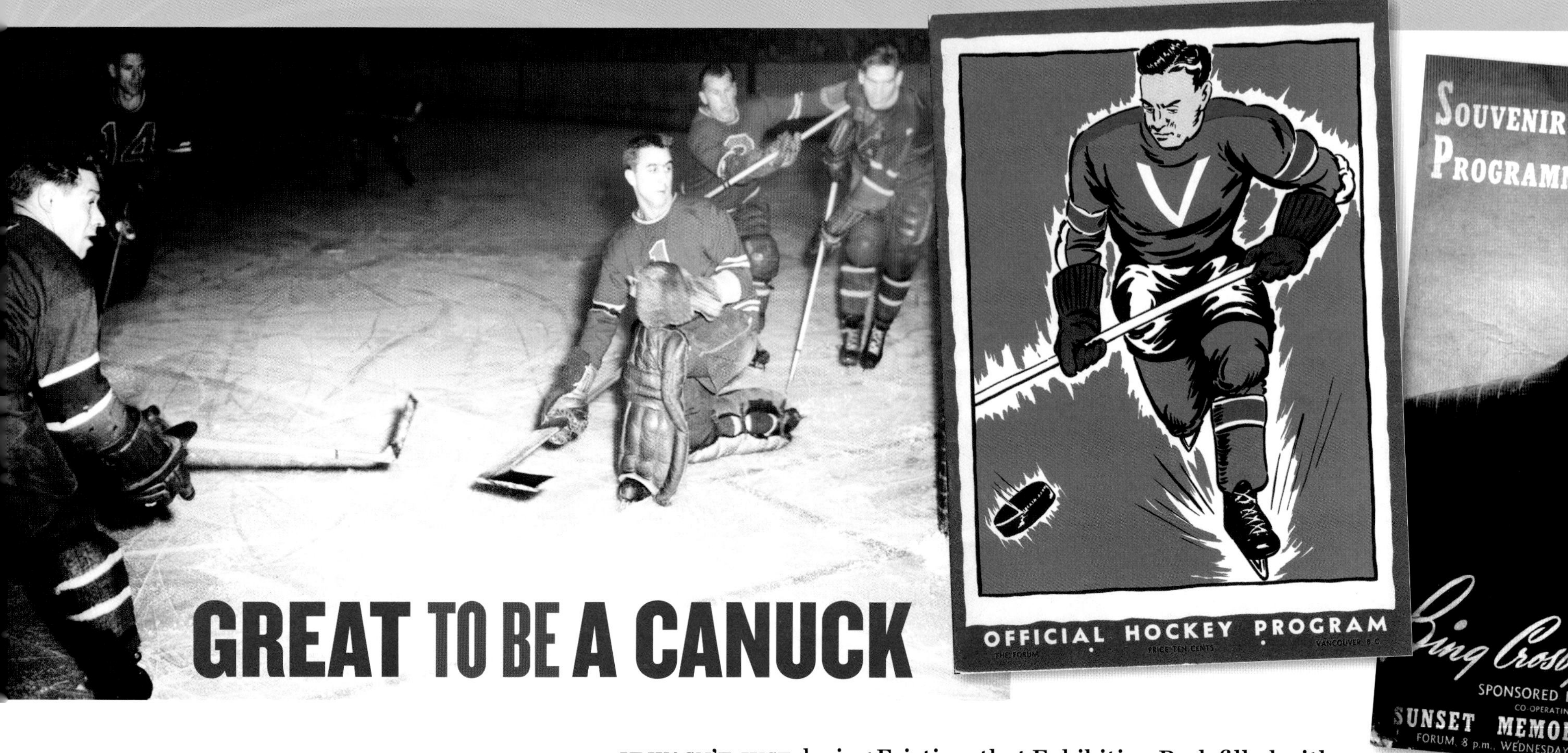

GREAT TO BE A CANUCK

IT WASN'T JUST during Fairtime that Exhibition Park filled with activity. The Pacific Coast Hockey League launched a hockey franchise in Vancouver in 1945. They called themselves the Canucks and played at the PNE's Forum where lacrosse games also drew large, noisy crowds. The Canucks were flushed with early success, winning the league championship in 1946. The public was hooked. There was no looking back — hockey and the PNE were married.

VANCOUVER WAS SMALL IN THOSE DAYS

"I WAS BORN in Vancouver in 1931 and I enjoyed the HAPPY memories of Happyland and the Shoot-the-Chutes ... I learnt how to skate at the old 'Forum' and watched Lacrosse games. Vancouver was small in those days."

Fairgoer, *PNE Memory Book*, 1999

CANUCKS 9, LOS Angeles 6. It was nightmarish in the first period of last night's Pacific Coast Hockey League game and deservedly the Vancouver Canucks were trailing Los Angeles Monarchs 4–1 at the end of that peculiar frame. But the Canucks blew the Monarchs off the ice in a terrific second period assault that netted three goals in six minutes and then, in the final frame, the Vancouver champions marched on to their decisive triumph ... Apart from the 15 goals which were chalked up during the wide open engagement, at least three fights among the more than 5,000 spectators added to the hilarity of the action-filled evening. Then too, some stupid person tossed a bottle on the ice and it was hoped the police nabbed him.[31]

The Vancouver Daily Province

CLOCKWISE FROM TOP LEFT: The final game at the Forum between the Vancouver Canucks and the Skyhawks, 1948. The first Canucks program, 1945. The Canucks claimed a championship in 1946. Lacrosse drew big crowds to the Forum, 1948.

NEXT PAGE, CLOCKWISE FROM TOP LEFT: Bing crooned on stage and raised money for a local charity in 1948. Big-time American performers such as Jimmy Durante headlined the Fair. The outdoor theatre was a favourite Fairtime destination, 1940.

A LITTLE HELP FROM MY FRIENDS

WHILE IN TOWN, Bing Crosby's gig helped raise funds for the Sunset Memorial Centre. Edgar Bergen hauled his hilarious wooden sidekick, Charlie McCarthy, over to Children's Hospital to entertain kids who couldn't make it to the PNE.

ALTHOUGH FUNDRAISING EFFORTS to build the Sunset Memorial Centre commenced in 1945, it wasn't until Crosby took the stage at the PNE Forum on September 22, 1948, that enough money was raised to complete the structure ... The entertainer consented to broadcast his Philco-sponsored network radio program, The Bing Crosby Show, from the Forum (with special guest Ray Milland) and donate all proceeds to the fund.[32]

Backstage Vancouver

CHEEKY CHARLIE MCCARTHY treated little patients ... to some gay moments today and gave them the best medicine a doctor could order ... Every time Charlie opened his trap-door mouth, he tickled the kiddies ... He poked his head at a two-year-old girl and asked her if she had a penny or a stick of gum. He screamed at the nurses, 'Hey, when is lunch around here?' One child stared with such fixed interest at Charlie that he asked: 'Are you going to bite me?' ... The impudent imp was dressed in a gay George Washington costume, which he also wears at his PNE show.[33]

The Vancouver Sun

> **"I have danced at the PNE outdoor theatre from 1949!"**
> Fairgoer, *PNE Memory Book*, 1999

JIMMY, EDGAR AND CHARLIE

WHEN THE FORUM wasn't filled with roaring hockey and lacrosse fans, it was giving top billing to Hollywood performers.

WITHOUT A FAIR for five years, Vancouverites swarmed to the first post-war fair, pushing week-long attendance to 600,000 ... Particular importance was placed on 'big-name' American personalities, with acts such as Jimmy Durante and Edgar Bergen headlining the fair ... the exhibition was clearly changing with the traditional focus on industrial displays and agricultural competitions ... replaced by entertainment extravaganzas.[34]

The Pacific National Exhibition: An Illustrated History

A REVUE-TYPE OF entertainment starring Edgar Bergen was presented during the first four days of the exhibition. A great deal of valuable advertising and publicity was undoubtedly obtained by the appearance of such a well-known figure as Mr. Bergen ... There is of course the possibility that the presence of a 'name' star induced some people to attend the PNE.[35]

PNE Bulletin

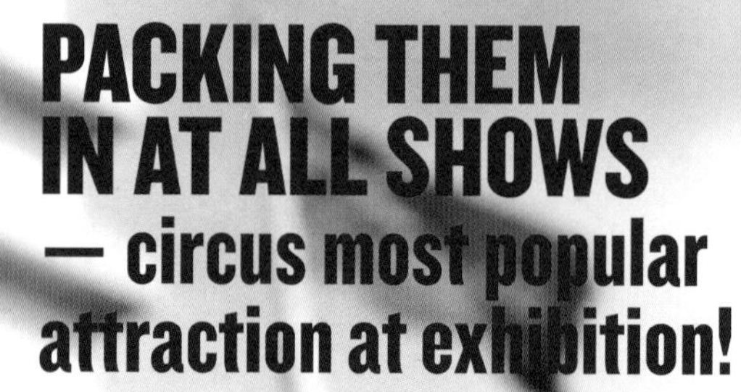

PACKING THEM IN AT ALL SHOWS — circus most popular attraction at exhibition!

Headline, *Vancouver Sun*

EVERY KID'S DREAM

THE CIRCUS IS every kid's dream. The big top had been a major part of the Fair from opening day in 1910, but the fantasy got a lot bigger when the Shrine Circus opened at the Forum during the 1948 PNE.

THE SHRINE CIRCUS brought in a $30,621 net profit ... and a public opinion poll taken by PNE officials showed the circus was preferred 10–1 over other shows ...[36]

The Vancouver Daily Province

The breath-takin'est, death-defyin'est circus.[37]

"Fair Just Keeps Getting Better and Better," John Mackie

MOMENT OF MAGIC

For a birthday treat, Leonard Wilson and his brother Billy travelled with their mom on a bus from Whalley's Corner in Surrey to see the first PNE Shrine Circus in 1948. For the young boy the three-ring spectacle was a moment of magic that he kept alive for more than 50 years.

'POPCORN!' 'PEANUTS!' 'PROGRAMS! Get your Programs here for the PNE Shrine Circus!' The voices rang out and I stared at everything, mesmerized as Billy kept yelling at me to hurry.

As I had done since we had left Whalley's Corner earlier that day, I ran to catch up to Billy and Mama. To get to a place like the Pacific National Exhibition by a certain time in August of 1948 was twenty-percent planning and eighty-percent luck. Mama was giving my brother and me a special treat, a day at the circus. A late birthday present for Billy, his birthday was in May, and an early present for me, my tenth birthday was the next day and we were equally excited.

... After making the necessary transfers to the tram, then buying our tickets to get into the PNE, then into the Circus, most of the seats were already filled and the show had already started by the time we arrived. Searching for seats, Mama led us higher and higher, and Billy kept calling me to hurry, but I was so fascinated with what was happening, I ignored him. I stumbled on the stairs as I watched and laughed at three clowns at one end of the main floor shouting and chasing each other with water guns. A lady riding a white horse came galloping out of the other end of the arena. As the horse's hooves thundered she swung her legs skyward and rode around the arena standing on her head. I could smell the wonderful aromas of popcorn, cotton candy, peanuts and candied apples as vendors brushed past me in their rush to satisfy screaming customers.

'Ladies and Gentlemen, boys and girls of all ages!' The building darkened and spotlights circled the crowd finally resting on a man in a black suit, standing in the center of a huge ring. His voice echoed over the loudspeaker, 'Now for your enjoyment in the center ring, swinging on thin cables one man will attempt the death defying acts of the trapeze.'

Racing, the spotlights swung upwards to silhouette a man in sequined trunks standing on a metal bar near the top of the building. The crowd buzzed with anticipation as the man waved and began swinging, floating effortlessly back and forth.

Billy kept calling my name but I couldn't take my eyes off the man on the trapeze. The announcer yelled, 'The World's Greatest Aerialist, Donny Dorsey is going to demonstrate his amazing ability for your pleasure this afternoon. Unlike any other performer in the world though, Mr. Dorsey is going to perform without a net so it is important we have complete silence.' All the floodlights concentrated on the man and except for the muffled sound of a drum, the building was silent.

... 'Come on you little brat!' Billy grabbed me by the shoulder, jerked me around and practically dragged me up the stairs. He hissed through gritting teeth, 'You're gonna get it for not coming when you're called' ...

The rest of the circus was a blur of beautiful colours and heart stopping thrills. There was a man with a whip in a cage with lions and tigers. Another man and a beautiful lady had elephants doing amazing tricks. The lady with the white horse returned, galloping at top speed doing incredible stunts.

During intermission, the man with the microphone called out numbers, and boys and girls ran down from all over the audience to receive a Mickey Mouse watch. I prayed he would call my number but I wasn't lucky.

The show continued with more clowns, animals, finally finishing with pretty ladies and strong men walking the tightrope. This time though, the people walking the thin wire did their act over a net and after walking back and forth using long poles to balance flipped off the wire into the net.

My Unforgettable Birthday, Leonard W. Wilson

LEFT FROM TOP: What's a circus without the clowns, 1952. There have to be elephants, 1965.
TOP RIGHT: Giant signs at the PNE's 1950 Fair offered a peak at what was inside.

One of These Beauties Will Reign as 'Miss PNE'

SIGNING THE REGISTER at the City Hall are candidates for the "Miss PNE" contest, winner of which will be chosen today and reign over the Pacific National Exhibition. Their signatures go down on the register which bears those of the King and Queen. From left, front: Helen Chernoff, Trail-Rossland; Mayor Charles Thompson; Joyce Warrington, Penticton; Maureen Smith, Victoria. Back: Florence Shannon, Vernon; Marjorie Hildebrand, Vancouver; Joyce Goodwin, Nelson; Jean Ross, Kelowna; Betty Boyd, New Westminster; Verna Bellamy, Chilliwack; Cynthia Norton, Prince Rupert; Gloria Sather, Kamloops, and Kay Ronco, Port Moody.

POISE, TALENT AND A GREAT SWIMSUIT

IN 1948 THE PNE started a blockbuster beauty contest. The contest soon sparked a host of small-town pageants, province wide, with local winners travelling to Vancouver to vie for the Miss PNE crown. The lucky Miss PNE represented the Fair at a variety of civic functions, rode the PNE float at regional fairs and reigned as the Queen of the Pacific National Exhibition. She also held the unofficial title of Miss B.C.

The prettiest girl in British Columbia likes men to be quiet, even a little shy. Beautiful Margaret Brain, 17-year-old Queen of Prince Rupert, said Tuesday after she was crowned Miss PNE 1948, that she would rather sit home with a boy she could talk to than go night-spotting with a 'smoothy'. Margaret will have an opportunity to try out her theories on ... Hollywood hero Alan Ladd ... She will hop a plane for a filmdom screen test and four jammed days of Hollywood hobnobbing as her contest prize.[38]

The Vancouver Sun

GIFTS CONTINUED TO be showered on the first Miss PNE after she returned to her hometown to resume working as an operator for the B.C. Telephone Co.

WHEN PRINCE RUPERT'S beauty queen, Margie Brain (now Ciccone), returned in triumph from Vancouver where she had been crowned the first Queen of the Pacific National Exhibition ... she was on the bridge of the *Catala* with Capt. Ernie Sheppard as the vessel pulled into her hometown, where she was met by city dignitaries and a parade through town.[39]

Steaming Through Northern Waters

Even the PNE president, H.M. King, mentioned the second Miss PNE in his annual report in 1949.

THE ANNUAL 'MISS PNE' Contest ... was another outstanding success. Fourteen girls from communities all over the Province participated in the finals, and Miss Marjorie Hildebrand of Vancouver was chosen for the title at the contest in the Forum on the opening day. We stressed culture, talent, and ambition along with feminine beauty and charm and all members will agree the contest produced a picture of B.C. girlhood at its loveliest.[40]

PNE Bulletin

CLOCKWISE FROM TOP LEFT: Miss PNE candidates get a photo op during the second year of the contest, 1949. A beauty queen in the parade. The first Miss PNE, Margaret Brain, waves to the crowds in 1948. **NEXT PAGE:** With a demure gasp — the winner of the 1953 contest is announced.

We stressed **CULTURE, TALENT, AND AMBITION** along with **FEMININE BEAUTY AND CHARM** and all members will agree the contest produced **A PICTURE OF B.C. GIRLHOOD AT ITS LOVELIEST.**

CROWNS,

SASHES, PERFECTING "THE WAVE," OPENINGS, PROMOS AND ANIMALS:

scenes from the lives of PNE beauty queens

On air with Jack Cullen in the 1950s.

The coronation, 1956.

Sandy Friesen, Miss PNE 1984, getting acquainted with the Fair's livestock.

Three contestants at the PNE Parade, 1970.

Miss PNE 1954 admiring well-layed eggs.

Miss PNE enjoying a 7 cent Coke.

Miss PNE's duties included inspecting exhibits and contests such as Mr. PNE, 1965.

Taking in the Fair at the Hastings and Renfrew gate, 1950s.

B.C. TELEPHONE CO.
"I USE LONG DISTANCE TO GET QUICK ACTION"
BRITISH COLUMBIA
LONG DISTANCE
TELEPHONE NETWORK
LEARN HOW TO USE THE DIAL TELEPHONE
HOW THE DIAL AND NON-DIAL TELEPHONES WORK TOGETHER IN VANCOUVER
FREE
LONG DISTANCE
CALLS
2

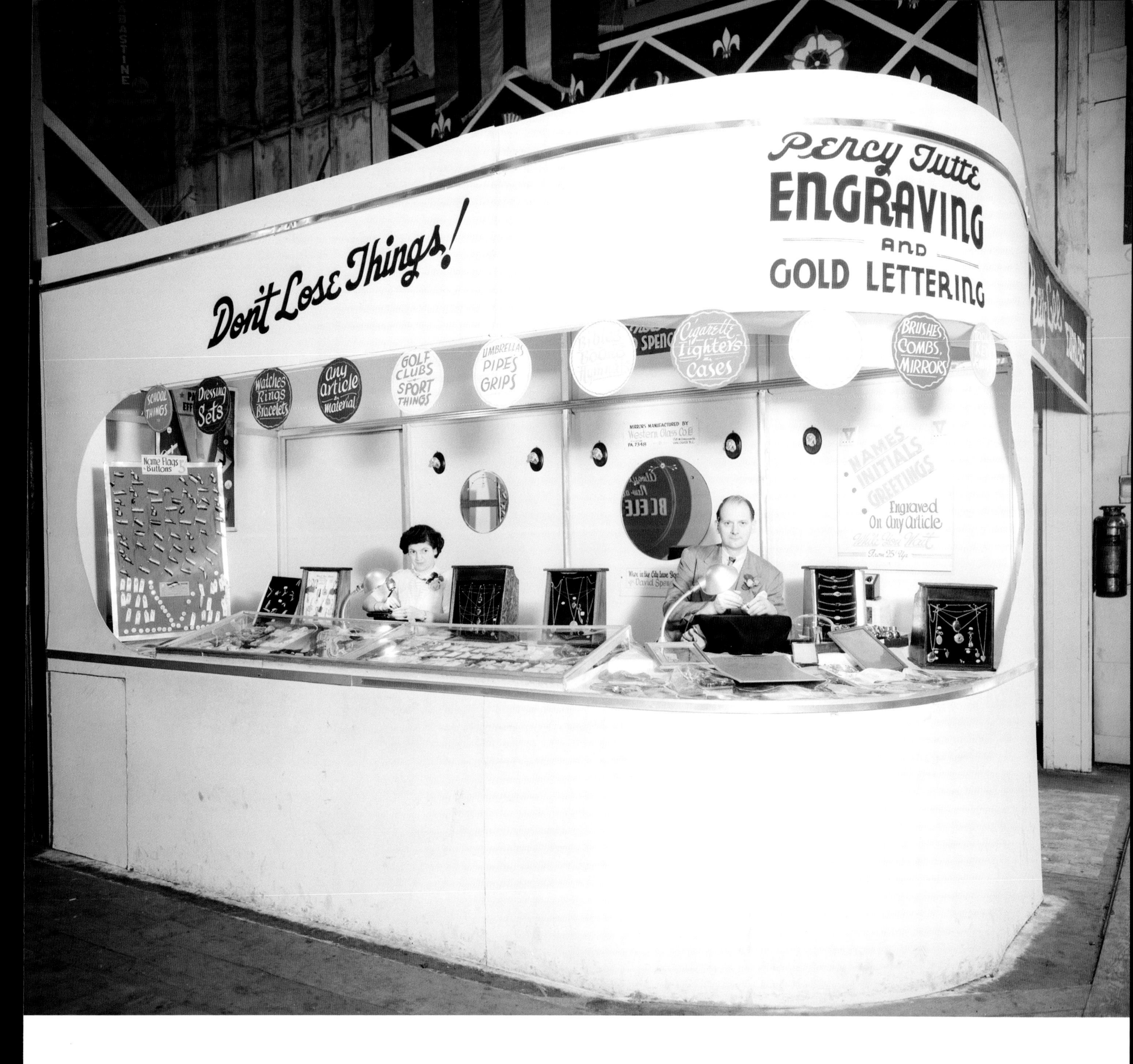

WHAT'S NEW AT THE FAIR?
The B.C. Telephone Company's display demonstrates how to use the long distance telephone, 1940. Percy Tutte's engraving display, 1941.

Another One Program PRIZES
WIN A 52 AUSTIN
Buy YOUR PNE PROGRAM Now!
Buy your

CHAPTER 5

1950–1959

LET US ENTERTAIN YOU

'50–'59

Fairgoers swarm the Fair's main gates in 1952.

NEON, MALLS AND ROCK 'N' ROLL

The 1950s signalled change for Vancouver; the city was shedding its sedate reputation as an outpost of British loyalists and turning into a faster-paced, brightly lit, multicultural urban mosaic. After a decade of economic depression, followed by wartime privations, people hankered for good times. There was a boom, in babies and in buying. People had more time and money on their hands and opened their wallets. It was a spree that fuelled the postwar economy and gave Canadians their first big taste of full-on consumer culture.

FACTORIES HUMMED, AND retail goods poured into stores and then into new suburban homes. There was a new buoyancy. Hobbies were hot, travel was enticing and team sports were big. Trade shows took centre stage, offering something for everyone and filling space at the PNE.

The boom extended to buildings too, as long retail strips sprang up along Kingsway, central Broadway, East Hastings and south Granville. Canada's first suburban shopping mall, Park Royal, opened to great fanfare in West Vancouver in 1950. Oakridge Shopping Centre in Vancouver was completed in 1959. This was the era of the suburb, the commute and a new concept called the industrial park. Bedroom communities mushroomed and rooftops sprouted forests of television antennae as the city got its first CBC affiliate station, CBUT.

Perhaps what best signalled the change in mood was neon. Brilliant artwork sprouted on downtown streets, announcing anything that could fit on a sign, from the tiny Only Seafood Restaurant on Hastings to the gaudy stretch of Granville Street's Theatre Row. One report has put the number of neon signs in Vancouver during the '50s at 18,000.

IN PERSON
AND HIS ALL-STAR SHOW
EMPIRE STADIUM VANCOUVER
THIS SATURDAY AT 8 P.M.
BOX OFFICE AT STADIUM
OPEN SATURDAY 10 A.M. TO SHOWTIME
ELVIS PRESLEY
Tickets at Kellys, Seymour & Georgia, PA. 3351, 10 a.m. to 5 p.m. daily. $1.30, $2.50, $3.50. (Inc. Tax)

CLOCKWISE FROM ABOVE LEFT: Fun was endless at the Fair. A performer poses on her steed outside the livestock building, 1953. Kids have fun on the boat ride, 1953. It's never too early for a majorette to get in on the parade, 1953. Kids get their PNE hats, 1953. A poster announces Elvis's historic Empire Stadium concert in 1957.

The ultra-chic Cave Supper Club sported a smart marquee, announcing top-notch acts from the U.S. that featured Frank Sinatra, The Mills Brothers, Mitzi Gaynor and Rosemary Clooney. The Panorama Roof Ballroom at the Hotel Vancouver, Izzy's and a host of other supper clubs made Vancouver a hot spot on the nightclub circuit.

In no time, PNE buildings were also festooned with neon, setting fairground nightscapes aglow. The new Empire Stadium at the east end of the site hosted the 1954 British Empire and Commonwealth Games. During the games, the world held its breath; John Landy and Roger Bannister had recently broken the four-minute mile, and many were glued to new TV sets to see whether they could do it again in Vancouver. They did — with the North Shore mountains as a spectacular backdrop.

The stadium soon became home for the new BC Lions football franchise and hosted Grey Cup events in 1955 and 1958. At the other end of Exhibition Park, soccer fans filled the PNE's Callister Park bleachers. Hockey in the Forum and boxing and wrestling in the Garden Auditorium packed them in too.

By the middle of the decade Happyland was about to make way for a brighter, faster and bigger midway: Playland. Those who mourned the passing of the venerable Shoot-the-Chutes rejoiced when the new Roller Coaster opened in 1958.

This was the decade when rock 'n' roll dethroned bebop and jazz. The PNE took centre stage again when it became the scene of one of the city's most talked about events — the night Elvis played Empire Stadium. In no time, the PNE was synonymous with entertainment, once again turning Exhibition Park into everyone's destination of choice. As one civic leader saw it, the 180 acres on Hastings had become a matchless "town within a city."

CLOCKWISE FROM TOP LEFT: In 1953, the PNE and the city unveiled plans for a new stadium. A hopeful young man tries his luck with one of the 5 cent diggers. New rides like the Round-up abounded at Playland in the 1950s.

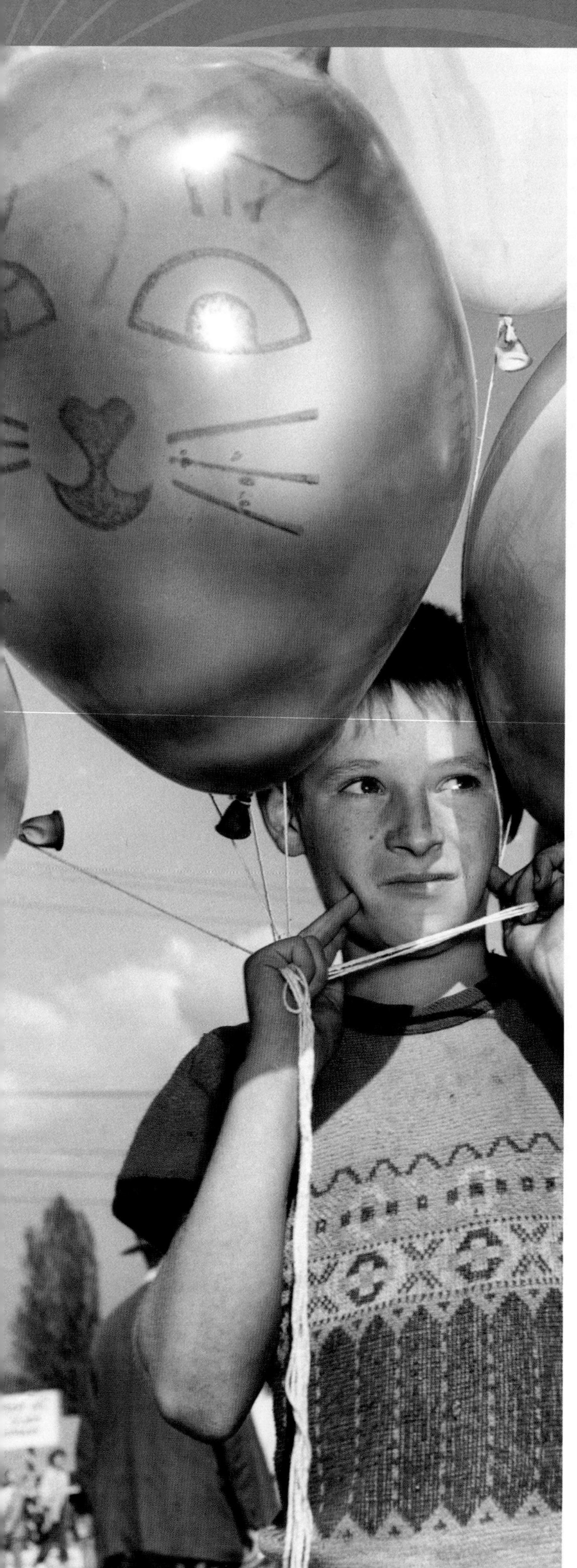

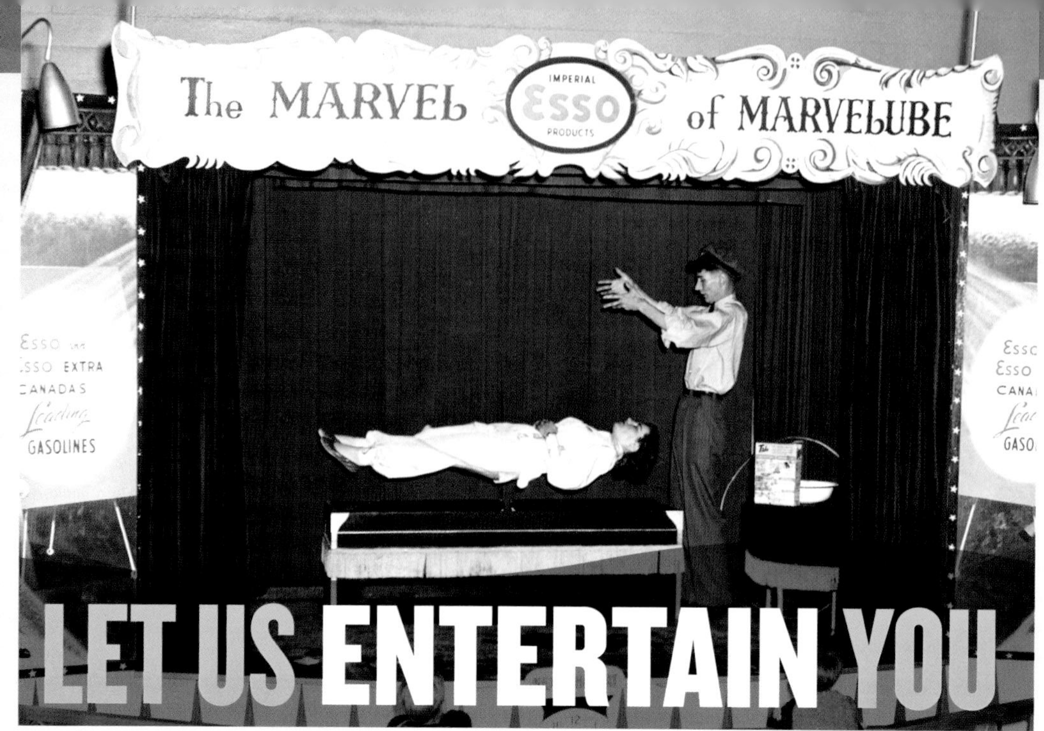

LET US ENTERTAIN YOU

ENTERTAINMENT AT THE PNE was big after the war. Agricultural and industrial displays were major showcases for the city's and province's booming economies. But people were looking for more. And they got it — a smorgasbord of sporting and musical events that would have staggered the imaginations of the V.E.A.'s founders.

AT THE 1950 fair country and western star Wilf Carter headlined a 'western musical extravaganza' (reserved seats, 75 cents to $1.25), followed by a big square dance at the Forum.[1]

The Vancouver Sun

THE SHRINE CIRCUS was such a hit with the public that the PNE offered daily shows for the duration of each Fair.

A THRILLING ACROBATIC stunt is the ride by eight equestrians atop five horses keeping a steady, even pace. This pyramid at the PNE-Shrine-Polack circus ... is by the Giustino-Loyal-Repensky group.[2]

The Vancouver Sun

A BIG DRAWING card in the evening continues to be the Western Music Round-up and Extravaganza. With the finals scheduled for Saturday, an Arabian violinist seems to be heading the 'fiddling' field in this $17,000 feature. He is Ameen Ganam, lead violinist in the CBC orchestra, Edmonton.[3]

The Vancouver Sun

"I USED TO come here as a child with my grandmother and parents on the buses. We kids in the interior of British Columbia got free PNE passes. I have missed very few fairs since 1950!"

Colleen Shaw, *PNE Memory Book*, 1999

FROM LEFT: For kids, fun at the Fair always included balloons, 1953. The Marvel Magic Show wowed audiences, 1953.
NEXT PAGE, INSET: The circus served up amazing feats of daring, such as tightrope artists who walked the wire in ice skates, 1953.

'Mr. Reporter, can I join the circus please?' She was candy-floss-coated and her arms were bulging with souvenirs ... The Vancouver Sun picked a tiny eight-year-old girl to help judge the 2 hour long extravaganza. She was Donna, from the Loyal Protestant Home for children in New Westminster. And she was just one of a crowd of 4,500, most of them children, who LAPPED UP THE FANFARE, THE NOISE, THE CLOWNS AND THE EXCITEMENT OF OPENING DAY AT THE CIRCUS.'[4]

The Vancouver Sun

Pride and smash hit of the Pacific National Exhibition and one of the truly Canadian displays this year is the ROYAL CANADIAN MOUNTED POLICE MUSICAL RIDE. The nightly 20-minute ride by the 32 mounted men on superbly-trained and superbly-conditioned steeds is as Canadian as the Eskimos in the Arctic exhibit.[5] *The Vancouver Sun*

WORLD TRAVEL BECAME a lot easier and more affordable in the 1950s, so the PNE made sure that exotic places got top billing.

A KISS ON the cheek and a lei of Hawaiian flowers were what Miss PNE (Delle Calhoun) got from Bill Lincoln when she welcomed a group of Hawaiian entertainers who arrived Saturday to perform at the PNE which opens Wednesday. Lincoln is one of the Hawaiians who may be seen daily at the exhibition.[6] *The Vancouver Daily Province*

ONE OF THE outstanding features was the Western Air Command Band and Drill Team which appeared for the first four days of the Exhibition prior to going to San Diego where they won international honours.[7] *PNE Bulletin*

THOUSANDS OF PLEASURE-LOVING PEOPLE AGREE — THERE'S A WORLD TO SEE AT THE P.N.E. ... Visit the giant 80 x 76 foot Challenger relief map of the Province; listen to the Band Concerts, watch the world's champion Tree Climber; then let yourself go for the time of your life at the Shrine–P.N.E. Circus, the Race Track, the free Outdoor Theatre. IT'S THE BIGGEST, HAPPIEST FAIR IN THE WEST ...[8] Poster ad in *The Vancouver Sun*

CLOCKWISE FROM TOP LEFT: The RCMP's famed Musical Ride, 1958. Girls on a Tilt-A-Whirl. In the 1953 PNE parade a majorette toes the line on Hastings, in front of the Marine Building. A military band serenades the Fair from the Outdoor Theatre, 1950.

GET ON YOUR HOBBY HORSE

WITH THE CANADIAN economy on a roll, people had money and time to spend on a host of at-home pursuits. If you were looking for a hobby, the PNE was the place to find it.

CIRCLING THE INTERIOR of the big building are glass cases of the most ornate, intricate and clever samples of household arts. All the colours and textures of fabrics and fancy work are there. There are crocheted doilies, place mats and table cloths, fine as gossamer. There are knitted and crocheted baby clothes and carriage robes to gladden the heart of any mother. There are rugged Indian-type sweaters, cuddly shearing toys, cozy slippers, brilliant quilts, delicate-looking but warm afghans made of soft wool in rich, warm colours.[9]

The Vancouver Sun

HE DOESN'T KNOW who counted them, but Ben Williams will insist that there really are four million toothpicks in that model circus in the hobby show at the PNE. Just like a proud father with his first-born, Mr. Williams, general manager of the fair, will stop his duties any time to take visitors on a personally-conducted tour ... Visitors were astounded at the six-foot ferris wheel, and the merry-go-round with its toothpick horses and carriages.[10]

The Vancouver Sun

THE WOOL BUREAU of Canada, Paton and Baldwin Limited, and the Hudson's Bay Company co-operated with us to present a Fashion Show of wool and wool fabric garments; this phase of the show was supplemented by an educational exhibit of the Canada Department of Agriculture featuring the wool industry.[11]

PNE Bulletin

THE INTEREST SHOWN in our Home Arts Show was indicated again this year by a further increase in entries in various classes. The new feature of giving demonstrations of actual judging of exhibits was appreciated ... The working displays were, as expected, of great interest. These included the two days of pottery making; two days demonstrating needlework art; two days of demonstrations by the Weavers' Guild, on a table loom, and some judging demonstrations and the knitting bee.[12]

PNE Bulletin

FROM TOP: In the 1950s the PNE showcased the arts, crafts and hobbies — everything from totem pole carvers to crocheters.

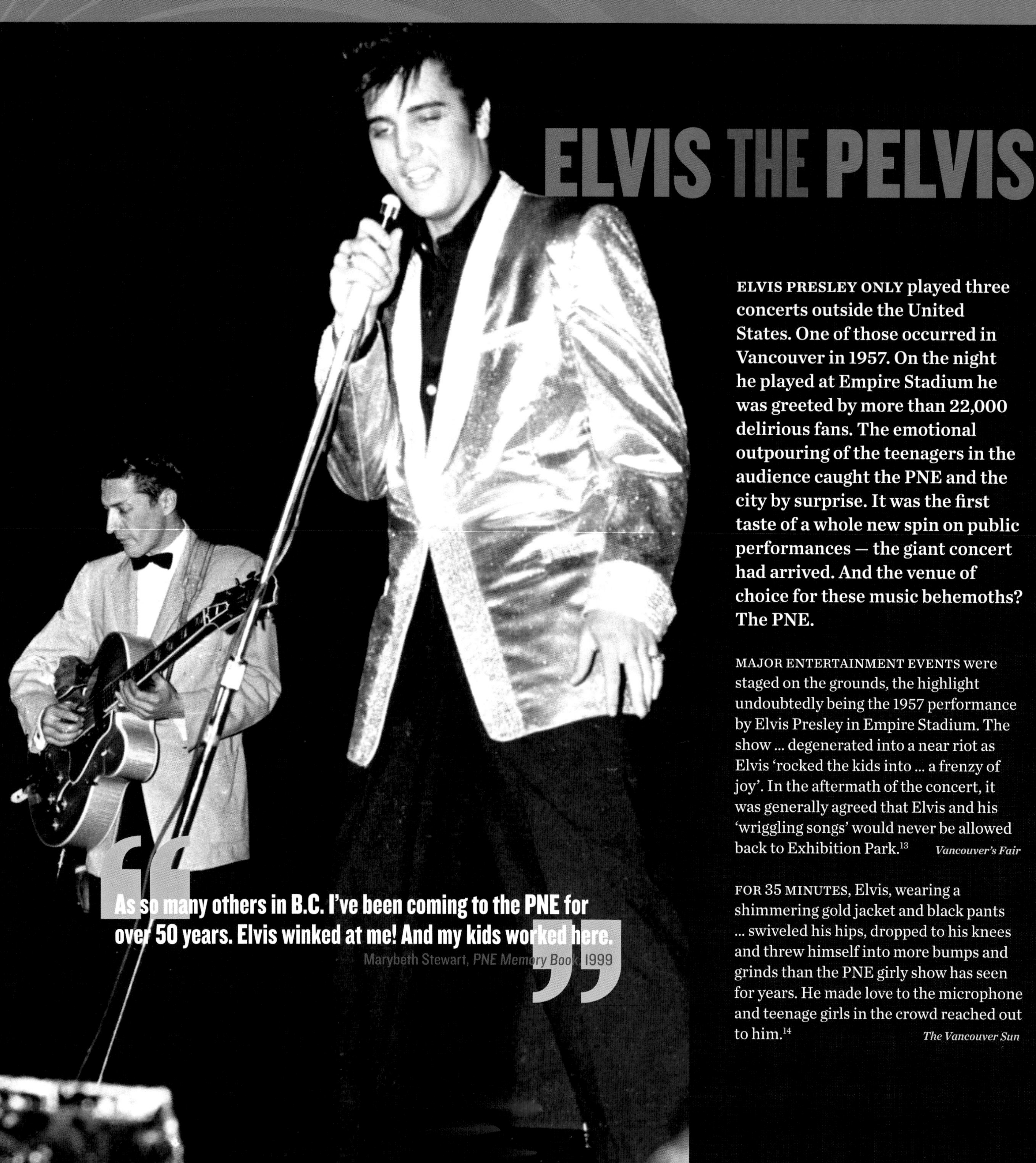

ELVIS THE PELVIS

ELVIS PRESLEY ONLY played three concerts outside the United States. One of those occurred in Vancouver in 1957. On the night he played at Empire Stadium he was greeted by more than 22,000 delirious fans. The emotional outpouring of the teenagers in the audience caught the PNE and the city by surprise. It was the first taste of a whole new spin on public performances — the giant concert had arrived. And the venue of choice for these music behemoths? The PNE.

MAJOR ENTERTAINMENT EVENTS were staged on the grounds, the highlight undoubtedly being the 1957 performance by Elvis Presley in Empire Stadium. The show ... degenerated into a near riot as Elvis 'rocked the kids into ... a frenzy of joy'. In the aftermath of the concert, it was generally agreed that Elvis and his 'wriggling songs' would never be allowed back to Exhibition Park.[13] *Vancouver's Fair*

FOR 35 MINUTES, Elvis, wearing a shimmering gold jacket and black pants ... swiveled his hips, dropped to his knees and threw himself into more bumps and grinds than the PNE girly show has seen for years. He made love to the microphone and teenage girls in the crowd reached out to him.[14] *The Vancouver Sun*

"As so many others in B.C. I've been coming to the PNE for over 50 years. Elvis winked at me! And my kids worked here."

Marybeth Stewart, *PNE Memory Book*, 1999

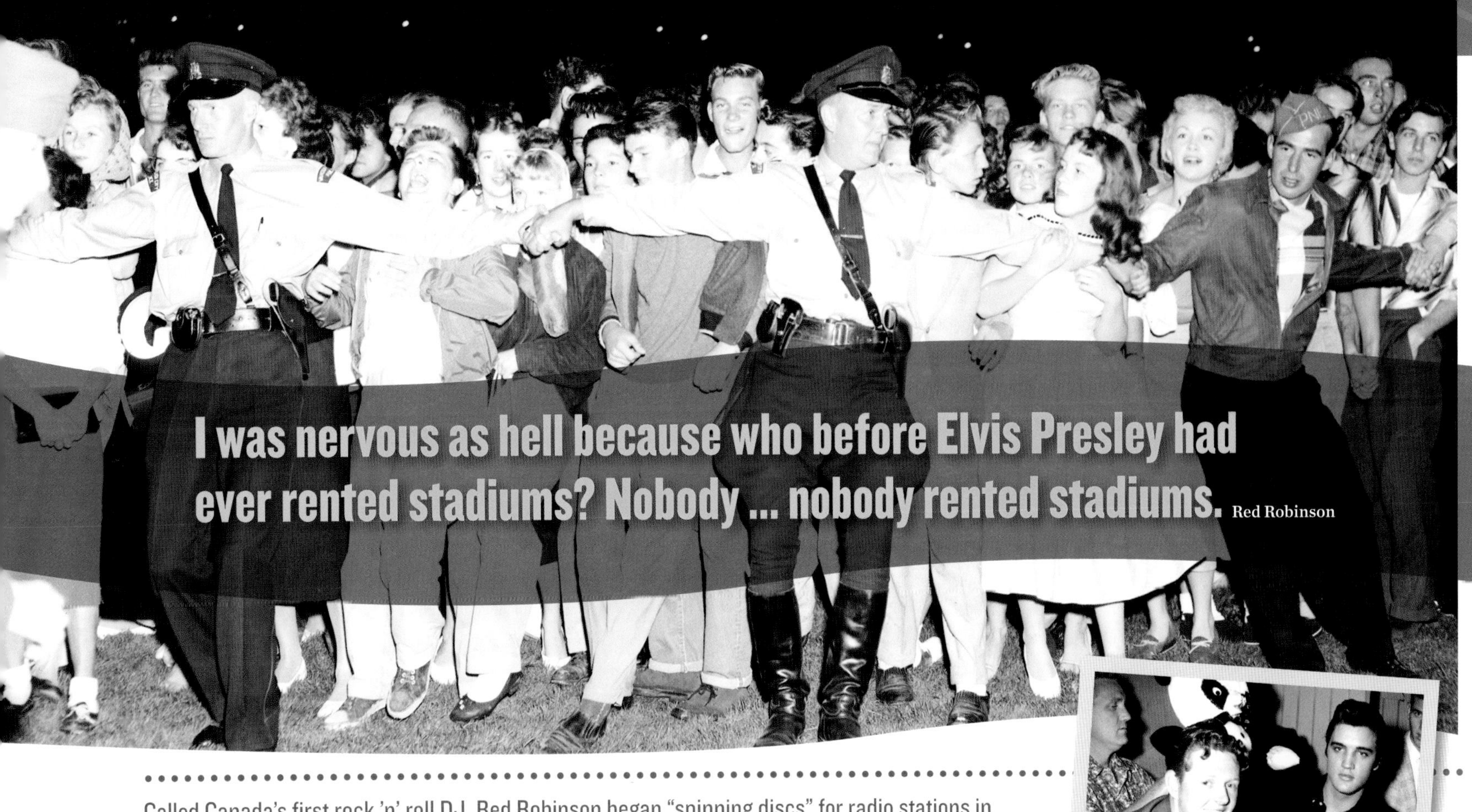

I was nervous as hell because who before Elvis Presley had ever rented stadiums? Nobody ... nobody rented stadiums. Red Robinson

Called Canada's first rock 'n' roll DJ, Red Robinson began "spinning discs" for radio stations in 1952 at the age of 15. Five years later he found himself the master of ceremonies for the Elvis Presley concert. After picking up Elvis from the train station, Red escorted him to the Georgia Hotel where he would be staying and later to Empire Stadium where he would perform.

HE LOCKED ME TO A SHOWER ROD

"HE WAS A nice, down-to-earth guy, about six feet tall and built like an NFL quarterback — he struck me as a big, strong guy. I waited with him in the B.C. Lions' dressing room in the pit of Empire Stadium while the warm-up acts were underway. He paced up and down. I was used to emceeing shows by this time but I was nervous as hell because who before Elvis Presley had ever rented stadiums? Nobody. Maybe Bing Crosby or Bob Hope for troops overseas, or at big conventions, but nobody rented stadiums.

While we were waiting, Elvis walked over to where two police officers were standing by the door of the dressing room. He asked, politely, because Elvis was always polite, if he could borrow their handcuffs. Then he walked back over to me. 'I can see you're nervous and I am too,' Elvis said to me. 'Do me a favour and put your arms up over that shower rod there.' Then he said something about learning a routine for the movie *Jailhouse Rock* and handcuffed me to the curtain rod. 'Now you're locked in here,' he said and threw the key across the floor where I couldn't see it. I wasn't scared at first. Until Elvis started looking for the key and couldn't find it. He got the cops looking for the key too. I was thinking, Jesus, I have the most important star in the world and I'm not going to be able to introduce him because he locked me to a shower rod.

Well it was all a joke. Elvis finally started laughing. He had the key all the time. I found out later Elvis was known to be a practical joker."

At the end of the show, Elvis escaped through a trapdoor in the stage. He waited under the boards with Robinson while an Elvis stand-in made a dash for a limo. It worked. The crowds followed the stand-in. The real Elvis was able to climb out of his hiding hole into another vehicle that whisked him back to his hotel. Robinson went to his radio station for his late-night show and played Elvis records until 2 a.m. At the end of his shift, Robinson got a call on his private studio line. It was Elvis. He wanted to thank Robinson personally and say goodbye.

FACING PAGE: Elvis brings down the house at his 1957 Empire Stadium concert.
FROM TOP: Teenagers went wild for Elvis during his visit to Vancouver. When he was just starting out, well-known radio personality Red Robinson emceed his show.

MIRACLE MILE

IN 1954, THE province, city and PNE staged one of the biggest sporting events ever held in Canada — the British Empire and Commonwealth Games. The games received international coverage and local viewers had the chance to watch the events on TV, broadcast by the CBC's new station, CBUT, launched just in time for the games. An outdoor stadium was built. A naming competition produced monikers such as Totem Bowl and Evergreen Bowl. In the end, it became known as Empire Stadium.

SECURING THE BRITISH Empire Games was a major coup for Vancouver and the Pacific National Exhibition ... To allow for construction of the stadium, the P.N.E. had to close down the golf course and a recently built driving range.[16]

The Pacific National Exhibition: An Illustrated History

The highlight of the games, and one of the most memorable moments in sports history, occurred at the Empire Stadium in the finals of the one-mile race. The first man to break the four-minute mile, Roger Bannister, was challenged by Australian John Landy. THE CONTEST WAS A CLASSIC CONFRONTATION, with Bannister pulling ahead in the stretch and with BOTH COMPETITORS BREAKING THE FOUR-MINUTE BARRIER.[15]

Vancouver's Fair

FROM LEFT: At the 1954 British Empire and Commonwealth Games, Roger Bannister (England) beat John Landy (Australia) in the Miracle Mile. People scooped up memorabilia from the historic games. Bannister and Landy dash for the finish line.

When Premier Gordon Campbell was a boy growing up in Vancouver, the PNE seemed a marvel to him. His father introduced him to some of the wonders of Exhibition Park.

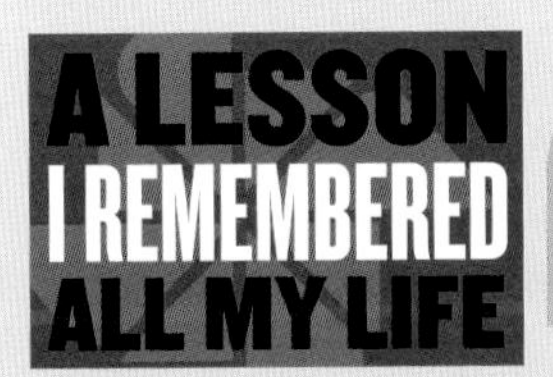

In 1954, my dad came home and told me about the miracle mile. He described how Landy looked behind him when he was still leading Bannister. 'When you're in a race, you never look back,' Dad said. 'You wait until you have crossed the finish line, then you have time to look back.' It's a vivid memory for me and I can still hear him saying that. It's a lesson that I have remembered all my life and used in politics.

The PNE had a couple of firsts for me. I saw my first B.C. Lions game at Empire Stadium. My dad had tickets at the 55-yard line. I can still remember how exciting it was hearing the roar of the crowd.

I also went to my first political rally at the Forum. Prime Minister Diefenbaker was addressing a crowd and there were about 3,000 people in the audience. I was maybe 9 or 10 years old. It seemed big and noisy. I was a small person in a big crowd.

The PNE is important. It defines us as a place. A lot of significant things have happened there.

THERE'S NO BUSINESS LIKE TRADE SHOW BUSINESS

Merchants have always known that a good product demonstration and pitch helps sales. But the age-old art form was limited in scale and magnificence. The '50s changed all that when trade shows became giant public spectacles. The PNE saw the potential; it had the space for these larger-than-life shows enticing car and boat enthusiasts, sports buffs and fashionistas.

Not only is the PNE big business at fair time ... It is big business the year round. Ben Williams, general manager of the PNE, referred to the scores of money-making events that are featured throughout the year at the Exhibition Park.[17] *The Vancouver Province*

Calling attention to the first Northwest Sport and Vacation Show ... were these Kiwanis 'bathing beauties,' who urged President A.D. Richardson to get into the swim, or at least the canoe.[18] *The Vancouver Daily Province*

Other one-time events staged in P.N.E. facilities included a 'warehouse sale' held by Wosk's Department Stores in the Showmart Building in 1958, one of the first retail shows held on the grounds.[19] *Vancouver's Fair*

I was about eight or nine [in the late '50s] when Dad first started taking me and my brother Jim to the PNE's car and boat shows. It was a big deal for the two of us, piling into the car right after school on a weekday afternoon and driving all the way in from New Westminster. Jim was keen on cars then, but it was the boat show that got me.

I remember arriving at the fairgrounds and seeing the buildings lit up like it was Christmas. We went through the towering front gates and joined a huge crowd moving through the Forum, Showmart and Garden Auditorium. It was dark and cold outside. Then, we'd pass through one of the doors into dazzling light that showed off everything from sporty little outboards to giant yachts. There was something about the smooth, sleek lines of those impossibly big boats, towering over us, perched so precariously on blocks or trailers that made it seem all the more amazing.

Some people gawked and pointed. Others looked like they were in serious negotiations with smartly dressed sales people who talked effortlessly about their product. A couple of times we'd get invited to step up into some of the swankier boats and would peer into galleys and heads. I always made a grab for the glossy brochures, so I could take the fantasy home. John Alexander

ABOVE: The Boat Show was one of the earliest and best-known consumer shows at the PNE.

A TOWN WITHIN A CITY

IN THE DAYS before big performance venues downtown, many of Vancouver's biggest popular-culture moments happened at the PNE. With the Forum, the Garden Auditorium and new buildings — Empire Stadium and the B.C. Building — the PNE soon turned into B.C.'s premier entertainment district.

REAL AUSTRIAN DANCES are only part of the reason students from Austrian universities are touring Canada and the U.S. Their music, poetry, drama and good fellowship are all designed to give North America an introduction to Austrian culture. The group ... will perform at the Garden Auditorium at 8:15 p.m. under the Canadian Folk Society auspices.[20]

The Vancouver Daily Province

THE NEW MOVIE theatre in our British Columbia Building was opened for the first time this year. The National Film Board ... presented 110 shows to a total audience of 33,844 persons.[21] *PNE Bulletin*

Throughout the year Exhibition Park still functions as a 'town within a city'. Its 180 acres constitute a small 'boom-town' where day and night events vie for public attention and parking space. Often two or three are staged at the same time and often they are of provincial or national import such as car and boat shows, conventions, conferences, religious and organizational meetings. And always there are indoor and outdoor sports of one type or another: hockey, ice-skating, roller-skating, soccer and national football, wrestling and boxing. During the daylight hours scores of young men attend at the trades and technical schools that run continually through the fall, winter and spring months. In the administration building, utilizing the entire lower floors, the Vancouver Police Academy conducts classes that transform raw recruits into trained members of Vancouver's finest. The ever-changing and expanding B.C. scene, with its exploding population and industrial and residential growth, is setting the stage of Exhibition Park for a continuing role of unprecedented magnitude in the future of this province.[22]

PNE President's Report

ABOVE: An aerial view of the PNE in 1957.

To my mind the Exhibition has much in common with a University. Both teach the Art of Living but from different angles. The University teaches chiefly intellectual knowledge and scientific studies. THE EXHIBITION ... TEACHES THE ART OF LIVING THROUGH 'INTERESTING COMPELLING EXHIBITS'.[23] Letter sent to the PNE

CLOCKWISE FROM TOP LEFT: The huge ski jump, built for an international competition, dominated the PNE grounds in 1958. At the 1953 Fair, the entrance to the Shrine Circus and Austin automobiles on display. The Fair in 1952. Crowds gather in front of the 1957 PNE Prize Home. If your your feet were tired, Jitney Rides were a fun way to get around the Fair in 1950.

FUN AT THE FAIR
Two girls share a 1950s midway moment. Popular kids' TV programs such as *Fun-O-Rama* offered daily free shows at the Fair, 1965.

FREE

PNE "fun-o-rama theatre"

Every day during the Exhibition

GARDEN AUDITORIUM

Starring at 2 P.M.

★ JOE BODRIE *The fastest gun alive*

★ DENNY *The smallest and youngest elephant ever trained*

★ CHATTER THE CHIMP *The most unusual comedy star*

2:30 to 4:00 P.M. ★ CARTOONS

Brought to you by your good friends

Pillsburys

FUNNY FACE DRINKS

LOWNEY'S

Sunbeam

ENRICHED BREAD

NABISCO Shreddies

braves Children's Shoes

WATCH! FUN-O-RAMA! – 4 p.m. Every Playday

ON EXCITING KVOS-TV Channel 12

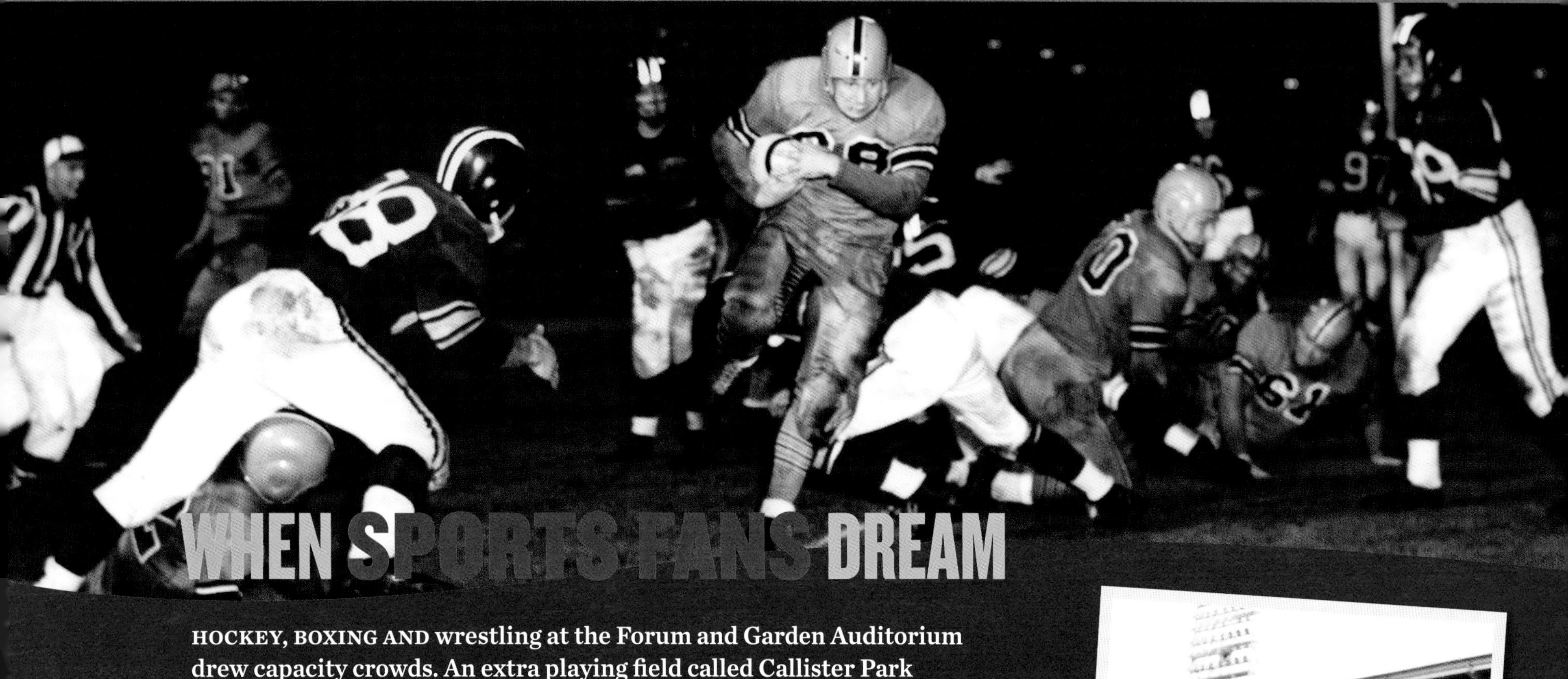

WHEN SPORTS FANS DREAM

HOCKEY, BOXING AND wrestling at the Forum and Garden Auditorium drew capacity crowds. An extra playing field called Callister Park became part of the PNE and was home to the city's soccer elite. Once Empire Stadium was completed, Vancouver had an impressive home for its new professional football franchise.

A GROUP OF eager Vancouverites formed the city's first professional football club in 1953. But they needed to convince the Western Interprovincial Football Union (WIFU) that the city had what it took to stage big sporting events — it boiled down to providing a place that could seat lots of paying customers. In no time, the PNE had the solution.

VANCOUVER WAS GRANTED a conditional franchise, on the requirements of a 15,000 seat stadium, selling 6,500 season tickets and guaranteed travel expenses of the visiting teams. All the pieces began to fall into place when it was announced that Vancouver would host the 1954 British Empire Games, and that it would mean the building of a new stadium — Empire Stadium.

BCLions.com

WHATTA LIFE! Middleweight and light heavy champion, Leo Logan, reposes on a stool as gal friend Norma Mantine wipes sweat from his brow. Logan won both titles Friday night in the PROVINCIAL BOXING CHAMPIONSHIPS AT EXHIBITION GARDENS. Oh yes. The girlfriend weighs in at a petite 108.[24]

The Vancouver Daily Province

FROM TOP: The first BC Lions' touchdown in a game against the Winnipeg Blue Bombers, at Empire Stadium, 1954. BC Lion number 88 at practice. Boxing at the PNE was a big draw — here Kenney Lindsay and Jackie Turner square off at the Gardens in 1948.
NEXT PAGE, FROM TOP: Rain or shine, the Lions' cheerleaders were always ready to go. CKNW radio's Bill Good Jr. was always on hand for the games as a child. At the other end of Exhibition Park crowds packed Callister Park for soccer games.

EXCITING STUFF FOR A TEENAGE FOOTBALL FAN

Bill Good Jr., co-anchor of the local CTV evening news, has long been a fixture on the Vancouver television and radio scene. News and sports runs in his blood as his father, Bill Good Sr., was also a famous journalist and sportscaster. He introduced his son to the PNE at an early age.

"I REMEMBER GOING to hundreds of football games over the years at the old Empire Stadium. My dad covered the BC Lions and he did a post-game radio show at CKNW called 'Touchdown Topics.' I used to sit in the car and listen to it while I waited for him to come out and see what guests he would be delivering to their downtown hotels. I'd meet people like footballers Rollie Miles and Jackie Parker. It was pretty exciting stuff for a teenage football fan. My mother used to go along in the early days to the Lions' games and we'd sit together. Then I gravitated to going with friends and eventually I covered the Lions myself.

I was probably 10 or 11 when I met hockey players Maurice 'The Rocket' Richard and Gordie Howe when I was with my father — that was before the Pacific Coliseum, back in the old Forum.

When I came to CTV we used to broadcast live from the PNE for seven years. I've shaken thousands of hands at the Fair.

We took our kids several times to the PNE. It's like going to Disneyland, only it's closer and you tend to do it more often. It's something most families enjoy. Now my kids are taking their kids. My oldest boy has two daughters. It goes full circle."

SOCCER FANS SATURDAY WILL SEE ONE OF THE GAMES THAT THEY HAVE BEEN WAITING FOR FOR ALMOST THREE MONTHS — New Westminster Royals' Frank Ambler and Dave Brown playing against their old club, North Shore, at Callister Park ... Against North Shore, Saturday, however, Royals' manager Malcolm Peacock says BROWN AND AMBLER WILL GIVE HIS LINE THE PUNCH THEY NEED TO BEAT THE REDS.[25] *The Vancouver Daily Province*

THE PRINCESS AND THE PNE

IN 1951 A young princess, soon to be crowned Queen and with husband in tow, thrilled citizens with an afternoon visit to the PNE.

ONE OF THE outstanding highlights of this year was the visit of Their Royal Highnesses, Princess Elizabeth and Prince Philip, to Exhibition Park. Their Royal Highnesses visited a Folk Festival display in the Garden Building, and from there, an exhibition lacrosse game staged by the Inter-city Lacrosse Association in the Forum.[26] *PNE Bulletin*

LEFT TO RIGHT: Princess Elizabeth, with Prince Philip, on their 1951 Canadian tour that brought them to Vancouver and the PNE. Returning eight years later as Queen, Elizabeth, along with Philip, visited the PNE again and attended an event at Empire Stadium in July 1959.

A "SPANKING NEW" MIDWAY

IN 1953, THE B.C. Building was completed. The imposing modernist structure offered manufacturing exhibits and a movie theatre and became the new home of the famed Lipsett Museum. But the crowd pleaser was the giant new Challenger topographical map of B.C. Then, in 1957, work started on an all-new amusement park — Happyland came down and Playland went up.

The coloured map, made of 968,428 separate pieces of plywood, took seven years to build.

PREMIER W.A.C. BENNETT, Mayor Fred Hume and PNE directors took a record two minute-twenty second trip the length of B.C. Wednesday and saw every tiny bay and inlet; mountain peak and river; city and village from a cloudless 140,000 feet up. They got the rocket's-eye view without leaving Exhibition Park, too, and the same opportunity will be afforded almost everybody when the PNE's new $1,400,000 British Columbia building is thrown open to the public. Premier Bennett was dedicating the building and the vast relief map of the province that covers the floor of the rotunda. The coloured map, made of 968,428 separate pieces of plywood, took seven years to build. Horizontal scale is one inch to the mile and the vertical scale of one inch to 1000 feet ... Special tribute was paid to George Challenger and his son Robert who planned and built the huge map.[27] *The Vancouver Province*

CONSTRUCTION OF PLAYLAND began in December 1957, and it was completed in time for the 1958 exhibition.[28] *Vancouver's Fair*

To celebrate B.C.'s Centennial, Canada's second largest exhibition has done a major face lifting job. A key portion of the improvement — a spanking new midway. AND AN EXCITING NEW ROLLER COASTER WHICH WILL SOON BE AS FAMOUS AS THE PNE'S OLD GIANT DIPPER.[29] *The Vancouver Sun*

FROM TOP: Crowds view the Challenger Map, 1955. The new midway in 1959.

ANOTHER PM, ANOTHER OPENING

NICKNAMED "DIEF THE CHIEF," Prime Minister John Diefenbaker arrived in town to open the 1959 Exhibition. Like an earlier PM, Wilfrid Laurier, he found his day at the Fair filled with humorous mishap.

FROM THE SECOND he stepped on the grounds everything went wrong — except John. Surrounded by a series of freak accidents, and mobs of people, the prime minister remained as cool as a summer shower. And the day was HOT. To drive him from the entrance to the Outdoor Theatre where he was to open the fair, PNE officials had hired a horse-drawn carriage from Victoria expressly for the purpose. But John never got the buggy ride. Someone stole the reins. A cream-coloured Cadillac was substituted and the prime minister and his wife Olive, pulled up in front of the platform. But the cheers he heard weren't for John. A motorcycle aerial act, 'The Kings and Queen of the Air,' were just completing their breath-taking finale on a high wire 120 feet above his head. Then, when the crowd turned to cheer the prime minister, the dare-devil team took their bow. But nobody was watching them ... At the platform, PNE general manager Bert Morrow asked the audience to rise for the Royal Canadian Air Force Band's playing of *O Canada*. The audience of 14,000 rose. After 15 seconds of silence Morrow said, 'The band has apparently left.' They had.[31]

The Vancouver Sun

THROUGH THE COMEDY of errors that marked his PNE visit, Prime Minister Diefenbaker's good humour prevailed. He gave a rousing speech to open the Fair, praising the PNE's "Salute the Orient" theme for that year.

I HAVE NEVER BEEN SO PROUD AS I AM TODAY OF BEING A CANADIAN AND OF BEING PART OF THIS WONDERFUL EFFORT BY THE PNE to bring a closer understanding between the nations of the world. It is by endeavours such as this one, where the peoples of many nations, creeds and customs meet on common ground, united by a common purpose, sympathy and understanding, that FIRM AND LASTING PEACE WILL BE ACHIEVED IN THIS WORLD WHERE THE AGE-LONG BARRIERS OF GEOGRAPHY NO LONGER EXIST.[30]

PNE Bulletin

ABOVE: Prime Minister John Diefenbaker and his wife, Olive, open the 1959 Fair.

BIRTHDAY BASH

BRITISH COLUMBIA CELEBRATED its centenary in 1958. Displays and events at the PNE were lavish; among them a giant rocketry display that fired the public imagination after the Soviet Union's 1957 launch of *Sputnik*.

A SILVERY, 108-FOOT, three-stage rocket will 'rise above' Exhibition Park to focus attention on the Pacific National Exhibition's 'outer space' theme this year. PNE directors have termed the display 'startlingly different' from anything previously shown at the exhibition ... The rocket, an aluminum replica of the one that sent the first *Sputnik* into orbit around the world, is rising seven storeys above the ground. It will be the most dramatic section of 'Project X,' which directors have kept under wraps for the last six months. Exhibition visitors will also be able to see an 'Honest John' tactical air missile from Fort Lewis, Wash.

The surface-to-surface missile ... has a 16-mile range. With the missile will be a 41,250-pound launcher and a crew of 6 men to explain its workings. It is the latest missile to be taken off the secret list by the U.S. At the rocket's base will be a space science show from New York. The exhibit will show a rocket in flight, complete with blast-off, and reproducing the beeping voices of satellites circling the earth.[32] *The Vancouver Sun*

ABOVE AND INSET: Rockets on display at the B.C. Centennial celebration, 1958.
RIGHT: A roving "Pioneer" promotes the Centennial celebrations at the 1958 Fair.

COASTER CITY

From the 1915 Coaster to today's big-thrill ride, Vancouver has had a love affair with these HEART-PUMPING, SCARE-INDUCING, ROCKETING, ROLLING RIDES.

A group of traveling monks found a whole new reality, 1990s.

The Dipper in 1923.

The Giant Dipper in 1932.

The roller coaster in the 1950s.

It's a long way down, 1950.

Another group thrill, 2005.

Everybody! Do "the wave," 2006.

Throw up your arms, scream and laugh, 1993.

There's nothing like a sunset from the coaster, 2008.

QUARTERBACK CLUB
CKNW

CHAPTER 6

1960–1969

A WHOLE NEW GENERATION

'60–'69

By 1964, the space race had produced gadgets like this jet pack that was demonstrated at the Fair.

HIPPIES AND HIGH RISES

The postwar boom took hold in the 1960s, affecting Vancouver in many ways. Inspired by the ideas of forward-thinking architects like Arthur Erickson, the city's downtown grew ever more skyward with the construction of concrete and glass office towers and modern highrise apartment buildings filling the densely populated West End. Baby Boom children came of age and headed west as Vancouver lured transient youth from across the country and gained the title "Hippie Capital of Canada."

KITSILANO'S FOURTH AVENUE transformed from a working-class neighbourhood to our version of San Francisco's Haight-Ashbury district, crowded with university drop-outs and draft dodgers escaping the United States' unpopular war in Vietnam. Never before had youth so flagrantly questioned authority and conventional wisdom. The mini-skirt craze began, bikinis appeared on the beaches and some women abandoned their bras as they adhered to the "burn your bra" slogan, so popular with the new women's liberation movement. In the late 1960s, a group of radicals calling themselves the Don't Make a Wave Committee decided to take on the American military-industrial complex by trying to prevent the testing of nuclear weapons in Alaska; they later renamed themselves Greenpeace.

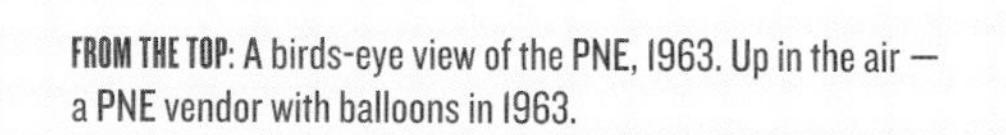

FROM THE TOP: A birds-eye view of the PNE, 1963. Up in the air — a PNE vendor with balloons in 1963.

—Bob Dibble Photo

PACIFISTS demonstrating against war in Viet Nam slumped in path of PNE parade in 100 block West Hastings, only to be carted off in police paddy wagons. Incident was only one to mar parade.

These movements impacted the PNE as protesters made their presence felt during the parade and the Fair. When police asked them to leave, they did so quietly. Exhibition organizers heeded these youthful concerns, though, and made adjustments to their programs. They also began to cater to the new tastes in music with Teen Dances and Teen Fairs. The Beatles shook Empire Stadium in 1964, leading the way for a series of pop and rock star appearances at the PNE through the next decades. Other big music stars included Frank Sinatra Jr., Rosemary Clooney and a Motown musician they called Stevie Wonder in the days before the affectionate epithet "Little" was added to his name.

In 1963, Her Excellency Señora Eva Sámano de López Mateos, the wife of Mexico's president, became the first woman to officially open the PNE. Thomas Fyfe, the PNE president, presented Mexico's First Lady with a uniquely Canadian artifact — an Inuit carving. The PNE maintained its multicultural thrust, started in the 1950s, with ongoing international entertainment and exotic foods from faraway lands.

Forestry and mining continued to underpin the provincial economy. In 1960, the PNE started a new Timber Carnival with loggers showing off their brawn by trying to be the fastest to scramble up long poles and even faster on the way back down. These, as well as tricky log-rolling competitions, became instant hits with fairgoers.

Sports fans also had much to cheer about. In 1964, the football season culminated in Toronto with Joe Kapp quarterbacking the BC Lions football team to its first Grey Cup win. Hockey fans rejoiced in 1969 when they learned that the Vancouver Canucks were joining the National Hockey League. The Pacific Coliseum had just been completed the year before, able to accommodate around 16,000 spectators and readily adaptable for exhibition and trade show purposes.

After four years of planning, the PNE celebrated Canada's 1967 centennial year with a Festival of Forestry and a big birthday party bash at Empire Stadium. The PNE showed it was not only up to showcasing a city, province and nation, but that it attracted a myriad of cultures to Vancouver from around the world. International cultural acts and influences, including music and culinary arts, flooded into the Fair each year.

CLOCKWISE FROM TOP LEFT: Vietnam protestors at the 1965 PNE parade. Kids at the Fair in 1966. A logger shows his might at the 1969 Timber Carnival.

Our PNE Has 'GROWED UP' Since Sir Wilfrid's Day.[1]

The Vancouver Sun

"CAAANAAADA, NOW WE ARE TWENTY MILLION"

THE PNE TURNED 50 in 1960, and Vancouver, the province and Canada celebrated big milestones too. Vancouver had its 75th anniversary in 1961, 1966 marked the centenary of the colonies of Vancouver Island and British Columbia amalgamating, and in 1967 Canada turned 100. What better place than the PNE to stage some splashy festivities?

BACK IN 1910, when the Pacific National Exhibition was born as the Vancouver Exhibition, an estimated 68,000 persons turned out for the official opening by ... Sir Wilfrid Laurier. They paid 50 cents each to get in, wandered through exhibits set up among the trees, 'oo-ed' and 'ah-ed' at the four-square, turreted and glass-domed 'Exhibition Building' ... This year, its golden anniversary, the PNE expects to draw an attendance of at least a million persons. If the PNE pulls in its million patrons this year, it will be the third largest fair on the North American continent, behind only Toronto's Canadian National Exhibition and the Dallas Fair, in Texas.[2]

The Vancouver Sun

FOR SOME YEARS, the PNE had been looking for a peg on which to hang a theme that would honor the seas, the lifeblood of Vancouver's existence, growth and prosperity. The 75th anniversary was a natural one and in the early spring, the PNE announced that it would salute Vancouver's birthday with a Marine Festival.[3]

PNE Bulletin

IF ANY SINGLE production at the Marine Festival impinged a dramatic punctuation mark on the theme centre, it was Willie the Whale ... Willie with his interior tastefully highlighting a fairyland walk-through featuring King Neptune, upstaged every theme attraction at the Fair. Thousands queued daily to tour his tummy and his sly and roving eye was a come-one for every professional and amateur photographer at the Park.[4]

PNE Bulletin

THE PACIFIC NATIONAL Exhibition this year [1966] saluted British Columbia's Centenary with a 14-day 'Centennial Jamboree' — the brightest, boomingest, most boisterous PNE in history.[5]

PNE Annual Report

FROM LEFT: Cover of the 1960 Fair program. Prime Minister Lester Pearson was on hand for the parade in 1965. The PNE's 50th Anniversary float in 1960.

PREMIER W.A.C. BENNETT was on hand to open the Exhibition's 1966 B.C. centennial celebration. He also inaugurated other important parts of the PNE that saluted the province's first hundred years.

PREMIER BENNETT OFFICIALLY opened a magnificent collection of paintings, the 'Confederation Life Association's Gallery of Canadian History' which was located throughout the 14 days of the 1966 PNE on the ground floor of the Modern Living Building.[6]

PNE Annual Report

THE YEAR 1967 will long be remembered as the year of the 'Big Birthday Party' with celebrations staged throughout the land. Exhibition Park was no exception ... Nowhere was the spirit of this Centennial year more in evidence than at the Birthday Party staged at Empire Stadium on July 1st, which proved to be one of the most successful Dominion Day celebrations in the whole of Canada.[7]

PNE Annual Report

FROM LEFT: Premier W.A.C. Bennett gets up close and personal with a parade clown, 1966. Miss PNE for 1966 poses with the big birthday cake for the province's 100th anniversary, 1967.

A TOP-NOTCH PLACE FOR ANIMALS AND OTHER THINGS

TO GREAT FANFARE, the PNE opened its new agricultural arena in 1963: the Agrodome. With a 3,200-person capacity, the state-of-the-art facility was the envy of livestock and rodeo venues across Canada. During the year, it hosted an array of other big events.

Rodeo Glamour

YOU CAN BET your silver spurs that not only the animals will be colorful out at the Pacific National Exhibition's spanking new agricultural building. The 3,200-seat Agrodome, which is being opened this evening by Agriculture Minister Harry Hays, will be 'city corral' for some pretty spectacular riding during the next two weeks — and some of the most eye-opening garb you ever did see on western folk as well. No longer restricted to the dusty tones of barnyard and rangeland, you'll see cowgirls and cowboys in startling pinks and purples, brilliant oranges and greens.[8] *The Vancouver Sun*

HOW DOES HE DO THAT?

"IT WAS CHRISTMAS 1963, and the Moscow Circus was in town. I had no idea I was going until Mom popped it on me on Christmas Eve. It all seemed a very exciting and a terribly exotic way to celebrate Christmas — have dinner then drive to the Agrodome to catch an evening performance. We were all abuzz too because these were Russians coming to town — in 1964 they were still pretty scary to contemplate.

When we got to our seats, the Agrodome was done up like a giant circus tent with the great round dome rising over us. Down on the sawdust there were all kinds of acts. The one I remember vividly was the tightrope walker who climbed up a thin-looking rope that was on a 45 degree angle. He had nothing but his toes to get a grip on the steeply angled rope.

There was no net. I wondered, 'How does he do that,' and watched, holding my breath until he reached a tiny platform way up under the dome."

Norma Butler

CLOCKWISE FROM TOP LEFT: Bessies on parade — livestock muster for the Agrodome opening, 1963. Tightrope walking at the circus, 1964. Crowds in front of the new Agrodome.

BRINGING THE FARM TO THE CITY

BY THE MIDDLE of the century, urban culture was the norm in Canada. Fewer folks lived in small towns and on farms, and the general populace was getting a bit unclear about where their food came from and how it was grown. The PNE saw another opportunity and reintroduced the farmer to the city-dweller with an expanded Agricultural Show.

THE FUR AND feathers show was 'Easter in August' for the young and the living story of B.C.'s vast poultry industry for the more serious-minded. Here patrons peered into massive incubators to see chicks in their hundreds 'break-out' into life. They saw a bewildering variety of rainbow-hued game birds, family-conscious rabbits and hamsters, piercingly vocal cage birds, raucously arrogant roosters, placidly prolific hens, bellicose bantams and turkeys, garrulous geese and ducks, peacocks and guinea fowl.[9]

PNE Annual Report

ABOVE: The chicken or the egg? A curious youngster presses her nose to the chick incubator, 1966. (Inset) The Okanagan's wealth of produce on display at the Fair in 1969.

133
CUTEST
4-H
ANIMAL
PACIFIC NATIONAL EXHIBITION
VANCOUVER, CANADA
1969
PARKSVILLE-QUALICUM
4-H
CALF CLUB
The 4-H CLUB
OUR LADNER PURE BRED
JERSEY CALF CLUB WAS
FORMED IN 1937 AND SINCE
THEN HAS SEEN MANY
MEMBERS COME AND GO
WITH A RELUCTANCE TO LEAVE
BUT A HEART FULL OF GRAT-
ITUDE FOR WHAT OUR 4-H
CLUB HAS DONE FOR THEM.
FOR WE NOT ONLY LEARN
TO CARE FOR OUR CALF,
CANADA
LADNE
IMPARTS to its MEMBERS:
FAITH IN GOD.
FAITH IN OUR FELLOW-MEN.
FAITH IN CANADA.
FAITH IN AGRICULTURE
AND HOME-MAKING.
491

HEAD, HEART, HANDS AND HEALTH

THE 4-H CLUB of Canada — the four H's being head, heart, hands and health — was founded in 1913 and had been an integral part of the PNE from the start. The club played a big role in the 1960s, helping the PNE introduce city kids to progressive farming practices. By 1963, the PNE had added a multicultural component by sponsoring visits to the Fair by 4-H children from outside Canada.

FAIR AMBASSADORS FROM Jamaica ... Eulah Witters and Clement Morrison, top 4-H members of that newly-independent country and its first 'goodwill ambassadors' to travel abroad with messages and gifts of state. They spent the most hectic week of their young lives as official guests of the PNE 4-H Show.[10]

PNE Annual Report

THE PROVINCE-WIDE FINALS of 4-H ... brought 436 boys and girls to the PNE for a week-long show that featured a capacity of exhibits and filled our dormitories to overflowing ... Biggest single problem of the PNE 4-H officials right down the line is overcrowding![11]

PNE Annual Report

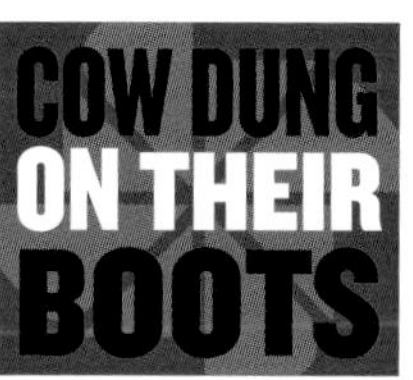

COW DUNG ON THEIR BOOTS

John Friesen has been in the Lower Mainland farming business for over 50 years. He has participated in and contributed to the PNE's 4-H festival for many years. His children attended 4-H events. John is currently the chair of the Agriculture Advisory Committee to the PNE Board and president and chair of B.C. Youth in Agriculture.

"WHEN I WAS 11, I lived with my family on a dairy farm in Ladner. I was in the Holstein calf club in Delta. At the end of summer, we had our calf-raising achievement day in Delta and then after that we went to show our calves at the PNE. It was the highlight of the year for me. It actually still is for most 4-H kids today. They love going to the PNE show.

The week I stayed at the PNE, all of us 4-H kids bunked together in the Hastings Community Centre across the road from the livestock barns. I remember getting up at five o'clock every morning and walking across Hastings Street to the grounds to look after my calves. The others did that too. Then we'd hike back to the Community Centre. By the end of the week, it got pretty rank in there because all the boys came back with cow dung on their boots and sometimes on their clothes. We'd throw our dirty clothes into a big pile until we went home, because that's what kids do!

I started showing cattle again when my son turned 11 in 1973 and he was part of 4-H. In 1976, we had purebred cattle and showed them right across Canada. I always liked coming back to the PNE though. The Agrodome is as good a showplace for cattle as any in the country."

FACING PAGE, CLOCKWISE FROM TOP LEFT: One 4-H member gets the nod from judges for the cutest cow, 1969. Parksville-Qualicum 4-H members proudly display their trophies, 1962. A lamb gives 4-H kids an assist with food delivery, 1965. Ladner boys with their prized heifers.
FROM TOP: Giving the cow a final brush before the competition, 1969. One 4-H kid finds time to play with a nosy heifer.

A 4-H Saanich Holstein contender gets a spruce up before the show, 1960.

A proud 4-H-er gets in the picture with his prize-winning twin calves, 1953.

FARM IN THE CITY

SOME OF THE BEST TIMES AT THE FAIR AT THE PNE ARE SPENT WITH THE ANIMALS.

Girls show a couple of prize roosters, 1953.

Two young comic book fans brush up on their reading between 4-H events, 1953.

Youngsters get a kick out of feeding the animals, 1948.

A 4-H participant proudly shows his prize rabbit, 1988.

Showing off the sheep, 1988

Hands up, who wants to feed the goats?

Getting in some cuddle time with the rabbits, 1948.

WHAT'S A FAIR without food? The PNE satisfied the expectations of regular fairgoers with its usual bonanza of hot dogs, hamburgers, pop and cotton candy. But the city was showing more culinary sophistication, so organizers started developing innovative food shows. People were soon lining up to try samples of local fare and exotic cuisines from around the world.

ANOTHER INNOVATION IN Canada was the PNE Food Circus in the Food Building. In keeping with this year's continental theme, it sold taste treats from nations around the world. A large space was set-up with tables and chairs as a type of sidewalk café.[12]

PNE Annual Report

ACRES OF FOOD it's called, and acres of food it is ... You'll need at least an hour if you're going to make your visit worthwhile. Stop at each booth to chat with the home economists and food demonstrators. Pick up samples of the delicious foods prepared from our own B.C. products ... Plan to take in some of the onstage cooking demonstrations too. Every hour, on the hour, home economists and demonstrators show how easy it is to be creative with B.C. products. The stage, located at the north end of the food exhibits, is equipped with two modern kitchens decorated in cool citrus tones of lemon, orange and lime green.[13]

The Vancouver Sun

Cheryl Prepchuk is the chief executive officer of the Greater Vancouver Food Bank Society. The Food Bank is helped every year by the PNE in its drive to bring food to needy households. The PNE has also been part of Cheryl's life since she was a child.

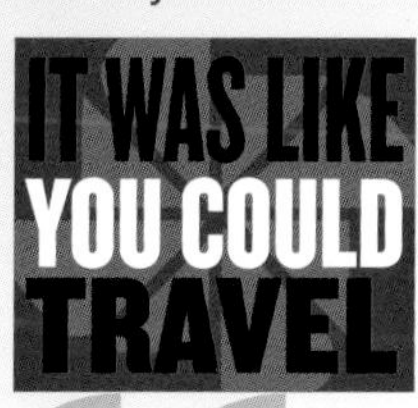

"WHEN I WAS a kid growing up in the East End, I went every year to the PNE. It was an explosion of fun and was the biggest thing that happened, especially for those of us in the East End who didn't necessarily get away on vacation. This was like having a holiday in the heart of the city.

My favourite thing was the food building. There was something about it, even though it was always hot, steamy and smelly with a bunch of different food odours. It always epitomized to me what Vancouver was — a concoction of all kinds of people, all kinds of food and all kinds of cultures. The building was a city within a city. You could walk around and have foods from a variety of countries. It was like a microcosm of the city as it was growing. Everything co-existed so perfectly in the food building.

The food building was like being in another country — you could travel vicariously through the different foods. Taste a curry and be instantly transported to India."

FROM TOP: A day at the Fair isn't complete without cotton candy, 1969. Taste treats at the Fair run the gamut from flapjacks to kebabs.
NEXT PAGE: Cotton candy and hot dogs are Fair essentials.

Mom shows how to feed a sheep, 1982.

Kids lifting kids, 1982.

Feeding time at the Petting Zoo, 1982.

He ate my program! A culinary caper at the Petting Zoo, circa 1980.

"HEY MOM, I'm hungry!" No problem at the PNE fair grounds, which are fair to bursting with delicious foods appealing to all sizes and types of appetites. Debbie and Jim Ansell try super-size hot dogs.

The perennial kids' favourites: cotton candy and candied apples, 1963.

Vancouver's finest take a donut break.

Get a cone at Ernie Dougherty's legendary soft ice cream stand.

A foodie's feast at the Fair might include Asian, then a slice of pizza, followed by classic fish and chips, topped off with a plate of perogies, sausage and a cabbage roll.

FOOD! GLORIOUS FOOD!

At the Fair, everyone bends their food rules: find the whale's tail, locate those cute little donuts or track down that new thing, Yakitori.

Get a grip on some chopsticks and dig in to your favourite food from Asia.

Grab a slice at Pizza Bäckerei.

Steve Parsons takes a bite at Jimmy's Lunch, a PNE staple for decades.

If it were up to kids — cotton candy, of course.

Help an elephant visitor to the Fair at snack time.

TIMBER!

THE FOREST INDUSTRY was (and still is) the single most important employer in the province. Times were changing and a skilled, technical workforce was in big demand. But it was the near mythic lumberjack, a potent symbol of B.C.'s and Canada's roots, that seized the public imagination. The PNE launched a festival to spotlight the industry and celebrate these heroes of our forests. Eager for logging glory, competitors from around the world flocked to the Fair.

THE TIMBER CARNIVAL, which shows the province's forest heritage in thrilling action, drew more than 7,000 to its three shows on its first day.[14]

The Vancouver Sun

IN 1966, THE Timber Carnival grew into a newer and bigger attraction. It was developed in time to celebrate the centenary of the union of the two colonies that would make up B.C.

THE PNE FESTIVAL of Logging opened today to the scream of power saws and the ring of axes ... Working loggers from all over B.C. are competing for $15,000 in prize money at the festival. The 'Greatest Logger of Them All' trophy will be presented at the end of the fair to the logger with the most points.[15]

The Vancouver Sun

THE BIRLING HERRLING brothers demonstrated Sunday that it takes more than muscle to be a logging champion. The four brothers from Sooke — aged between 9 and 13 — placed first, second, fourth and fifth in the novice birling competition at the festival of forestry's North American logging championship at the PNE.

'We're real proud of our boys,' says father Dick Herrling, a faller for Butler Brothers in Sooke. 'When they put on a little muscle I imagine they'll be going into the other events.'[16]

The Vancouver Sun

LOG BIRLING, AXE THROWING, BLOCK CHOPPING, OBSTACLE POLE BUCKING, POLE CLIMBING, POWER SAW BUCKING, and POLE FALLING all were performed in the new three-acre Feature Attraction Area in the heart of Exhibition Park. Some 210,000 spectators watched the FESTIVAL OF LOGGING WHICH WAS A PRIME FEATURE OF THE 1966 PNE.[17]

PNE Annual Report

PREVIOUS PAGE, CLOCKWISE FROM TOP LEFT: Lumberjacks with their trusty tools, 1960. The Chainsaw Competition at the 1967 Timber Carnival. A lumberjack handsaws his way to victory. Log rolling was a big favourite in 1969.
THIS PAGE, FROM TOP: One lumberjack shows his skills with an axe, 1969. The Squamish Timber Queen at the 1969 carnival.

THE — GEORGE — BELL — TROPHY
"THE GREATEST LOGGER OF THEM ALL"

CELEBRATING THE LOGGER

For its full century the PNE has found ways to celebrate B.C.'s forest industry and the awesome skills of loggers. In 1960, the PNE launched its popular Timber Carnival and it expanded on the theme in 1967 with the Festival of Forestry. Winning logger, Chris Arnet (facing page), gets a kiss from Miss PNE, Judy Collyer, in 1966. A pole climber easily scoots up 100 feet at a show in the 1980s.

> "I've been coming since 1949 (the year I was born). I love it but I miss the PNE parade. My best memories are of DANCE PARTY where I had a BLAST. I remember Glen Campbell singing on stage while we danced!"
>
> Jacquie MacDonald, *PNE Memory Book*, 1999

OH, TO BE A TEEN

THE PNE POURED on new attractions to keep fairgoers entertained. Teen power was at its zenith in the 1960s and it was adolescents who drove fashions in clothing, style and music.

THE PACIFIC NATIONAL EXHIBITION added a number of features ... to draw teenagers to the fairgrounds. A teen dance was held in the Garden Auditorium in 1963 ... Two years after the dance was inaugurated, a separate 'Teen Fair' was opened in conjunction with the exhibition. Held in a cordoned-off area ... the attraction included disc jockeys, record sales, hair stylists, and other booths and displays of interest to teens.[18]

Vancouver's Fair

DANCE PARTY, FEATURING top deejay Buddy Clyde, is a nightly event in the Garden Auditorium. Buddy is bringing top recording stars including 12-year-old Stevie Wonder.[19]

PNE Program Guide

RESPONDING TO DEMAND, in 1967 the PNE added a new event to its roster — Teen City.

THE 'NOW SCENE' was held in the 50,000 square feet of instant excitement at Teen City. Thousands of swingers flocked in and it was go-go-go! ... Some 20 big-name-bands took part including the Papa Bears, Mojo Company, Black Snake Blues and Tom Northcott ...[20]

PNE Annual Report

Teen-agers call it the FREAK-OUT PARLOUR ... a cube-shaped, light-tight room hung with shiny plastic. A pulsating strobe light blinks from the ceiling. MUSIC BLARES FROM LOUDSPEAKERS. Walking into it is like becoming part of a jerky movie of the 1920s. Movements are disjointed, colours change under the violet light of the strobe, and the penetrating music makes thought impossible. SENSES OF THE VISITORS ARE POSITIVELY ASSAULTED. Most first-timers just stand and stare. Then experiment with arm and hand movements. Then start dancing.[21]

The Vancouver Sun

CLOCKWISE FROM TOP LEFT: Teens hit a PNE dance floor with new moves in 1963. Cool glasses set the mood for a young dancer, 1965. At the PNE in the '60s go-go dancers were hot-hot. Stevie Wonder on stage at the Fair, 1963. Three guys at the Teen Fair are happy to watch, 1962. A detail from the front entrance to the Fair's Freak-Out Parlour.

A TICKET TO RIDE

PLAYLAND WAS HOPPING too, with new rides and a makeover that gave the grounds a "Space Age" feel.

THE ASSOCIATION IMPLEMENTED a park-wide 'Space-Age Look' development plan in 1965 ... The most noticeable additions ... were a 1450-foot long sky-ride that could take fairgoers from Playland to the exhibition buildings on the west side of the grounds and a 330-foot space tower.[22]

Vancouver's Fair

A SPECTACULAR 300-FOOT high Spiro-Tower elevator ride into space was the exciting high point for visitors to Playland during the 1968 Pacific National Exhibition. Gently rotating three times on the way up, the picture windows allowed each passenger an uninterrupted panoramic view of not only the 184 acres of Exhibition Park, but of the most beautiful city in Canada.[23]

PNE Annual Report

GONE WITH THE WIND

Debie Leyshon has worked at the PNE for more than 40 years. She has two favourite stories from her days working in guest services. This is one of them.

"BACK IN THE 1960s and '70s, the Sky Ride was a popular attraction at the PNE: a chairlift-like structure that ran on cables across the grounds high above the crowds. You could get a great view of the fair, people milling below, food stands, other rides and the mountain and ocean view as it slowly carried you from one end of the exhibition to the other.

One summer day, an elderly woman and her gentleman friend were taking in the sights from the Sky Ride. Polyester fibre, afro-style wigs were faddish at the time and she was wearing one. Suddenly a gust of wind swept the wig off her head and down to the ground. There was nothing she could do but wait until she got to the end of the ride. She was fuming that her companion got a glimpse of her without the wig.

Mad as heck, she went to guest services and demanded her wig be found or get compensation of $19.95 to cover what she had paid for it. Her friend stayed quietly by her side; he didn't seem to be at all bothered by what she looked like without the wig. But he was a little embarrassed by all the kerfuffle. We scoured the grounds looking for the wig. Food vendors were asked about anything suspicious falling from the sky. The lost and found was searched. We never did find that wig."

CLOCKWISE FROM TOP LEFT: Playland through a fish-eye lens. Debie Leyshon, an employee of the PNE for over 40 years, got a push from her cousin in 1956. The Spiro-Tower, 1968.

SALUTES, TREASURES AND STARS

IN THE 1960S the Fair brimmed with new offerings of international talent that transported the fairgoer for a moment to another place and time.

AN INTERNATIONAL POTPOURRI OF ENTERTAINMENT ... saw artists from Mexico, Honolulu, U.S., Australia and Canada melded together in a two-hour show themed to the PNE's 'Salute to the Pacific' year. ACCLAIMED BY CRITICS AS THE GREATEST 50 CENT BARGAIN IN VANCOUVER.[24]

PNE Annual Report

IN 1968, THE PNE staged "Treasures of the Orient."

THE FORUM GAVE visitors a unique experience as nine of Japan's master artisans and craftsmen created their art treasures before the admiring eyes of the throngs which crowded this huge, free exhibit of talent appropriately entitled 'Treasures of the Orient'. These Japanese artisans, the first time ever seen outside of their native land, flew direct to the PNE to give demonstrations of stenciling, paper work, screen panel-making, decorating and wood carving of figures, animals, masks and many other creative art forms.[25]

PNE Annual Report

FOR THE FIRST four days of the Grandstand Show, it was headliner Frank Fontaine, the zany 'Crazy Guggenheim' of the Jackie Gleason television show. The next five days saw the exciting television, recording and supper club star Frank Sinatra Jr. ... And for the final five days, that all-time favourite crooner and actor Nelson Eddy and his charming partner Gale Sherwood were the featured attractions in a festival of nostalgic song and music.[26]

PNE Annual Report

CLOCKWISE FROM TOP LEFT: The Fair at the PNE brought the world to our doorstep with First Nations performances (1964), Malaysian dancers (1963), Japanese log rollers (1966), a visit by Miss Yokohama (1969), and an Oriental Revue (1967).

THE FAB FOUR

AUGUST 22, 1964, was a big day in Vancouver — The Beatles hit town. News of their performance at the PNE spread like wildfire. Crowds of young people screamed; parents were mystified.

THE BLARING, BRASSY Pacific National Exhibition parade and chanting, screaming Beatle fans rocked downtown Vancouver today. Some kept a vigil outside the Hotel Georgia where the four tousle-haired Liverpudlians were due to check in later in the day for an Empire Stadium performance tonight ... Hefty guards were hard put to keep the youngsters, mostly girls from about 11 to 16, from getting into the lobby ... The Howe Street entrance was boarded up with plywood that quickly became covered with lipstick.[27]

The Vancouver Sun

IN LESS THAN half an hour, The Beatles' performance was stopped when the crowd mobbed the barricades. The moment was captured by columnist Jack Wasserman, one of *The Vancouver Sun*'s best-known journalists.

ALL'S WELL THAT ends well. So The Beatles' appearance Saturday night was a success. Nobody was killed. That happy statistic is the result of a combination of circumstances. A thin blue line of unarmed policemen pulled off the greatest job of crowd control I've ever seen here in 20 years. And they were LUCKY!

The crowd screams were indescribable. They were of a range, volume and pitch roughly equivalent to the sound one would imagine coming from half a dozen DC-8 jets taking off at one time.[28]

The Vancouver Sun

NICE BRITISH BOYS

In the early 1960s, Jack Lee wrote sports news for *The Vancouver Sun*. He also worked in his spare time writing press releases for the PNE. One day he was asked to pick up, as he describes them, "some guys called The Beatles." His top-secret job on concert day: to drive them down Georgia Street, over the Lions Gate Bridge, along the Upper Levels Highway and back over the Second Narrows Bridge, then drop the four at the back door of Empire Stadium.

"THE BEATLES WEREN'T yet as big as they were about to become, but it was evident they were a popular group. When I talked to them in the car on the way from the airport and in the dressing rooms at Empire Stadium, they were nice — so self-effacing, so casual, so 'un-famed' — they weren't full of themselves. We talked about soccer and football, and why we North Americans called another game football when the British knew soccer by the name football, and what the hell was soccer anyway? They were just nice British boys."

CLOCKWISE FROM TOP LEFT: Beatlemania hit Vancouver in 1964. The Fab Four played Empire Stadium and teenagers went wild.

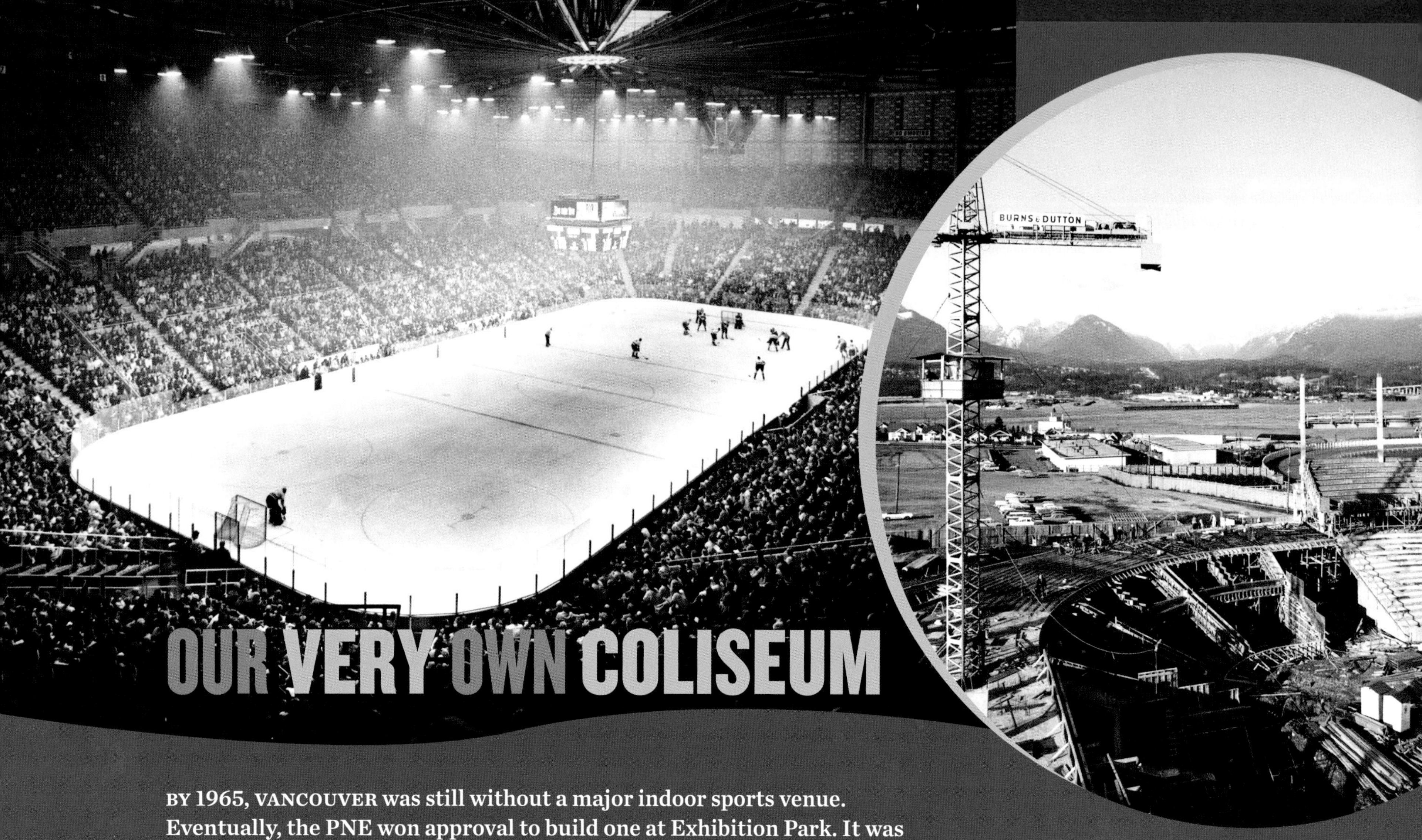

OUR VERY OWN COLISEUM

BY 1965, VANCOUVER was still without a major indoor sports venue. Eventually, the PNE won approval to build one at Exhibition Park. It was named the Pacific Coliseum and with this facility the Vancouver Canucks qualified for the big leagues.

JANUARY 8, 1968, marked the official opening of the PNE's newest and most expensive facility, the Pacific Coliseum. To herald the occasion, the PNE decided to stage an Old Timers' hockey game featuring former National Hockey League greats. An NHL franchise was finally secured in 1969, and in the fall of 1970 the Vancouver Canucks skated onto Coliseum ice for the first time.[29] *The Pacific National Exhibition: An Illustrated History*

THE BUILDING HAD to be up to National Hockey League standards, able to accommodate 16,000 spectators, and be readily adaptable for exhibition and trade fair purposes.[30] *Vancouver's Fair*

THE COLISEUM OPENED in January 1968, presenting Ice Capades under joint Rotary-PNE sponsorship. Response from the public was tremendous and a new attendance record was set for this show. Shortly afterward, the Vancouver Hockey Club moved in and their 'Canucks' have been drawing good crowds ever since.[31] *PNE Annual Report*

CLOCKWISE FROM TOP LEFT: The Old Timers' hockey game at the new Pacific Coliseum, 1968. Construction of the Pacific Coliseum, 1966. A taste of things to come at the Coliseum: ice skating, wrestling, the circus, basketball, concerts, and of course, hockey, 1968.

GOING BY THE NUMBERS

AFTER THE GROUNDWORK was laid in the 1950s, the PNE launched into its golden age in the 1960s. As early as 1962, millions of people were coming to Exhibition Park throughout the year for entertainment, education, culture and just plain fun. The target of one million visitors to the Fair was reached in 1963. The numbers said it all — the PNE was bigtime.

It's a Fair Job for All Concerned

HOW WOULD YOU like to supervise a staff of 15,000 people to operate a business that will run for only 17 days? Your plant — including buildings, private roadways, parking and fencing — is worth about $25 million, not including 184 acres of valuable urban property ...

If things go as projected, you'll deal with 1.25 million customers ... There will be 600 display booths at the fair this year ... About 10 tons of hamburger will be formed into two-ounce patties in on-site operations. Another 12 tons of wieners for the hot dog route ... And about 10,000 pounds of locally caught cod will be filleted and prebattered for fish and chips ...

There will also be about 1,000 hotel rooms occupied by PNE visitors, who will pour close to $40 a day into the city.[32]

The Vancouver Sun

MORE THAN 2,400,000 men, women and children from all over the world passed through the gates, turnstiles and doors of Exhibition Park's many facilities in 1962. They came to compete and display, to sell and buy, to learn and to earn and to relax and enjoy. They came to party and they came to pray. And they came in a never-ending stream throughout the year to tour Canada's most unique citadel of factual and artifactual culture — the B.C. Building ... The visitor's book shows that tourists from more than 40 countries were among them.[33]

PNE Annual Report

Sports Hub of Western Canada

WITH ITS INTERNATIONALLY known, 32,000 seat Empire Stadium; its ever-busy 5,080 seat Forum; its versatile 3,000 seat Garden Auditorium and its 5,018 seat Callister Park, [the PNE] catered to more than 600,000 people in the world of sports alone, in 1962.[34]

PNE Annual Report

THE 1963 PACIFIC National Exhibition, August 17 to September 2 ... 1,018,461 people, and you, were there! It was a year to remember; a year of FIRSTS ... The PNE surged over its 10-year attendance target of 1,000,000 ... for the first time City Council passed a resolution of commendation of the PNE for its outstanding contribution to the community.[35]

PNE Annual Report

The Vancouver Canucks of the Western Hockey League played their first full season (1968–69) in the new palatial Pacific Coliseum and attracted 362,699 PAYING CUSTOMERS TO THEIR EXHIBITION, LEAGUE AND PLAY-OFF GAMES, A WHL ATTENDANCE RECORD.[36]

PNE Annual Report

FROM TOP: At the turnstile the PNE greets Mrs. R. Atlee, the 1955 Fair's first visitor. Playland in 1967.

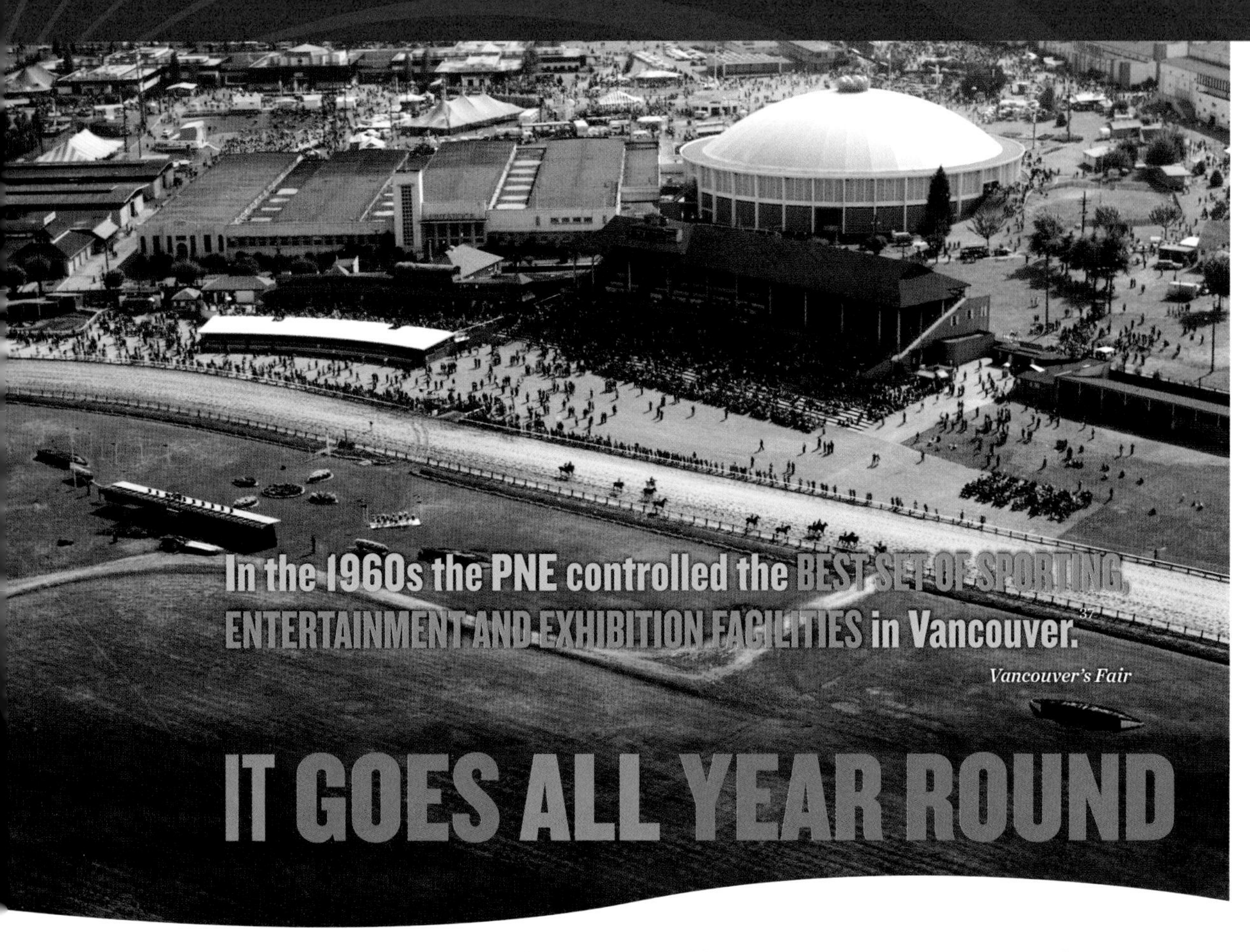

In the 1960s the PNE controlled the BEST SET OF SPORTING, ENTERTAINMENT AND EXHIBITION FACILITIES in Vancouver.

Vancouver's Fair

IT GOES ALL YEAR ROUND

BY THE 1960S Exhibition Park had become Vancouver's — and B.C.'s — largest full-tilt, year-round entertainment, sports, cultural and community facility. In terms of sheer size and types of facilities, no place in Western Canada could compete.

PNE films free for all

UPCOMING WINTER PROGRAM of the PNE Sunday Travelogue is a 'world-beater' in terms of free entertainment. Photographers who filmed the documentaries literally beat the world for their material. Sponsored by the PNE, the films will be shown in the Little Theatre in the B.C. Building from the beginning of October through every Sunday to the end of April.[38]

PNE Fairtalk Newsletter

AS PART OF the Centennial, the B.C. government held an international trade fair designed to highlight the importance of the import and export trade to the provincial economy. Held afterwards on an irregular basis through the 1960s, the International Trade Fair provides yet another example of the growing diversity of activities at Exhibition Park.[39]

The Pacific National Exhibition: An Illustrated History

IN 1960, THE Ascot Jockey Club, tenants at Exhibition Park, merged operations with the B.C. Jockey Club ... The merger left Exhibition Park as the site for all Lower Mainland thoroughbred racing and led to an expansion in the number of racing days and to the reconstruction of track facilities.[40]

The Pacific National Exhibition: An Illustrated History

PERFECT! IF YOU HAVE TWO LEFT FEET

In the early 1960s, the popular Hadassah-WIZO Bazaar was staged at the PNE. This pre-Christmas/Chanukah sale event offered a huge variety of household goods such as new and slightly used clothing, shoes, bridal boutique ware, jewellery, toys, food and baking, books and handicrafts. The bazaar was a major fundraiser for projects in Israel and Canada for socially disadvantaged and educationally challenged youth.

"I WENT TO my first Vancouver Hadassah Bazaar in 1964, shortly after my husband and I moved here with our young family. People loved it, including me. When I walked into the Forum building I said hoo-wee; I was overwhelmed. There was so much unbelievable stuff. One of my friends said, 'Oh my goodness, I can get outfitted for the whole year here.'

I eventually became one of the volunteers who worked for the bazaar. We used to lease three buildings — the Forum, the Food Building and Showmart. We had a big shoe department and one year a woman bought a pair of boots there. When she got home, she realized she had two left boots. The next year she came back to us with those two left boots. 'I knew you'd be back and so I held on to these,' she said to us. We told her to go ahead and find another pair to replace the ones she had mistakenly picked up the year before. Well, if she didn't find the two right boots to match the ones she had."

Fay Riback, Canadian Hadassah-WIZO member, interview 2009

FROM LEFT: Hasting's Park racetrack with the Agrodome and Livestock buildings behind, 1963. Hadassah Bazaar volunteers hoist the White Elephant Sale sign for one of the PNE's most popular community events.

CLOCKWISE FROM TOP LEFT: A young vendor at the Playland Midway has the world on a string, 1969. One Fair attraction in 1964 was the Flying Car. Some vendors sported their own signs, 1969. Playland in 1962.

FAIR FRIENDSHIPS
The Fair at the PNE is a great time for guys to bond — over a soft drink or a quartet of prize sheep.

198

EXHIBITION PARK
DIAMOND JUBILEE FAIR
THE PNE IS FOR THE KID IN EVERY
PNE
PNE

CHAPTER 7

1970–1979
AN EMERGING GEM

’70-’79

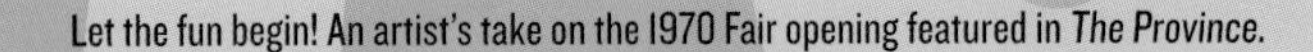
Let the fun begin! An artist’s take on the 1970 Fair opening featured in *The Province*.

THE "ME DECADE" AND DISCO

Vancouver has always had a knack for vision and reinvention. In the 1970s, with funding from Ottawa, the city transformed part of the south shore of False Creek into a model community. The gem at the centre of this urban makeover, placed on a grimy industrial island, became one of North America's most innovative public spaces — Granville Island. Out with smoke-belching sawmills, factories and small foundries; in with a public market, an art school, theatres and restaurants. As the rest of the province continued on its seemingly endless raw-resource bonanza, Vancouver started moving past its industrial roots.

IN THE 1970S, compliments of another real estate market boom, property values doubled. It was a good time, again, for speculators and land developers. Downtown bustled and the skyline bloomed with skyscrapers, changing the look of the city faster than at any other time besides the 1920s. Commercial property development dug in too, and before long the city (and eager shoppers) welcomed the Pacific Centre. Huge malls popped up in Burnaby, Surrey, Richmond and Coquitlam, as Greater Vancouver geared up for suburban sprawl.

TOM JONES
ANNE MURRAY
THE PNE GOES BIG-TIME ... PAGE 3
RAY CHARLES

FROM TOP: Concerts at Empire Stadium offered impromptu audience performances. In 1971 the lineup at the Fair at the PNE included Tom Jones, Anne Murray and Ray Charles.

Not everyone was happy about all the construction dust and noisy prosperity, though. When the iconic Birks building came down and a bank tower shot up some people started to question the race to big city status. Groups organized and people demonstrated.

Still, it was the "Me Decade," and despite its rapid growth Vancouver was in a mellow mood. Pet rocks, mood rings, *Star Wars* toys and handmade macramé plant holders abounded. The cheery yellow Happy Face smiled on everyone from everything.

The human potential movement hit town and people lined up for courses in self-awareness and workshops offering feel-good moments. People rearranged themselves inside and out: men strutted their stuff in pastel leisure suits and women rocked in hot pants. Everyone was perched on platform shoes and poured into skin-tight jeans. It was the start of the designer label craze, with fashionable behinds sporting brands like Jordache and Sassoon. For those less impressed with labels, Wreck Beach became the notorious destination for the clothing-optional crowd, helping the city gain its offbeat status as Canada's Lotus Land.

If people weren't "soul searching" or shopping, they were looking to boogie. Downtown, at clubs like Oil Can Harry's, disco reigned. Couples crowded the floors to learn "The Hustle," do "The Bump" and try out those new *Saturday Night Fever*–inspired moves. People felt sophisticated. Many cheered when Vancouver finally joined the rest of the world and got its first neighbourhood pub in 1972.

Entertainment was big and it was a money-maker. Concerts became huge events, and the PNE was the place to catch them. Thousands took in Bachman Turner Overdrive (BTO), Joni Mitchell, John Denver, Johnny Cash and jazz greats Ella Fitzgerald, Count Basie and 'ol' blue eyes' himself, Frank Sinatra, at the Pacific Coliseum and the Agrodome.

Mass sporting events were hot too. For fans the PNE was ground zero. The Vancouver Canucks joined the National Hockey League and called the Pacific Coliseum home. The North American Soccer League's new Vancouver Whitecaps franchise packed the bleachers at Empire Stadium — when they weren't being filled by the BC Lions home games.

CLOCKWISE FROM TOP LEFT: Disco ruled at the Fair in the 1970s, with intriguing combinations of themes and DJs. The PNE Sky Glider ride, 1973. Brazil's soccer star, Pelé, playing for the New York Cosmos, holds the ball for a kick from Franz Beckenbauer during a practice session at Empire Stadium, 1977. Sonny and Cher headlined at the 1973 Fair.

GO CANUCKS GO!

AFTER A LONG wait, Vancouverites' yearning for big-league hockey was answered on October 9, 1970, when the Vancouver Canucks played their first NHL game in front of a packed house at the Pacific Coliseum. It was a coup for the PNE, vaulting it to first place as the province's biggest and best multi-purpose venue for professional sports. Hockey fans across B.C. and Canada got to see the Pacific Coliseum on television as games were regularly broadcast on CBC's popular *Hockey Night in Canada* show. From the start, Canucks games were smash hits.

ALTHOUGH PASSED OVER in the N.H.L.'s first major expansion in 1967, a decision greeted with considerable bitterness in the city, a franchise was finally granted in 1969 ... and in the fall of 1970 ... the Vancouver entry in the N.H.L. skated onto the ice of the Pacific Coliseum to begin its first season in the league.[1]

Vancouver's Fair

IT WAS ESSENTIALLY a night of contrast. There were the Vancouver Canucks, glistening in whiter-than-white, contrasting colorfully with the Los Angeles Kings who, like the fabled Assyrian, 'gleamed in purple and gold'. ... There was Canada's singing 'pet' Juliette, back in the old home town and sparkling silver and white to get everyone on their feet with a lavish production of the national anthem ... And there was Mayor Tom Campbell ... to ceremoniously face off the first puck at the first Vancouver National Hockey League game ... There was dear old Fred (Cyclone) Taylor, at 87 still a sprightly figure to receive the biggest cheer of all, as he stepped on the ice in pre-game ceremonies to recall the memorable day in 1915 — when he led the Vancouver Millionaires to a dramatic Stanley Cup victory. But it was the players the fans had come to see — not Mayor Tom, not old Cyclone, not even Miss Juliette. Each Canuck was greeted with a roar of applause as he came within range of the CBC cameras for his initial moment of glory.[2]

The Province

WELL THEY GOT Vancouver's National Hockey League show on the road Friday night, but somebody better fire the script girl! The good guys lost. Not even the official blessing of Premier W.A.C. Bennett could inspire the Canucks in their first-ever league appearance at the Pacific Coliseum and the ... paying customers had to settle for a 3–1 Los Angeles victory.[3]

The Province

BUT IT WAS THE PLAYERS THE FANS HAD COME TO SEE — not Mayor Tom, not old Cyclone, not even Miss Juliette. EACH CANUCK WAS GREETED WITH A ROAR OF APPLAUSE as he came within range of the CBC cameras for his initial moment of glory.

PRETTY EXCITING STUFF FOR A YOUNG GUY LIKE ME

The emergence of a new sports team, especially one as big as the Vancouver Canucks, presented sports journalists with wonderful opportunities, as Bill Good Jr. discovered.

"BY THE TIME the Pacific Coliseum was opening, I was a young sportscaster. I did the first telecast of the Vancouver Canucks for *Hockey Night in Canada*. It was my first telecast for *Hockey Night in Canada* too. The Canucks played the Los Angeles Kings and lost by a score of 3 – 1.

It was a beautiful new building and it was a great time, with the Vancouver Canucks finally being in the NHL. It was great to work with legendary journalist Jim Taylor and a guy called Jack Bennett who came out every year from Toronto for the Vancouver broadcasts. Bennett was a huge name in broadcasting in Ontario and well known across the country so it was pretty exciting stuff for a young guy like me."

ABOVE: The Canucks first-ever goal as a team in the NHL against the L.A. Kings, at the Pacific Coliseum, 1970.

THE PARTY WAS a little late getting started, but no one noticed or cared amid the massive hero's welcome afforded the Vancouver Whitecaps, newly crowned monarchs of North American soccer. The Caps, for those who spent the weekend in a cave, made 2–1 believers of the Tampa Bay Rowdies Saturday, bringing home Vancouver's first professional silverware since the 1964 Lions' Grey Cup. And the town turned out by the thousands Sunday afternoon to shout out its pride and demonstrated just how wound up it gets over a winner.[6]

The Province

SOCCER FEVER

HOCKEY WASN'T THE only sports passion in Vancouver. On December 11, 1973, Vancouver soccer fans woke up to the news that the city had a team in the North American Soccer League. Enter the Vancouver Whitecaps. Their home? Empire Stadium at the PNE, of course.

The Whitecaps played their first-ever match on May 5, 1974, when they fell to a 2–1 home defeat to San Jose Earthquakes. Though an Empire Stadium crowd of 17,343 saw their side lose that day, defender Neil Ellett wrote his name in the history books by scoring the Whitecaps first-ever goal in the league.[4]

whitecapsfc.com

She is the mother of Vancouver's premier soccer family but only once has she seen her sons play professionally. Usually Mrs. Clelia Lenarduzzi sits in her Dundas Street home listening to the roar of the crowd at Empire Stadium through her open door. Last night, there was a special roar from the 24,216 fans watching their favorite Whitecaps blitz San Jose Earthquakes 6–0 ... a round of thundering applause which even Mrs. Lenarduzzi might have realized was something special. It was of course the greeting for her youngest soccer son, 18-year-old Danny Lenarduzzi, making his professional league debut. And it was perhaps significant on this night when the Lenarduzzi Soccer Circus came to town that the man he replaced on the field was older brother Sammy. Said a breathless Danny afterwards, 'I was certainly nervous going out there for the first time ... but it worked out fine. I'm only sorry Sam had to come off but he had taken a knock on the knee.'[5]

The Province

CLOCKWISE FROM TOP LEFT: The Whitecaps' Derek Possee acknowledges the crowd at a game. Bob Lenarduzzi playing in the Whitecaps' NASL debut game, against the San José Earthquakes, 1974. Whitecaps' ball. Trevor Whymark of the Whitecaps takes the trophy, 1979.

HOMETOWN BOY MAKES GOOD AT THE GREY CUP

IN THE YEARS 1971 and 1974, Empire Stadium hosted the contest to see which football club would take home the Grey Cup. Unfortunately the home team, the BC Lions, didn't make the playoffs in either year. But the 1974 contest saw hometown boy Don Sweet play for his fans as a Montreal Alouette, which won 20–7 over the Edmonton Eskimos.

WHEN DON SWEET was growing up in Vancouver he used to fantasize about kicking field goals before a huge crowd at Empire Stadium — wearing the uniform of the B.C. Lions. Well, the Lord Byng high school graduate had half his dream come true Sunday. And it really didn't matter that he was wearing the red, white and blue of the Montreal Alouettes. Sweet's four field goals were a Grey Cup record. He also added a convert and a single point for a total of 14 points. That was the most points in a Grey Cup game since Winnipeg's Gerry James scored 14 in the Blue Bombers 1961 overtime win over Hamilton.[7]

The Province

FROM LEFT: Larry Highbaugh leaps for the ball during the 1974 Grey Cup contest with the Montreal Alouettes. Taking a dive on rain-soaked turf.

FLOATS LIKE A BUTTERFLY, STINGS LIKE A BEE

VANCOUVER FIGHT FANS got to see one of the greatest boxers of all time, Muhammad Ali, on the night of May 1, 1972. He fought the stalwart Canadian George Chuvalo at the Pacific Coliseum.

'I TRIED MY best to drop him, but he wouldn't go.' So said Muhammad Ali last night in the wake of a 12-round brawl with George Chuvalo that saw the former world champion win a unanimous decision — but little else to soothe his ego. Despite the fact that he spent the last half of the battle ripping and stabbing a deep gash in Chuvalo's forehead, with the Canadian's vision at times blurred with his own blood, Ali was unable to make good his pre-fight promise to floor Chuvalo for the first time in the tough veteran's career. In fact, there was far more to this fight than the mere matter of whether or not Chuvalo would fall, for despite the unanimous call from the two judges and the referee, this was a grimly-fought, bruising affair that gave Ali more than one bad moment. Testimony to Chuvalo's courageous stand against the 'new' Ali was the standing ovation given him by the ... Coliseum crowd.[8]

The Province

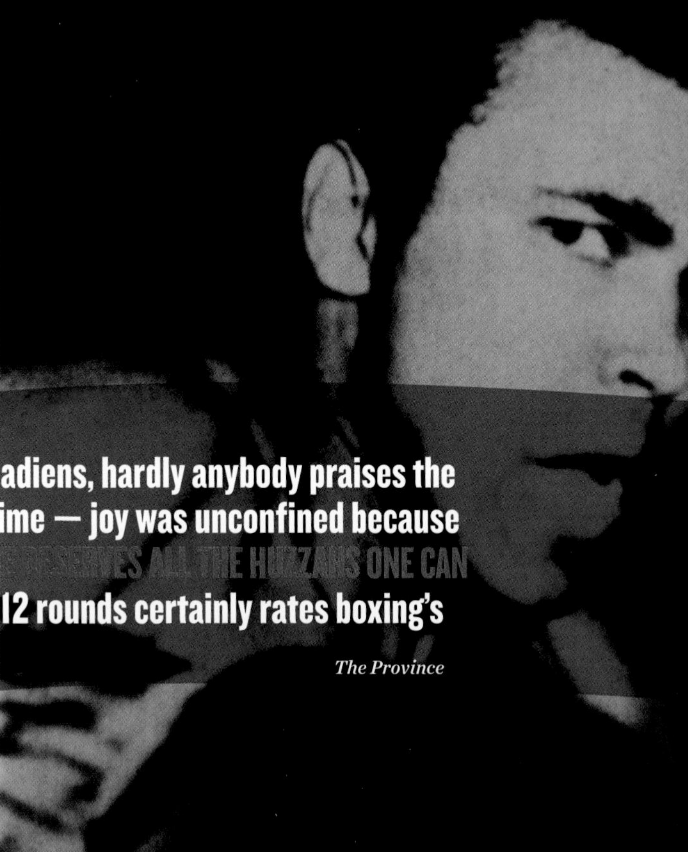

FUNNY. When the ... Canucks get subtly slugged, say about 6–0 by Montreal Canadiens, hardly anybody praises the losers just for finishing. But Monday night at the same scene, but a different crime — joy was unconfined because George Chuvalo was still standing when the final bell sounded. OF COURSE GEORGE DESERVES ALL THE HUZZAHS ONE CAN MUSTER FOR HIS COURAGE. Anybody who can take Muhammad Ali's best shots for 12 rounds certainly rates boxing's equivalent of the Victoria Cross, and his chin bones should be left to posterity.[9]

The Province

CLOCKWISE FROM TOP LEFT: Muhammad Ali floated out of George Chuvalo's reach at their 1972 Pacific Coliseum bout. Muhammad Ali.

Al Antonson worked at the PNE in the 1950s and '60s as an exhibitor for Nabob Foods. He was so successful at attracting people to his exhibit, he was hired by the PNE to develop its trade shows for both Fairtime and other periods throughout the year. His success grew throughout the 1970s and into the early 1980s.

I THINK THE AGRODOME'S LEAKING

"I REMEMBER THE very first Home Show. It was run by *The Vancouver Sun* and managed by people from New York. It was a very small fair in those days, but later was taken over by a larger Home Show based out of Toronto. Today it's still one of the biggest annual shows in Vancouver.

The B.C. Automobile Association put on the first international Auto Show. They got it right because it is still operating.

The Boat Show was started by the O'Loughlin family out of Portland, Oregon. Our public relations department really knew how to get coverage for that show, which sometimes rented all our major buildings. We even flooded the Agrodome for them one year. Before the show, the media thought that the Agrodome had sprung a leak! We got more than a few pages of press over that stunt.

Other small shows came along to fill in most of the first three months of the year. Some shows we experimented with and only hosted once. For example, one year we had a large Christmas Show at the Forum building. That was put on by a Toronto PR company. It lasted 30 days and attracted over 100,000 people. We had all of the Forum food concessionaires and made a lot of money from them that month."

YOU WANT A LAKE? YOU GOT A LAKE

AS FAR BACK as the 1960s, the PNE began positioning itself as *the* west coast stop on the trade show circuit. By the 1970s, events at Exhibition Park had become record-breaking sales extravaganzas, attracting hundreds of thousands of people throughout the year. The PNE was soon known as a premier "can-do" organizer. If someone wanted a special feature, they got it. Some of the splashier stunts garnered loads of media coverage.

As the P.N.E. moved to make more productive use of their facilities on a year-round basis, trade shows proved to be particularly valuable tenants. The Auto Show, Home Show, Boat Show and others were usually staged annually and attracted large crowds to Exhibition Park. The P.N.E. had the only set of facilities in Vancouver capable of handling such events.[10]

The Pacific National Exhibition: An Illustrated History

FROM TOP: Happy to accommodate trade show requests, the PNE flooded the Agrodome for the 1975 Boat Show. The 1972 Boat Show offered indoor balloon racing.

IT HAPPENS HERE ... ALL YEAR LONG

IN THE 1970S, when the PNE celebrated its diamond jubilee, it was clear for the first time that Exhibition Park's year-round activities had surpassed those of the 17-day fair. President Charles Jaggs made note of this fact in his annual report. It was a trend that would continue.

THE PNE'S YEAR-ROUND business accounted for 60.2 percent of 1970–71 gross revenue.[11]
PNE Annual Report

THE PNE TODAY hosts virtually every major trade and consumer show in Vancouver, plus a preponderance of banquets, receptions, and meetings. Rock concerts are an almost weekly occurrence; there are annual circuses, ice shows and similar 'spectaculars'. The PNE also is home for all sports, including soccer, recreational ice skating, minor, Junior-B and college hockey, figure skating, professional wrestling, horse shows, various touring events and roller skating. And, of course, there are the Vancouver Canucks ... and the B.C. Lions ... plus thoroughbred racing at the sumptuous Exhibition Park race-track. The B.C. Pavilion is a showcase of B.C. government and private industrial displays, plus the giant, handcrafted Challenger Relief Map of B.C. and the glittering B.C. Sports Hall of Fame attracts some 90,000 persons per year exclusive of the Fairtime period.[12] *PNE Annual Report*

CLOCKWISE FROM TOP LEFT: Crowds pack the racetrack, 1975. The Harlem Globetrotters brought court brilliance and humour to the PNE several times. The BC Sports Hall of Fame at Exhibition Park had lots to offer hockey fans in the 1970s. The Agrodome became a major staging venue for horse shows, 1973.

WHERE YAKITORI MEETS CANADA

While teaching English in Japan from 1972 to 1974, Bill McMichael developed a passion for Japanese food. He met and married his future wife, Hisae, there, and together they moved back to Canada.

"THERE'S A LOT of street food in Japan. One type that was a great favourite with a lot of the foreign teachers was known as kushi katsu, or food cooked on sticks (bamboo skewers). It's served out of small shacks in various neighbourhoods of Tokyo where I was living. Yakitori, which means barbequed chicken, is one of the kushi katsu foods served on the street. You can either eat it with a sauce or just with salt. We would order yakitori and drink beer with it. It made a very tasty meal if you were on the go.

Shortly after Hisae and I got back to Canada, I decided to go to graduate school, but I needed money to do it. It occurred to me that yakitori was easy to make. All you needed was a small grill on which to cook and you can process hundreds of these skewered chicken meals in no time. I decided to set up a small shack and see if this bit of Japanese cuisine would go with Canadians. It was not a thing you could easily get in Vancouver in the 1970s. There were not more than a dozen Japanese restaurants here and they mostly served teriyaki and sushi.

The PNE seemed like a good place to introduce yakitori and I figured I could make a few dollars to finance my schooling. My father and I built the shack and friends helped me move it. I called it "Tokyo Style Chicken Yakitori" and told everyone it was the first time yakitori had been served in the West. I was sure someone would dispute that claim, but to date, no one has.

It turned out to be an incredible success. We sold each skewer for 50 cents and a large pop was 75 cents. We were right on the main drag, next to the BC Pavilion. 'Boy, that smells good,' people would say or 'love that smell.' We sold thousands every day. All the guys from the Japanese food stands came down to check it out. They knew how to make yakitori, but didn't know if it would sell in Vancouver.

I cleared more than $2,200 in the three weeks of the fair, enough to pay for my graduate registration fees, with money left over for other expenses. It was a hoot running the stand. And I still like to tell people that I introduced yakitori to Canada."

THE MANY MOODS OF TURKEY

FOOD IS A quintessential, multi-faceted Fair experience: eating it (often in huge amounts) whether it is fast food or gourmet; watching it being cooked; learning how to prepare it; or finding out how much fun foreign cuisine can be.

The Many Moods of Turkey

THAT'S WHAT THE sign says over the array of turkey dishes on display: casseroles, stew, rigatoni, salad, boneless roast. But today's free sample is turkey fondue ... chunks of white meat rolled in pancake flour and dipped in pancake and instant potato batter.[13]

The Vancouver Sun

FROM LEFT: Bill's and Hisae's yakitori shack, 1976. A Fairgoer trying out a foot-long hot dog.
NEXT PAGE FROM LEFT: Some foodies felt like experimenting with exotic treats like the Tiki Dog, 1970. Others opted to learn a bit about new cuisines from experts like Mona Brun, who tackled the art of taco-making in 1974.

THE LIGHTS GO UP — organist Hazel Cunningham breaks into Roll Out the Barrel — Mona Brun turns on her mike — and THE COOKING DEMONSTRATION IS UNDERWAY. Twice a day throughout the PNE, Mona entertains a crowd at the B.C. department of agriculture's Country Fair, a new version of the old Acres of Food, in the Forum. Mona's demonstrations are definitely unique — RATHER LIKE A COMBINATION OF THE SLAPSTICK COMEDY OF THE GALLOPING GOURMET AND THE WRY HUMOR OF JULIA CHILD. If the mood — and/or the music — is right, Mona may even dance a jig or two. All in all, it MAKES A VERY ENTERTAINING WAY TO LEARN SOME PRACTICAL COOKING TIPS.[15]

The Vancouver Sun

EXHIBITION PARK VISITORS IN 1969–70, INCLUDING THE FAIRTIME PERIOD, ATE SOME 460,000 HOT DOGS AND HAMBURGERS, drank some 642,000 cups of coffee and 1.5 million cold drinks, and enjoyed 504,000 ice cream bars. The 42 PNE concession outlets (46 at Fairtime) also did a landslide business in other food items.[14]

PNE Annual Report

CELEBRATING THE SILLY

WHAT GOOD IS a fair without a bit of "carnival" mood and a few out-of-the-ordinary offerings to try out? The Fair at the PNE has a proud history of celebrating the silly. It's a congenial setting for Vancouverites to unwind a little and sample things that are a little odd, before cocooning for the long wet winter.

IN VANCOUVER, YOU can always tell when summer is coming to an end. It's marked by the opening of the Pacific National Exhibition ... The exhibition would be the final fling of the summer. But the decline of summer is also signaled by something else ... the slowdown of the silly season. There is something about the summertime that brings out the foolishness in people. It's the time of year when, whether it's because of hot weather or the release of tension during vacation, even normally staid people let it all hang out.[16]

The Vancouver Sun

PROVINCIAL LIQUOR OFFICIALS are expected to rule this week on whether the sale of high-alcohol 'herbal tonic wines' at the PNE violates the law ... The wines, which are sold at a health food stand, contain between 17 and 35 per cent alcohol by volume, compared with an average of 12 per cent for B.C. wines ... The tonic is one of a multitude of products being hawked by promoters at the PNE who promise to make the customer's life longer, better and more satisfying ... Also being sold at the PNE are Foo-Tie-Teng — 'The Elixer [sic] of Life' — which is touted as a rejuvenating drug which aids digestion, and Gotu-Kola, an herb which its promoters claim solves mental troubles, blood pressure, abscesses, arthritis and rheumatism.[17]

The Vancouver Sun

FOR $30, JOHN Watt will look into your eyes and tell you about your body ... The technique he practices is called iridology. Although medical science does not substantiate its claims, practitioners of iridology are convinced that analyzing the colors and fibers of the iris reveals valuable information on the body's condition.[18]

The Vancouver Sun

THERE MAY NOT be gold out thar at the PNE but if you look closely, you'll find a few minor gems. We did, when we went browsing among those fascinating stands that sell all the weird and wonderful household gadgets at every fair ... Who said consumerism had to be all serious? First of all we came upon the amazing window cleaner. The amazing *magnetic* window cleaner. This particular gem allows you to wash inside and *outside* windows at the same time, while standing securely indoors ... With this, you'll no longer have to wonder on which side of the window is the spot.[19]

The Vancouver Sun

CLOCKWISE FROM TOP LEFT: Michael and Michelle perform a few aerial stunts for Fair crowds far below. Meanwhile a couple of "grannies" share a laugh with their coffee, 1977.

THERE'S NO SIGHT sweeter to Dave Slater than a well-wrecked car, no sound more like music than steel grinding steel. It's all so much fun. Slater, an auto mechanics teacher at B.C. Vocational School, won the demolition derby team cup for the Satellite Motorsport club over the Seattle club Saturday at the Pacific National Exhibition. 'It's just fabulous, getting behind the wheel like that. Like today, we won that trophy, and to me, that meant a heck of a lot. They've been hanging onto that trophy for three years.' Dave prides himself on the preparation of his cars. He puts about 40 to 50 hours of work on them and they can last through three derbies. The doors and hood are chained down, the sides reinforced with steel girders or railway ties. Inside, the car is stripped down to the metal. The gas tank sits behind the driver with a metal fire shield in front of it.[20] *The Vancouver Sun*

THIRTEEN-YEAR-OLD VAN LOCK left the ring-toss game booth grinning from ear to ear. For his $1.50 spent on 18 throws at empty soft drink bottles Saturday, he won four large bottles of pop ... Further along, Thora McCloy hugged her large stuffed dolphin and equally huge Donald Duck, courtesy of her husband Ian's throwing arm at the knock-over-the-milk-bottles game.[21] *The Vancouver Sun*

RICHARD RODRIGUEZ HAD JUST FINISHED MORE THAN 170 HOURS ON THE PNE'S ROLLER COASTER — 3,310 trips worth of rolling and coasting — and the first thing he did after stepping out of the coaster car was have a drink of champagne. Wondrously, he kept it down. The 21-year-old Rodriguez stepped off Playland's rollercoaster at 8:25 p.m. Sunday and back into the pages of the Guinness Book of World Records by surpassing his earlier endurance record of 150 hours ... HE LOOKED HAGGARD AND A BIT SUNBURNT, AND HIS HAIR DEFINITELY HAD THAT WINDBLOWN LOOK.[22] *The Vancouver Sun*

FROM BOTTOM LEFT: Midway patrons could check out the winner of the bushiest beard contest, take in a hammering contest, catch the latest in sock-darning techniques, or watch in awe as Richard Rodriguez beat the Guinness World Record in 1979 for hours spent on a roller coaster.

THE BEST VIEW IN TOWN

A favourite moment for PNE Fairgoers is being swept up above the crowds and getting a bird's-eye view of all the excitement to be found across Exhibition Park. The Sky Glider (above, 1977) was a great way to travel the length of the park. Ferris Wheels (1976) have been a fixture at the PNE since opening day in 1910.

PEDAL TO THE METAL
Uneasy Rider, 1976. Learning to drive in the Bumper Cars, 1976.

CELEBRATING THE SUBLIME

THE CRAZY FUN at the Fair at the PNE transformed into surreal, high art when the PNE launched a big production of the well-loved children's story *Alice in Wonderland*. The show was one of many events that kept Fairgoers enthralled. Dog lovers and dancers came with their own special thrills too.

THROUGH THE LOOKING Glass and down to The Mall, Alice and company are paying a call; Then away with White Rabbit, Tweedle Dum & Dee, To the gallimaufry stage show at the PNE.[23]

Poster ad in *The Vancouver Sun*

You Call It, Girl!

"I CAN REMEMBER our many years of bringing our three daughters down to the PNE to perform with the Delta Sundancers Teen Square Dance Club. Small dressing rooms filled with fluffy crinolines. Excitement and fun and apprehension — especially when our youngest had to call! Loved the sewing competition/ fashion shows too! Both my mother and I have best of class ribbons for our entries. These memories make the fair 'real' to us; not just an amusement park to visit for a day."

Patricia and Dario Baisi, *PNE Memory Book*, 1999.

CURIOUSER AND CURIOUSER! I thought, as the gargantuan proportions of Theatre at the Fair's Alice in Wonderland show elbowed for space in what I once considered my rather expansive imagination ... With a 100-voice choir, 18-piece orchestra and 150-member chorus, not to mention principal actors, the locally written and produced musical-comedy adaptation of Lewis Carroll's children's classic opens Aug. 23 for 10 performances, at the Coliseum in conjunction with the PNE. I've talked with the producer, director, scriptwriter, songwriters, costumer — even the leading ladies. I've met the Mad Hatter in person and tried on his hat. But can you blame me for my skepticism when my interview notes go on at great length about a troupe of 50 dancing oysters and a croquet game with live croquet balls and shocking pink flamingos for mallets?[24]

The Vancouver Sun

ABOVE: The cast of Alice in Wonderland on the PNE's roller coaster, 1974.

Herb Williams started the ever-popular SuperDogs show in 1976. At the time, Herb owned championship show dogs and was involved with the Hall of Fame for Canadian Show Dogs.

WHEN STARS BARK

"WE HAD A gallery of pictures of the country's top show dogs. I suggested to the PNE that they have an event at the Fair showing some of these dogs and take the opportunity to show the pictures too. The program director asked me, 'What do these dogs do?' I told him these were just gorgeous dogs that walk around the ring. He said, 'I would really like to have dogs that run faster and jump higher than the average dog.' I said if that was what he wanted, I would do that.

So I contacted some of the dog agility and obedience teams that I knew and they were happy to participate. Five hundred seats were built for our first show. The first day, the seats were packed. Overnight the PNE decided to build another 200 seats. Unfortunately, the paint was still wet at show time the next day. A number of people had their clothes dry-cleaned at the PNE's expense! But the PNE was the first formal offering of the SuperDogs show, which is still exhibited all across the country to big crowds."

FROM LEFT: Herb Williams and some SuperDogs, 1999. Oscar Peterson at a PNE concert in 1973. Ella Fitzgerald, 1973.

ALL THAT JAZZ

IT WASN'T ONLY rock and roll that the Pacific Coliseum brought to Vancouver. The PNE's Star Spectacular program started attracting a wider range of artists. By 1973, organizers were bragging that the PNE had the world's greatest jazz show.

ELLA FITZGERALD, COUNT BASIE, Stan Getz, Cannonball Adderley, Oscar Peterson. This incomparable array of the world's jazz greats appears in person August 18, 7:30 p.m., at the Coliseum. Ella the Singing Superstar; the big sound of Basie's band; the sax brilliance of Stan Getz and Cannonball; the piano stylings of Peterson. Reserved seats: $6.00, $5.00, $4.00, on sale at the door.[25] *PNE Program*

WHEN PACIFIC COLISEUM ice wasn't crowded with hockey teams or ice shows, it was the centrepiece of a new form of musical entertainment in Vancouver: big stadium rock. In a city where weather is always a consideration, the big-capacity, indoor facility made booking the PNE's Star Spectacular packages easy work.

WITH THE COMPLETION of the new Pacific Coliseum ... the P.N.E. could turn from its accustomed practice of offering free entertainment, as it had often done in Empire Stadium, to charging admission. The entertainment packages put together for the Coliseum shows, designated the 'Star Spectacular,' were far from being a sidelight to the exhibition, as its predecessor had occasionally been ... The annual show became a highly publicized media event designed to attract people to the exhibition and to provide the P.N.E. with additional revenue.[26] *Vancouver's Fair*

THE PNE TURNED the Pacific Coliseum into a showcase for major entertainment during the Fair, bringing in some of the biggest names in show business yet ensuring that the public could see these acts at family prices. Fairgoers during 13 of the 17 days this summer ... could choose from shows featuring Anne Murray, Jimmie Rodgers, the R.C.M.P. Musical Ride plus the Young Canadians of the Calgary Stampede, Ray Charles, The Irish Rovers and The New Seekers. Prices per show were just $1.00 for adults and 50 cents for children 12 and under, plus PNE grounds admission. The PNE ... also brought in superstar Tom Jones for a 'one-nighter' at prices of just $7.50, $6.50, $5.50, plus grounds entry — half the price of a Jones concert in other cities.[27] *PNE Annual Report*

ABOVE: Tom Petty and the Heartbreakers playing the PNE, 1979.

STAR
ACULAR!

THIS IS THE FIFTH SEASON SINCE THE PNE ADMINISTRATORS FIRST TOOK A CRACK AT THE IMPRESARIO'S TRADE and their original idea is still in effect: they are out to provide ... grandstand shows appealing to the broadest of public tastes yet OFFERING SOLID ENTERTAINMENT VALUE FOR THE DOLLAR.[28] *The Vancouver Sun*

BIG STARS OF the day like Tom Jones brought their special brand of entertainment to Vancouver when they performed. He inspired torrid headlines and reviews the next day.

Welsh Singer and Torso Vibrator Extraordinaire

MADAM, TURN THE faces of your children to the wall, for this is not a tale for those of tender years ... You say he is merely a handsome singer with a moderately good voice and a lot of fancy moves. To his fans he is like lightning and Liberace, a natural phenomenon ... As Tom Jones's show begins to end it appears that literally hundreds of pairs of panties are being offered from various hands. They want him to touch. He takes a pair, wipes his forehead with them and then his body. He tosses them back. It happens again and again. Then the song ends. Tom says a hurried goodnight, charges to the exit and it is over. The lights go up. We stumble out into the night. By the time the parking lot is reached we don't believe what we have seen.[29] *The Vancouver Sun*

CLOCKWISE FROM TOP LEFT: Joni Mitchell, 1979. Johnny Cash, 1978. The Pointer Sisters, The Guess Who, Seals and Croft and Anne Murray played at the PNE in 1975. Heartthrob Tom Jones riveted audiences in 1979.

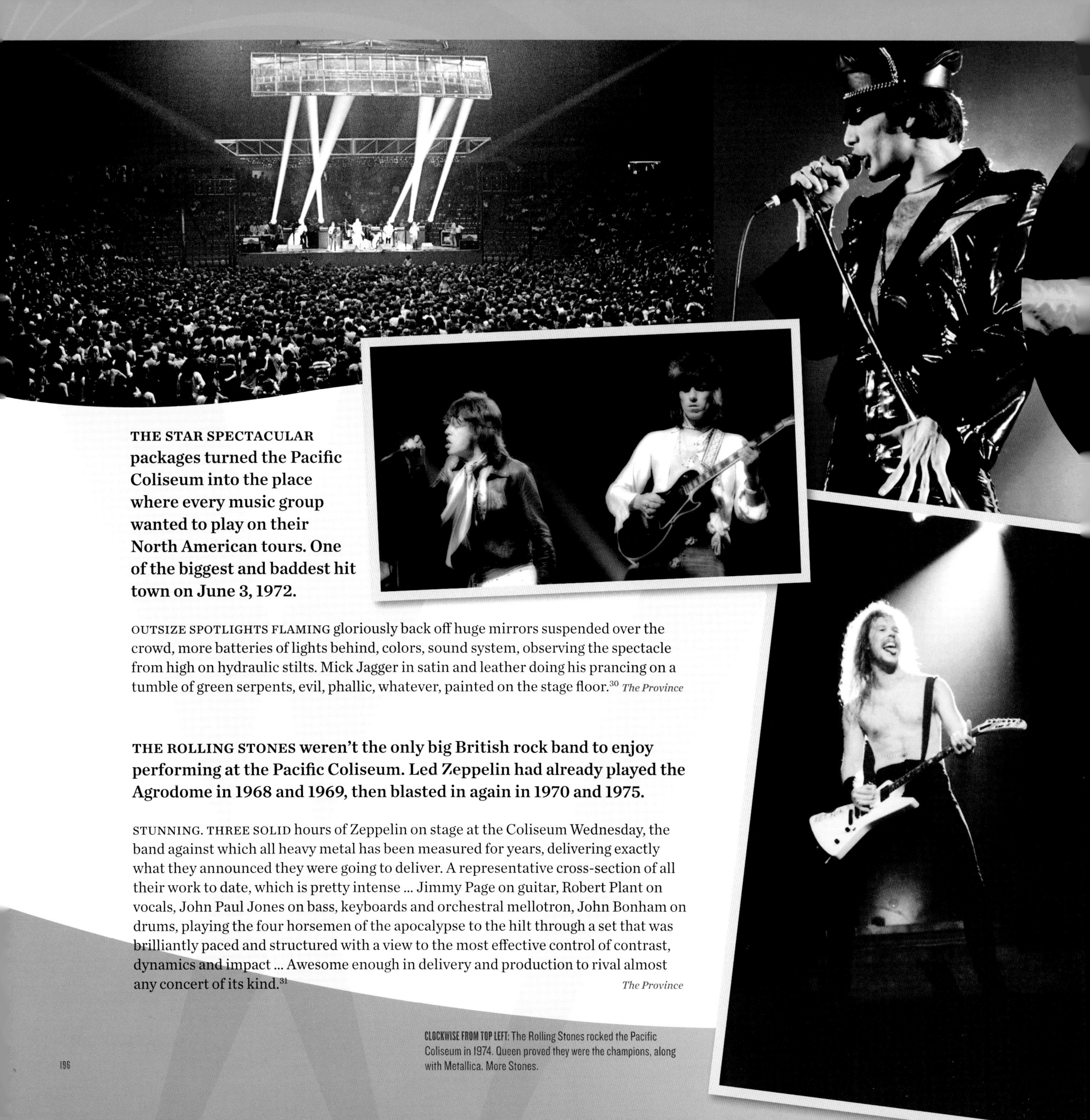

THE STAR SPECTACULAR packages turned the Pacific Coliseum into the place where every music group wanted to play on their North American tours. One of the biggest and baddest hit town on June 3, 1972.

OUTSIZE SPOTLIGHTS FLAMING gloriously back off huge mirrors suspended over the crowd, more batteries of lights behind, colors, sound system, observing the spectacle from high on hydraulic stilts. Mick Jagger in satin and leather doing his prancing on a tumble of green serpents, evil, phallic, whatever, painted on the stage floor.[30] *The Province*

THE ROLLING STONES weren't the only big British rock band to enjoy performing at the Pacific Coliseum. Led Zeppelin had already played the Agrodome in 1968 and 1969, then blasted in again in 1970 and 1975.

STUNNING. THREE SOLID hours of Zeppelin on stage at the Coliseum Wednesday, the band against which all heavy metal has been measured for years, delivering exactly what they announced they were going to deliver. A representative cross-section of all their work to date, which is pretty intense ... Jimmy Page on guitar, Robert Plant on vocals, John Paul Jones on bass, keyboards and orchestral mellotron, John Bonham on drums, playing the four horsemen of the apocalypse to the hilt through a set that was brilliantly paced and structured with a view to the most effective control of contrast, dynamics and impact ... Awesome enough in delivery and production to rival almost any concert of its kind.[31] *The Province*

CLOCKWISE FROM TOP LEFT: The Rolling Stones rocked the Pacific Coliseum in 1974. Queen proved they were the champions, along with Metallica. More Stones.

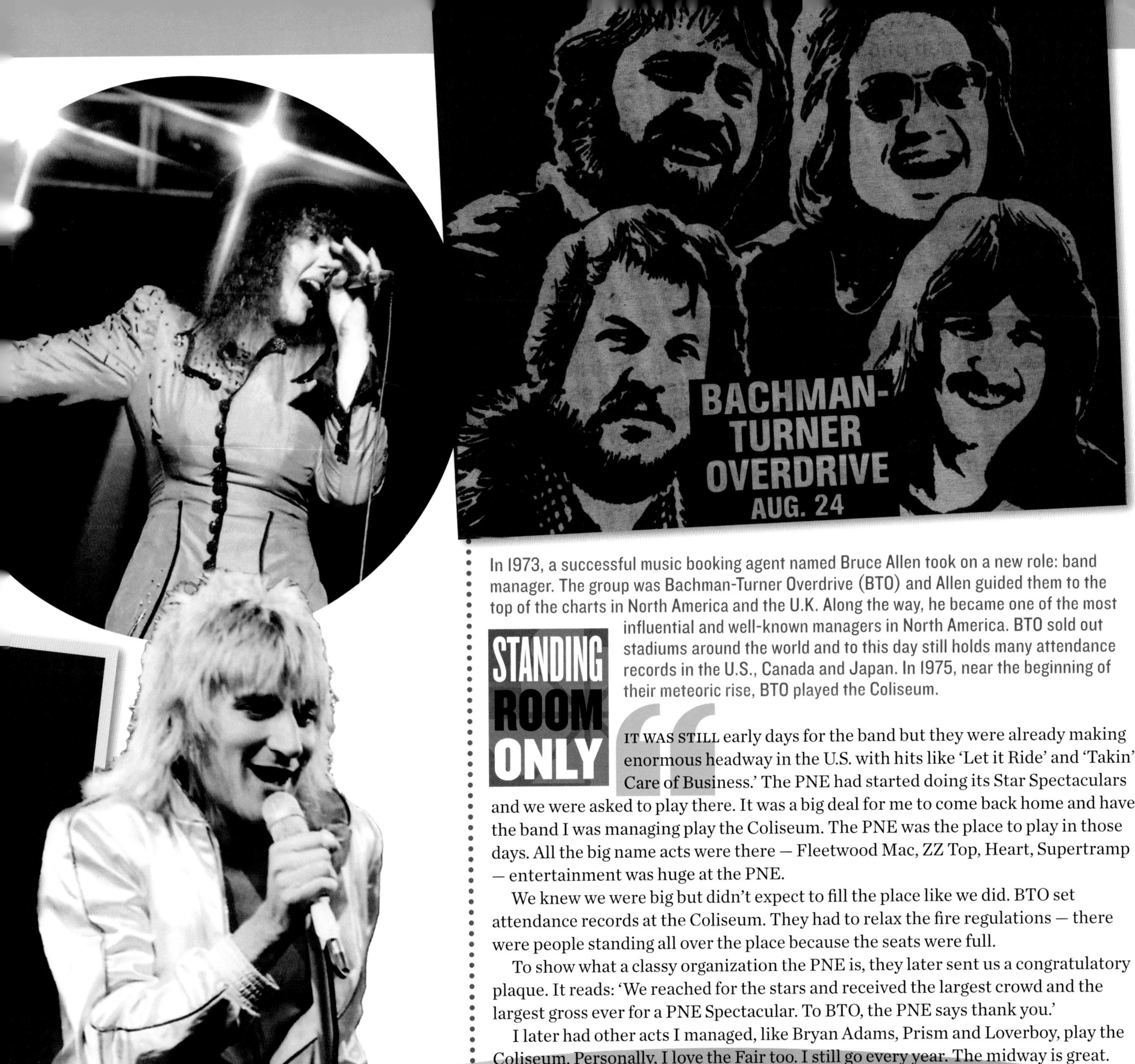

In 1973, a successful music booking agent named Bruce Allen took on a new role: band manager. The group was Bachman-Turner Overdrive (BTO) and Allen guided them to the top of the charts in North America and the U.K. Along the way, he became one of the most influential and well-known managers in North America. BTO sold out stadiums around the world and to this day still holds many attendance records in the U.S., Canada and Japan. In 1975, near the beginning of their meteoric rise, BTO played the Coliseum.

STANDING ROOM ONLY

"IT WAS STILL early days for the band but they were already making enormous headway in the U.S. with hits like 'Let it Ride' and 'Takin' Care of Business.' The PNE had started doing its Star Spectaculars and we were asked to play there. It was a big deal for me to come back home and have the band I was managing play the Coliseum. The PNE was the place to play in those days. All the big name acts were there — Fleetwood Mac, ZZ Top, Heart, Supertramp — entertainment was huge at the PNE.

We knew we were big but didn't expect to fill the place like we did. BTO set attendance records at the Coliseum. They had to relax the fire regulations — there were people standing all over the place because the seats were full.

To show what a classy organization the PNE is, they later sent us a congratulatory plaque. It reads: 'We reached for the stars and received the largest crowd and the largest gross ever for a PNE Spectacular. To BTO, the PNE says thank you.'

I later had other acts I managed, like Bryan Adams, Prism and Loverboy, play the Coliseum. Personally, I love the Fair too. I still go every year. The midway is great. I've cracked the 'Baseball in the Peach Basket' game — I figured out how to drop the ball softly into the basket. I don't win every time, but I have won so much stuff there. I like giving the fuzzy animals to kids and watch their eyes get big. One year I was a demolition derby driver. Now that was a trip. I did it for a promotion of some kind. That was fun.

CLOCKWISE FROM TOP LEFT: Heart wowed audiences with Dreamboat Annie in 1978. Bachman-Turner Overdrive broke attendance records in 1975. Then there's Rod Stewart.

All I've Got to Say Is ...

"THE PNE ROCKS!"

PNE Memory Book, 1999

Van Halen's David Lee Roth rocks the Pacific Coliseum, 1979.

CHAPTER 8

1980–1989

BIGGER AND BETTER

'80–'89

Erwin Swangard welcomes some small Fairgoers. Swangard was appointed a director of the Pacific National Exhibition in October 1976 and was elected its president in January 1977, positions he held for some 13 consecutive years.

ONTO THE WORLD STAGE

In 1986, Vancouver threw a party and the world showed up to celebrate. First, there was the city's 100th birthday on April 6, and then the main event from May to October — Expo '86. Vancouver played host to more than 100 countries and several million people. With transportation as the theme, the False Creek site brimmed with technology and bright visions of the future.

NOT TO BE outdone by all the international presentations, Vancouver built a SkyTrain demonstration to spotlight Canada's mass-transit prowess. The iconic white sails rose over the harbourside Canada Pavilion, and the twinkling orb of the Expo Centre's IMAX theatre (now Science World) became a favourite rendezvous for nighttime visitors. The PNE was part of the excitement, with its landmark staging of an Expo cultural extravaganza at the Pacific Coliseum.

By fall the crowds had gone home, but the city had been changed forever. In no time, the vacant Expo site was sold to Hong Kong billionaire Li Ka-shing and work eventually got underway on the largest urban redevelopment in North America. The centrepiece of the new False Creek neighbourhood was BC Place Stadium, which opened in 1983 after a spirited but unsuccessful bid by the PNE to incorporate a new big-capacity sports facility into its proposed Exhibition Park Multiplex project. With all this new development and with the world at Vancouver's doorstep, the PNE's Fair soon began offering citizens a taste of the future with a series of pavilions that showcased Pacific Rim countries.

FROM TOP: Fun at the Plaza of Nations at Expo '86. The Expo Centre under construction. The Centre was the largest theme pavilion at Expo and became Science World after Expo closed.

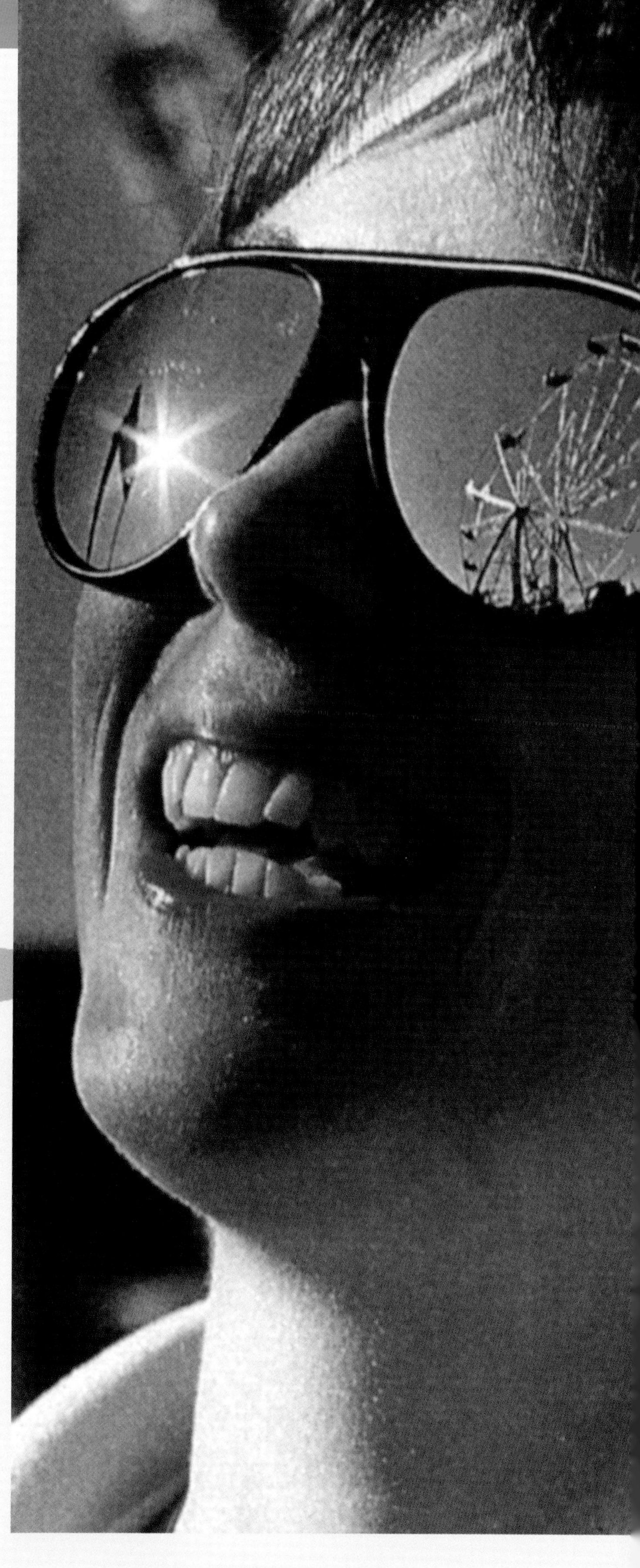

While big things were happening, a host of small things were changing the way people lived in their homes. Personal computers made their debut, along with videocassette recorders (VCRs), microwaves, cordless phones, telephone answering machines and compact disc players. Nintendo video games like Super Mario Bros. and Tetris became all the rage. Once again, the place to get a taste of the future was at the PNE with its smorgasbord of trade and recreation shows.

Punk and rap started making their way into the musical mainstream, but it was the hard rock bands with "big hair" who still ruled. Wrestling became big too, morphing into a riotous, theatrical sports event that drew huge, screaming crowds. The PNE's venues — the Forum, the Agrodome and the Pacific Coliseum — were tailor-made for those who wanted to jump to the music or roar for their favourite WWF (now the WWE) star.

Serious issues also got headlines in the 1980s — a double-digit unemployment rate, a recession, skyrocketing (then plummeting) housing prices and the devastation of AIDS. Good causes counterbalanced the "greed is good" sentiment of the times. The Vancouver Food Bank was established in 1982 and through the years the PNE was there with support — in one notable example, using its Fun Buses to pick up food donations at stops along the way to the PNE, creating a massive community drive in more ways than one.

Canadian athlete Rick Hansen launched his Man in Motion tour from Vancouver in 1985, pushing his wheelchair across four continents to raise awareness of spinal cord injuries and $26 million for research. An ecstatic public came out to cheer when he wheeled into the PNE grounds, near the end of his global journey.

CLOCKWISE FROM TOP LEFT: The Circle-Magic Theatre in The Forum, part of the BC Centennial celebrations during the Fair, 1986. Expo's look to the future included a mascot robot. Cool shades reflect hot fun at the PNE.

PNE's 40 buses to collect donations for food bank over long weekend

LENDING A HELPING HAND

WHILE MANY ENJOYED the good times in the 1980s, Vancouverites also dug deep into their pockets for worthy causes and to help those less fortunate. Charities echoed the community's concern and the PNE offered its services to fundraising drives.

BOBBY HULL, FRANK Mahovlich, Darryl Sittler and Yvan Cournoyer will highlight an exciting list of NHL players facing-off March 21st in the Pacific Coliseum at 7 p.m. They'll all be playing in the special 'Legends of Hockey: the East-West Challenge' hockey game to raise money for Rick Hansen ... The game is co-sponsored by the Pacific National Exhibition and the Vancouver Canucks. PNE president Erwin Swangard says his organization is delighted to be involved. 'We're very pleased to work with the Canucks on this extremely important event to raise money for Rick Hansen's tour,' he said.[1]

PNE Events

PNE PRESIDENT ERWIN SWANGARD PRESENTS A CHECK FOR $68,413 TO RICK HANSEN in a ceremony at Exhibition Park on the final day of the Man In Motion Tour. The money was raised from the 'Legends of Hockey' game.[2]

PNE Events

The Pacific National Exhibition will use THE LAST THREE OPERATING DAYS OF ITS 'FUN BUSES' TO HELP THE VANCOUVER FOOD BANK feed the increasing numbers of hungry people in the Lower Mainland.

PNE SPOKESMAN WAYNE Dizuta said Thursday that during the Labour Day weekend drivers on all 40 buses will pick up food bank donations at any of the stops along 14 routes throughout the Lower Mainland. The donations will be collected at a central depot on the fairground and delivered to the food bank warehouse after the long weekend. 'It really bothered us that there were so many people without food on the table, so we thought this would be a great opportunity to incorporate the buses we have on the road into a massive community drive,' Dizuta said ... In addition, the PNE collected about 10,000 cans during this year's parade.[3]

The Vancouver Sun

FROM LEFT: Rick Hansen's Man in Motion Tour got a boost with the PNE's contribution presented to Rick by Erwin Swangard. The PNE loaned 40 buses to help the 1984 Food Bank drive.

May 22, 1987, was a very special day for me. After two years, two months and two days of wheeling through 34 countries on the Man In Motion World Tour, raising awareness about the potential of people with disabilities, I was arriving back home in Vancouver.

"MY TEAM AND I made several stops around the city before our final homecoming celebration at BC Place Stadium, and one of the most memorable stops was the Pacific National Exhibition. The PNE has long been considered a showcase of British Columbia, a place that captures the spirit and enthusiasm of our city and its citizens. After being on the road for over two years with my team, arriving at the PNE was an amazing reminder of how great it was to be home again in B.C.! I was overwhelmed by the supporters who greeted us, and the crowds of kids who cheered us on. I was in awe when the original song "The Dream Will Live On," produced by McDonald's, was unveiled and very appreciative of people like Jack Munro and the union workers, who were selling wood to raise funds for the Tour. It was an incredible day, made even more special by the people who came out to encourage us and show their support." Rick Hansen, 2010 interview

STILL CRAZY AFTER ALL THESE YEARS

SOME TRADITIONS CATCH the public's fancy and just keep on going. The Fair's celebrated egg-laying contest, one of the many crowd-pleasers from early years, was keeping abreast of the times.

CELEBRITY EGG-LAYING CONTEST

Television and radio personalities will have a chance to lay an egg ... in fact they can lay half a dozen a day. The personalities are matched to a pen, each of which contains an equal number of laying hens. Each morning the number of eggs is tabulated ... and **THE WINNER IS AWARDED CASH WHICH IS DONATED TO THE WINNER'S DESIGNATED CHARITY.**[4]

PNE Media Notebook

CLOCKWISE FROM TOP LEFT: Rick Hansen meets one of his young fans at the PNE on the last day of the Man in Motion World Tour, 1987. Cabbage Patch Kids Day at the Fair, 1985. Workouts with headbands and big hair were hot at the 1985 Fair. Celebrities laying eggs and trivia contests pulled in big crowds.

YOU NEVER KNOW WHAT YOU'RE GOING TO FIND
Taking in the latest gadgets is a big part of a day at the Fair at the PNE. Through the years you might find a novel way to lose weight with the Darlyne Reducing Machine (1950), a pitchman demonstrating new ways to peel, slice and dice (1980s), or the perfect set of starry, glittery deeley bops to go with that very long straw (1980s).

THE BIGGER, THE BETTER

THE TRADE-SHOW BALL had started rolling in the 1950s, but the PNE really hit its stride in the '80s. Along with the usual blockbusters like the Auto, Home and Boat shows, an assortment of new shows kept Vancouverites on top of the latest modern conveniences, inventions and lifestyle choices. In 1989, the PNE launched its Christmas Fair, which drew big holiday crowds.

It Made Me Feel on Top of the World

"MY MOST MEMORABLE event at the PNE was going with my mom and dad every year as a child and visiting the show rooms. One of them was full of grand pianos. I always dreamed of learning to play a piano, but my parents couldn't afford the lessons. So when I was going through the building with the pianos, I would touch them and sit on the benches. It made me feel on top of the world. I never did get to learn how to play, but now both my kids play and they are trying to teach Mom! But I loved going through the building with those huge pianos and pretending I knew how to play."

Marianna Cianelli, Vancouver

NEVER BEFORE IN the 68-year history of the Pacific International Auto Show has there been such a lavish display of automobiles. When the 1988 auto show opens its doors Friday, January 15 for a 10-day run at the PNE, the value of five feature cars alone will total over $1 million. The Ferrari Testarossa, a flaming red beauty with maximum speed of 177.7 mph and acceleration from 0 to 60 in 5.7 seconds, is valued at $240,000. Two magnificent show cars, Probe V — a concept vehicle from Ford — and the Toyota FXV-II as seen at the Tokyo Auto Show, represent over one-half million dollars between them with many millions more spent on their development ... With more than 300 new vehicles displayed ... the auto show continues its tradition of providing the car-buying public an opportunity to view all that is new from the world's leading manufacturers in one location.[5]

PNE Events

Hunting and fishing show opens

THE OUTDOORS MOVES indoors at the PNE for the first annual Vancouver Hunting and Fishing Show ... For three days, Lower Mainland sports enthusiasts will have a chance to view the latest in hunting and fishing gear, sporting goods, camping equipment and all-terrain vehicles. Experts in fly and bait casting will be on hand to demonstrate various methods. There'll even be a mountain stream contained in a 20' X 50' tank, stocked with steelhead trout, where fly fishermen in hip waders will display their skills to the crowd. The Vancouver Hunting and Fishing Show is the first of its kind ever held here ... It's everything for the outdoor enthusiast.[7]

PNE Events

ESP Fair at the PNE Forum

THE ANNUAL PSYCHIC, holistic ESP Fair is presenting psychics from across North America ... Astrology, numerology, tarot, palmistry, healing, plus aura readings will be among the many disciplines featured ... the public will be able to listen to continuous free lectures and demonstrations on topics ranging from crystals, negative ions, past-life regression, tarot and personal growth.[6]

PNE Events

All new computer 'swap-meet' plays at PNE

CONSUMERS WILL HAVE an exciting opportunity to buy, sell or trade software at the Consumer's Computer Show '88 which opens October 22 in The Forum Building for a two-day run. 'The show is Vancouver's first annual new and used computer swap meet,' explained show manager Manuel de la Cruz. 'There's no other show in the Lower Mainland providing a marketplace for people to buy and sell computer equipment. We're filling a void that has been missing for a long time.'[8]

PNE Events

CELEBRATE THE GREAT TASTE OF B.C. WINES AT THE PNE!

SAMPLED ANY B.C. WINES RECENTLY? The Pacific National Exhibition offers two great chances at its Sixth Annual B.C. Wine Competition ... Join wine makers, retail merchants and other industry representatives at A GALA EVENING SALUTING B.C.'S EVER-IMPROVING WINE INDUSTRY. This year's competition is celebrating wines produced from grapes 100 per cent grown in British Columbia ... The following afternoon, visit the PNE Food Building between 5–9 p.m. and partake in 'TASTE THE BEST OF B.C.' — A CELEBRATION OF WINES AND FOODS PRODUCED RIGHT HERE AT HOME.'[9]

PNE Events

CLOCKWISE FROM OPPOSITE PAGE, TOP LEFT: The '80s were a decade of really big shows, including the 1986 Homeshow, an ESP Fair, the 1986 Hunting and Fishing Show, annual wine events and the 1985 Auto Show.

HULK HOGAN AND OTHER HEROES from the World Wrestling Federation stampede onto the PNE Coliseum stage Saturday, July 1 at 8 pm for **ANOTHER EVENING OF HARD HITTING ENTERTAINMENT.**[10]

PNE Events

WRESTLEMANIA

WHO KNEW THAT an ancient sport honouring strength and agility would become such a 20th-century show stopper? The PNE brought these roughhouse spectaculars to the ring for the legions of Vancouver fans who couldn't get enough of wrestlers' antics and displays of brute force. And it wasn't just burly men who came to the ring — women got in on the wrestling action too.

Exciting wrestling Dec. 6

THE WORLD WRESTLING Federation is to return to the Pacific Coliseum ... with a full card of professional action. In the main event Sgt. Slaughter battles it out against Nikolai Volkoff from Russia and following in a co-feature the former inter-continental champion Tito Santana will oppose the new champ Gregg 'The Hammer' Valentine in a rematch for the title. In other action, wrestling fans will see Angelo 'King Kong' Mosca take on the Iron Sheik from Iran and Billy Jack in the squared circle to deal with the likes of Moondog Spot. In addition, a special feature match-up will bring the newly crowned ladies champion Wendi Richter into the ring to defend her title against former champion 'the Fabulous' Moolah.[11]

PNE Events

My Heroes

FROM THE TIME I was a boy, I couldn't wait to watch wrestling on TV. The way those guys dressed and their outrageous talk kept me absolutely transfixed better than any cartoon show. They were huge and strong and I learned most of the moves. Wrestling became a serious pasttime for me but it also made me laugh when the characters swaggered around the ring and bragged. When I found out one of my heroes — Bret Hart — was coming to town, I begged my parents to let me go. They kind of hummed and hawed because they preferred stuff like books and serious movies. They didn't understand my love of wrestling but they humoured me.

One night, beside my dinner plate there was an envelope addressed to me. Inside were tickets to the show at the Coliseum! My dad was going to take me. I couldn't believe it. And what a fantastic show — choke holds, hammerlocks, head butts, full nelsons, scissor kicks — I was so excited to see it all.

My dad smiled a lot but I think that was because he liked seeing me so thrilled. He never did catch the wrestling bug like I did. I'm thankful both my parents were so liberal-minded and let me have my own heroes.

Dan Nelson, Vancouver

FROM LEFT: André the Giant hoists Miss PNE, 1983. Hulk Hogan's skill and flair give fans a thrill.

DAZZLING ON ICE

OVER THE YEARS, Ice Capades, the skating show that wows audiences, has been a major fundraising event for The Rotary Club of Vancouver.

FROM SKATERS TWIRLING thirty-five feet above the frozen surface to stunning precision footwork on ice, Ice Capades' newest revue, 'Dream World', explodes with universal appeal. The family ice extravaganza opens at the Coliseum for 9 performances ... Only the best can cut it here and the dazzling array of champions prove it as they take over the ice with a powerful display of athletics and grace. In keeping with the tradition of bringing top-ranked professional skaters to its audiences, Ice Capades is proud to announce the professional debut of the 1984 World Pair Champions, Paul Martini and Barbara Underhill. Together, they stole the spotlight at the World Championships in Ottawa ...[12] *PNE Events*

Only the best can cut it here and the dazzling array of champions prove it as they take over the ice with a POWERFUL DISPLAY OF ATHLETICS AND GRACE.

FROM LEFT: The Ice Capades always delivered, with stars Paul Martini and Barbara Underhill, Torvill and Dean and a cast of animated characters like the Super Mario Bros. Ice Capades skaters, 1988.

FINDING LOVE, PNE-STYLE

EVERYONE HAS A story about how they found love. For many, the PNE is part of their story.

A Special Secret

I WORKED AT the PNE in the Dogwood Restaurant and then later went on to be a ticket seller at the gates. One Seniors' Day, there was a huge line-up that went from the Coliseum to the bus loop on Renfrew Street. Because the line-up was so long, patrons started talking to each other. As they got to the gate, some of them started telling me, one after the other, that they knew a secret. 'Tee hee, I know something you don't,' was what one person said. After about five of these mysterious comments, I looked up and saw my boyfriend standing there with a single long-stemmed rose for me. Because we both worked different shifts, he and I had not seen each other in over a week (a long time when you are young and in love). My boyfriend had decided to lose some of his sleeping time to come and say hi to me ... It was one of the most romantic gestures that ever happened to me. Whenever I walk by the gates at the Coliseum, I remember that moment like it was yesterday.

Ella Gladstone, Burnaby, B.C.

Connecting on the Coaster

I LIVED IN Kamloops after I moved to Canada from Mexico. When I decided to take my first trip to Vancouver one thing I really wanted to do was go to the PNE. While I was waiting in line to get on the roller coaster, I met a man who asked me to join him in his car. He joked with me that I shouldn't be scared because he could protect me. I accepted his invitation and we had a blast. That was the start of our relationship. Up to this day we always go to the PNE to celebrate our anniversary because we have been together since then. I adore him and next year will be 10 years of loving each other. Thank you PNE for the loveliest present you could ever have given me. One day when we have the money we will get married right there, where we met.

Esperanza Raquel Reeb, Langley, B.C.

We Met in the Barn

MANY A COUPLE has met in a bar; not as many can say they met in a barn. The year was 1972. The girl was from West Vancouver, the boy was from East Vancouver. She was 15, he was 16. She was shy with mouse brown hair. He was a 'wheeling dealing' skinny redhead wearing Seafarer jeans. It was intrigue at first sight. Each of them had been assigned to work in the PNE livestock barn cafeteria. For her, this meant continuing the (at least) three-generation family tradition of working in food services. For him it meant free food, and hope that a skinny redhead might gain enough weight to make the local football team. That summer job of 17 days led to a second summer job and although he walked her to the bus stop on the last day of the second year, that would be it for quite some time. No Facebook, no Twitter, no email, and no cellphones in those days. As she boarded the bus, he said, 'I'll go on *Reach for the Top* for you.' He did, and she watched, but was too shy to connect with him afterwards (girls didn't call boys in those days). In 1989, 17 short years after the day they met in the barn, wedding bells rang.

Karol Traviss, West Vancouver, B.C.

CLOCKWISE FROM TOP LEFT: The PNE was the place for all kinds of love and commitment. A wedding on the coaster, getting close on the Wave Swinger or getting your girl that special reminder of a great day.

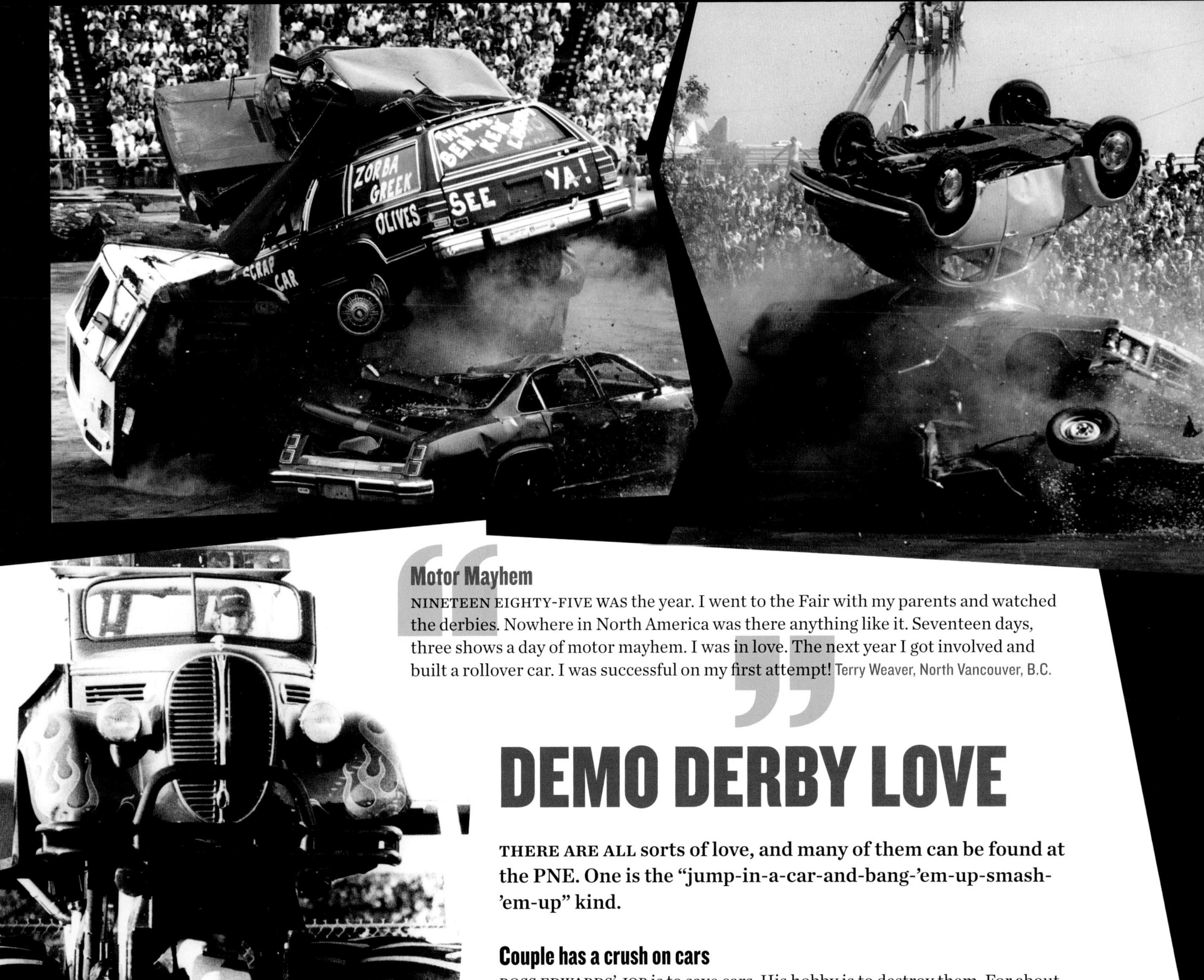

Motor Mayhem

NINETEEN EIGHTY-FIVE WAS the year. I went to the Fair with my parents and watched the derbies. Nowhere in North America was there anything like it. Seventeen days, three shows a day of motor mayhem. I was in love. The next year I got involved and built a rollover car. I was successful on my first attempt! Terry Weaver, North Vancouver, B.C.

DEMO DERBY LOVE

THERE ARE ALL sorts of love, and many of them can be found at the PNE. One is the "jump-in-a-car-and-bang-'em-up-smash-'em-up" kind.

Couple has a crush on cars

ROSS EDWARDS' JOB is to save cars. His hobby is to destroy them. For about 40 hours a week, Edwards is a tow truck driver for the B.C. Automobile Association. The rest of the time, Edwards, 31, is a demolition derby driver, competing in events such as the current Pacific National Exhibition derbies. He is the one behind the wheel of car 274. He says he doesn't like telling the stranded motorists he rescues that in his off-hours he smashes into other cars for fun. Once in a while, however, he lets on. 'And most of them are thrilled.' His wife Judy, 32, is also a derby driver. She drives car 174. During the day, she works as a computer tape operator.[13] *The Vancouver Sun*

ABOVE AND LEFT: Some found love in the '80s at the regular Demolition Derbies and Monster Truck competitions.

HOLLYWOOD NORTH

IN THE 1980S, Hollywood started hearing about this great town up the coast where you could produce your movie for a fraction of the Southern California price.

MOST PEOPLE KNOW about the annual Fair, trade and consumer shows, and rental facilities available for meetings, receptions, banquets and weddings at the Pacific National Exhibition. But, people would probably be surprised to learn that major motion pictures and a variety of television series are filmed here. Examples of films include *Rocky IV* starring Sylvester Stallone and *Reckless Endangerment* with Kelly McGillis and Jodie Foster, while television series include *Airwolf*, *Stingray*, *JJ Starbuck*, *Wise Guy* and *MacGyver*. 'The PNE has a unique physical set-up which enables film-makers to do a lot of different things,' says Dianne Neufeld, B.C. Film Commissioner ... 'PNE management is used to dealing with unusual requests for its facilities and, as a result, is very flexible. This attitude provides film crews with an atmosphere of creative latitude.' PNE archive report

BIG-HAIR BANDS

THE 1980S GAVE us big bands with big hair and outrageous outfits. The tough boys sported hairstyles that were teased into towering dyed coifs that seemingly defied gravity — all part of their act. Between these bands and other more mainstream groups, the PNE's facilities were booked solid.

PNE's 1988 concert business 'skyrockets'

THE PACIFIC NATIONAL Exhibition has released figures showing the PNE almost doubled its concert business [since the 1970s] ... The Pacific Coliseum was the site of 30 concerts in 1988 ... During 1986 and 1985, the PNE hosted 27 and 34 concerts respectively. Two major contributions to the PNE's success were the volume of pop acts touring throughout 1988 — especially in the summer months — and the continuing popularity of the Pacific Coliseum with acts and promoters ... 'Word is getting out, and Vancouver is becoming an influential city for the music industry,' explains Mark Norman, vice-president of Perryscope Concert Productions Ltd. 'It's now important to play Vancouver.' He also feels the Pacific Coliseum — as a building — enables a wide variety of performers to play there.[14]

PNE Events

Sinatra, Martin, Davis to appear at Coliseum

FRANK SINATRA, DEAN Martin, and Sammy Davis Jr. — three of the entertainment world's most outstanding performers — will perform in the round at the Pacific Coliseum ... Together, the three entertainers represent more than 130 years of experience in show business. They continue to draw critical and public acclaim wherever they perform. When these three get together on stage, as the song says, 'Anything Goes.'

PNE press release

KISS — THE living and screaming essence of rock & roll armed with slabs of hard chords, raging guitars, thundering drums and passionate vocals, jumps onto the Coliseum stage Friday, March 11, 1988. Opening act for the concert ... is Anthrax.[15]

PNE Events

HEAVY METAL FANS — seek your reward! Head to the PNE Coliseum Wednesday May 31, 1989 for twice as much metal and be rewarded courtesy of Metallica and The Cult.

PNE press release

WHEN ALL IS said and done, R.E.M. remains one of rock 'n' roll's most compelling, enigmatic and engaging bands. Their popularity was recently ensured when *Rolling Stone* magazine crowned them 'America's Best Rock & Roll Band'. R.E.M. performs at the Pacific Coliseum Saturday, October 14 , 1989.[16]

PNE Events

THE TOP TEN ACTS appearing at the Pacific Coliseum during 1988 by attendance were:

John Cougar Mellencamp (three concerts) – 47,916
Robert Plant – 14,785
Def Leppard – 14,705
George Michael – 13,863
Eric Clapton – 13,802
Sinatra/Martin/Davis – 13,204
Rod Stewart – 12,830
Aerosmith – 12,778
Prince – 12,300
INXS – 12,026[17]

PNE Events

George Michael, in his first solo tour, at Pacific Coliseum September 25

HIS CURRENT EIGHT-MONTH 'Faith Tour' will span four continents throughout 1988. And as fans at the Coliseum will see, it promises to be one of Vancouver's entertainment highlights of the year.[18]

PNE Events

CLOCKWISE FROM TOP LEFT: The PNE became the go-to place for Hollywood movie companies shooting films such as *Rocky IV*. At the Pacific Coliseum '80s all-star concerts included Aerosmith, Kiss, Eric Clapton, Pat Benatar, Robert Plant, and George Michael.

OPERA, PANDAS, STALLIONS AND MOTIVATIONAL SPEAKERS

THE PNE HOSTED a vast array of entertainments for the public, in addition to the blockbuster concerts and sporting events. To accommodate a large-scale production by La Scala, the PNE transformed the Pacific Coliseum into a vast opera house with a towering proscenium arch.

TEATRO ALLA SCALLA of Milan, Italy — the most famous opera in the world — will perform six performances of Giuseppe Verdi's *I Lombardi* between August 24 and September 4 at the Pacific Coliseum. The announcement was made recently at an Expo '86 news conference. During the announcement ceremony, PNE president Erwin Swangard said La Scala was another example of the excellent working relationship existing between Expo '86 and the Pacific National Exhibition ... The tour of La Scala is promoted by the Commissioner General of Italy.

PNE press release

THE MUSICAL POMP and pageantry of Scotland comes to the Pacific Coliseum ... with Black Watch — Scotland's senior highland regiment — celebrating its 250th anniversary. The show highlights a spectacular display of music, marching and highland dance, and also includes the massed bands of The Argyll & Sutherland Highlanders.[19]

PNE Events

FROM TOP: Showtime at the PNE went from La Scala's staging of *I Lombardi* to the Great Circus of the People's Republic of China.

GONG GONG — ONE OF ONLY TWO PERFORMING GIANT PANDA BEARS IN THE WORLD — will highlight The Great Circus of China when it opens at the Pacific Coliseum November 30, 1988. But Gong Gong is more than just a circus performer. He is touring across Canada representing the Canadian Panda Project — a special fund-raising program for The China Wildlife Conservation Association ... The Great Circus of China is pure oriental circus; it is a 2,000 year-old Chinese folk-art tradition that will entertain the entire family with TRAPEZE ACTS, UNICYCLE AND BICYCLE ACTS, PORCELAIN PLATE SPINNING, FOOT JUGGLING, HOOP ATHLETICS, JUGGLING AND CHAIR BALANCING.[20]

PNE Events

Superstars of Success

OUTSTANDING MOTIVATIONAL, INSPIRATIONAL and achieving excellence speakers including Earl Nightingale and Dr. Joyce Brothers will speak at the Pacific Coliseum Tuesday, November 15 during a one-day event. Billed as the 'Superstars of Success', the line-up is as follows:

DON BEVERIDGE
The Achievement Challenge

JOE GIRARD
How To Sell Yourself

DICK CAVETT
To Be Determined

DR. JOYCE BROTHERS
Success – A State of Mind

EARL NIGHTINGALE
Think and Grow Rich

OG MANDINO
Greatest Secrets of Success [21]

PNE Events

The aristocratic, royal, light and nimble Lipizzaner stallions will entertain horse-lovers when they perform at The Agrodome June 25, 1988.[22]

PNE Events

FROM TOP: Animals got star billing too — Gong Gong visited from China and the Lipizzaner stallions from Austria wowed the crowds.

Vending teaches you how to work with people and deal with them. YOU COULDN'T FIND A BETTER PLACE TO WORK THAN THE PNE.

Nedj Macesic

FAIR BUSINESS

THE PNE WAS big business year-round in the 1980s. Reports showed how important Exhibition Park and the Fair were to the economies of Vancouver and the province. The PNE was also acknowledged as a major employer, especially of youth getting ready to enter the workforce.

Study shows PNE is outstanding contributor to B.C. economy

A JUST COMPLETED independent economic impact study on the Pacific National Exhibition by the influential management consulting firm of Laventhol & Horwath shows operations at Exhibition Park will contribute the staggering amount of $420.2 million (1987 dollars) to the economies of the Greater Vancouver Regional District (G.V.R.D.) and the Province of British Columbia — an increase of $7.9 million compared to 1985! The figures are about five times greater than those of B.C. Place and the Vancouver Trade and Convention Centre combined for 1987.

PNE archive report

Working and Having Fun

THE SUMMER I graduated from high school, my friend Greg and I both decided we wanted to do something fun and we needed a little money too. Naturally we thought of the PNE. I got a job as a games worker at the balloon-popping booth. It turned out to be a great summer. It was like meeting the circus. The nostalgia of the Fair didn't wear off either. I worked with other people who were having fun and I was surrounded by guests who were enjoying their once-in-a-year Fair visit. It all contributed to us having a great time. My PNE job turned out to be the best job-related experience for my current job as a casino dealer, which helps me pay my way through university in Kamloops.

Matthew Wright, Kamloops, B.C.

FACING PAGE: Selling popcorn at a game, 1987. **FROM TOP:** Getting some valuable job skills — Lisa Herbert selling tickets (1987), and Edward Periera working at one of the parking lots (1985).

Vendors gain valuable work experience at the PNE

PEANUTS! POPCORN! ICE CREAM! ... If you're one of the thousands of visitors to attend a hockey game, concert or any other event at the Pacific Coliseum, you've probably noticed the vendors, dressed in their white shirts with the familiar red PNE pinwheel logo, selling drinks, ice cream, chips, peanuts and other products. 'Vending is a difficult job,' says Barb Robideaux, vendor supervisor. 'Most vendors are shy in the beginning, but they soon build their confidence through dealing with the public. They learn how to handle money and make decisions. It's a very formative job.'

Kerry Chow, 18, has been vending at the PNE for the past five years. 'You've got to hustle to make a living,' he says, 'and you soon learn to handle money without any goof-ups. A good vendor can sell anything. Salesmanship makes a difference.'

Nedj Macesic, 23, started vending when he was 15 and still works events on a part-time basis. On reflection, Macesic admits he was pretty green when he started vending but he says the job taught him how to interact with people and build self-confidence. His advice: 'Vending teaches you how to work with people and deal with them. You couldn't find a better place to work than the PNE.'

Former vendor Loris Pavan shares Macesic's enthusiasm. His vending job helped finance his education and prepare him for his business career. 'Vending taught me all about the entrepreneurial spirit,' he explains, 'I learned to be creative and motivated.'[28] *PNE Events*

TALENT SEARCH

IT COSTS THE PNE MORE THAN $3 MILLION IN WAGES AND SALARIES TO PRODUCE THE ANNUAL FAIR. **Much of this is effectively a subsidy for community events involving people across the province. For instance, in 1982 it cost the PNE $884,000 to put on western Canada's largest Agricultural Show; more than $250,000 on promotion and sponsorship of international trade;** $92,000 TO HOST THE LARGEST 4-H GATHERING IN NORTH AMERICA ATTENDED BY 1,300 YOUNGSTERS FROM 180 B.C. 4-H CLUBS; $90,000 TO STAGE THE TALENT CONTEST WHICH IS OPEN TO COMPETITORS ACROSS THE PROVINCE; **and $70,000 to produce the Miss PNE Pageant involving contestants representing 40 B.C. communities.**[24]

PNE Events

BACKING B.C.'S COMMUNITIES

THE PNE IS a quiet, effective partner in the lives of many communities and not-for-profit organizations throughout Vancouver and the province.

YEAR-ROUND, THE PNE subsidizes the operation of many amateur sports. Charging only nominal rental rates for 86 amateur sports events in Empire Stadium ... in 1982–83 it actually cost the PNE $120,000. Renting the South Forum to minor hockey and figure skating at Vancouver Park Board rates cost the PNE $132,000 in 1982. The PNE also provides the parking areas south of Hastings Street as a Park 'n' Ride lot to the City virtually free.[25]

PNE Events

CLOCKWISE FROM LEFT: Aspiring artists got their chance to shine at the Fair. Andrew Barr at the keyboard in 1989. A young 4-H winner phones home with the good news. Greg Joy at the annual Vancouver Secondary Schools Track and Field Meet set a Canadian high school record with this jump at Empire Stadium.

PACIFIC OVERTURES

BY THE LATE 1980s, the Fair at the PNE was sponsoring large international pavilions in the Forum building. The first exhibit came from China in 1988, followed by the Republic of Indonesia's pavilion in 1989. For the mere price of admission to the Fair, people could sample the sights, sounds and tastes of Pacific Rim countries.

THE PAVILION PRESENTED by the Republic of Indonesia — the Pacific Rim participant at this year's fair — will be the feature attraction at the 1989 PNE ... the display will include: A commercial show involving 80 Indonesian companies ... exhibiting products. Included will be bicycles, cocoa, cosmetics, rattan and wood furniture, spices and sporting goods; cultural dancing; twice-a-day fashion shows; an Indonesian restaurant, offering a delicious variety of foods from the country's different provinces. Free samples of the world-famous Java and other Indonesian coffees will be presented. [26]

PNE Media Notebook

THE CHINA PAVILION will be the feature attraction of FANFAIR '88. Presented by The People's Republic of China, their magnificent display will fill the entire 45,000 square foot Forum Building. Highlights of the display will include: ... the world-renowned 'Silk Road' fashion show. This show has been seen in Paris, London, New York and Moscow and will be seen for the first time in North America at the PNE. Other pavilion attractions include a major display of authentic Chinese artifacts, handicrafts, export commodities, textiles, arts & crafts, and unique demonstrations by Chinese artisans; a Chinese business show to showcase traditional consumer goods; and exciting travel opportunities showing Canadians what awaits them in China. [27]

FANFAIR '88: PNE Fair Facts

JUBILATION 75th PNE FAIR CANADA AUG. 19 - SEPT. 4 '89 VANCOUVER, B.C.

PNE International Festival 1988

CLOCKWISE FROM TOP LEFT: The PNE turned the spotlight onto the Pacific in the late '80s, with pavilions from Indonesia and China offering exotic cultural, food and fashion displays. Pins and ribbons marking the Fair are always popular.

BACK ON THE BULL

In the 1980s, photographer Craig Hodge decided to recreate the iconic 1920s photo of four young women posing with a prize-winning bull at the Fair's Agricultural Show. The updated versions involved a bevy of Miss PNE contestants and that year's reigning grand champion steer.

MISS LANGLEY

CHAPTER 9

1990 – 1999

A NEW LEASE ON LIFE

'90-'99

Dancers from the Ukrainian Pavillion thrilled Fairgoers in 1992.

A MODEL CITY

With its friendly streets, bounty of natural beauty, deepening multicultural diversity, and thriving arts and culture, Vancouver started winning accolades in the 1990s as one of the best places to live in the world. Residents bragged that you could play golf in the morning, go skiing in the afternoon and take in some theatre in the evening.

OTHER NORTH AMERICAN city centres languished as people fled to the suburbs, but downtown Vancouver defied the odds. It flourished. By 1995 the central city's population had increased by more than 100,000 since 1981. Curious about this phenomenon, city planners from around the world came to see how Vancouver kept its downtown so vibrant.

World leaders got to see the model city for themselves when U.S. President Bill Clinton and Russian President Boris Yeltsin held a media-saturated summit in Vancouver in 1993. Four years later, the city was again in the spotlight as Canada hosted a high-profile meeting of Asia-Pacific countries.

ABOVE: An illuminated Playland displayed against the majestic backdrop of Vancouver, 1995.

With all this attention, major new industries decided to set up shop in Vancouver. Movie production was a billion-dollar industry by 1999; and the PNE, with its large, flexible exhibition spaces, became favourite location for film shoots. As the dot-com bubble expanded, cutting-edge talent poured into Vancouver. The gleaming new towers downtown and funky lofts in Gastown were just the place to house prosperous young entrepreneurs.

New arrivals to the city came from everywhere, but most newcomers hailed from Asia, especially China and India. In a short time, neighbourhoods throughout the metro area were transformed. Store and restaurant signs sporting a cornucopia of different languages heralded the big cultural shift.

The PNE was plugged into Vancouver's new multicultural reality, staging Chinese and Vietnamese New Years celebrations along with Indo-Canadian concerts.

There were spectacles to thrill every citizen. Taking inspiration from the PNE Fair's successful evening fireworks display, the City of Vancouver decided to stage a waterfront fireworks competition. To the delight of organizers, some 300,000 people showed up on the first night in 1991 to gasp and applaud the spectacular pyrotechnics.

In 1994, the Vancouver Canucks went to the Stanley Cup finals for the second time in the club's history. Pacific Coliseum fans roared when the Russian Rocket, Pavel Bure, buried the puck in the opposing New York Rangers' net. But Bure's scoring prowess wasn't enough and the Canucks lost the series in the seventh game, causing unhappy fans to riot on Robson Street.

With the spendthrift '80s behind them, Vancouverites confronted the payback '90s by cocooning. They stayed home in droves to watch VHS and DVD movies, play video games or surf something called the Internet. Before long, new words like "World Wide Web" and "e-mail" were part of everyday conversation.

The stay-at-home movement stalled as people started hankering to reconnect — with each other and with their rural roots. The first contemporary farmers' market held at Trout Lake in 1994 was a hit and became an instant tradition. Similar weekend markets were soon popping up everywhere. None, however, compared to the PNE's annual summer agricultural extravaganza that brought in big crowds curious about what goes on down at the farm.

CLOCKWISE FROM TOP LEFT: American President Bill Clinton said the beauty of Vancouver inspired the historic work accomplished at the 1993 World Summit. Malkit Singh dazzles the audience with Bhangra beats fom the Punjab, 1995. Playland is bathed in light during a nightly fireworks display. Bob Lenarduzzi, Gloria Macarenko and chef Sev Morin get cracking for the celebrity cooking competition, 1990.

KIDS REALLY GO CRAZY over the cow Moo-ternity Ward (four births so far at the fair), and there are plenty of exotic animals, such as rare **SAN CLEMENTE GOATS.**[2]

The Vancouver Sun

Watching the Chicks Hatch

WHEN I WAS little, my grandparents would take me to the PNE every year and hold my hand as we walked through the rides and buildings. Every year we would make spin paintings, ride the merry-go-round and just before we left we would go to see the animals and watch the baby chicks hatch. Now I have a six-year-old and I make sure we do the same.

Roxanne Greer, North Vancouver

DOWN ON THE FARM, PNE-STYLE

AGRICULTURE HAS ALWAYS been the backbone of the PNE, just as its founders intended when they started planning the first Fair. For many Fairgoers, it's a big treat to see prize animals and learn how to grow championship vegetables and tasty fruit. The PNE has always provided farm folks and city folks an opportunity to connect and get to know one another. By the 1990s, the Fair was making these urban-rural connections one of the centrepieces of its agricultural show, occasionally throwing in a little extra entertainment for some added spice.

THE AGRICULTURAL SHOW offered city slickers and rural folk alike a fascinating look at various aspects of life on the farm, including the Mooternity Ward, Walk-through Beehive and, back for a second year, the International Horse Pull, featuring purebreds ... The 4-H Show at the PNE, one of the largest of its kind in Canada, welcomed 1,200 club members from across B.C. The Horticulture Gardens featured displays courtesy of 23 local garden clubs. And new in 1991, members of the Vancouver TheatreSports League tickled the crowds' funny bones with *The Stock Report*, a lively barnyard musical held five times daily.[1]

PNE Annual Report

CLOCKWISE FROM TOP LEFT: It doesn't get much cuter than that. Young hearts delight in cozy visits with their favourite barnyard animals.

MANY CITY KIDS' first encounters with farm animals are at the Fair. Sometimes the encounter is larger than life.

Big Bob is 1,600 kilos of gentleness, and that's no bull.

BIG IS A buzzword at the Pacific National Exhibition. The rides are Big, there are Big Deals at the Showmart and there are Big Stars at the Star Spectacular. And then there's Big Bob, an eight-year-old bull at the agricultural barns. Big Bob, a Limousin-Chianina cross, stands about 2.1 metres (seven feet) tall and tips the scales at 1,600 kg (3,600 pounds). His nostrils look big enough to inhale a grapefruit. 'He is impressive,' says John Dressler, the PNE's director of agriculture. 'To think that a big beast like that can be so kind and gentle is a real kick for city kids, or any kids.' Ten-year-olds Katie Hortobagyi of Sidney and Emily Strocen of Kamloops were suitably impressed. 'He's huge,' said Katie. 'I thought he was a horse,' said Emily.[3] *The Vancouver Sun*

CLOCKWISE FROM TOP LEFT: Now that is one big bull! Visitors are wowed by Big Bob the Bull, 1997. Sharing the same stripes, 1993. "Does it go any faster?" A budding farmer rides a tractor.

GREENING THE PARK, SAYING GOODBYE TO SOME "OLD FRIENDS"

IN 1991, MOMENTUM grew to increase green space at Hastings Park. The PNE planted new trees and flowers and created new picnic areas. Garden areas such as the Sanctuary, Momiji Gardens, Italian Gardens, a skateboarding park and a community sports field were added to the site. But to achieve these greening objectives meant saying goodbye to some old friends. Many mourned the loss of Empire Stadium, the B.C. Pavilion, the Food Building, Showmart, and the Sheep and Swine buildings. Buildings where generations had come to garner cherished memories were now gone.

Throughout this transition of the 1990s and early 2000s, the PNE's future on the Hastings Park site also remained tentative. Plans were being made to relocate the organization to make way for park space. Yet at the same time, a 1992 survey showed that, while people were happy with the landscaping efforts, the majority also wanted the PNE to stay at Hastings Park and continue to provide all the events it had historically offered — the same events made possible by the PNE's inventory of varied facilities, which had now changed dramatically.

IN 1993, ONE of the first structures to come down was Empire Stadium. The writer of a PNE staff newsletter, *Round Table*, wrote of his sadness.

Goodbye Old Empire

I JUST HAD to set aside some room to say goodbye to Empire Stadium. I'd heard it was coming down months and months ago; heck, I even wrote the news release saying it was going to happen. But I don't mind telling you, the morning I saw them tearing up the roof and crunching the cement, there was a lump in my throat ... I've had a chance to spend some time with a few people who have known Empire for many years, some who were there at the very beginning. The conversations all have the same pattern, we share a few memories — compare the great players, the great games, laugh at the oddities that took place. And then there's a pause, a sadness — we look at the rubble and it finally sinks in, Empire Stadium is no more — goodbye old Empire, thanks for the memories, we will miss you.[4]

Round Table

THERE IS A wonderful collection of art deco buildings ... that contain and form the site — they help make sense of the site. We shouldn't dislocate people's memories and traditions; they will be missed.[5]

Donald Luxton, heritage consultant

LEFT TO RIGHT: The flourishing Momiji Gardens frame the Forum in the background. A fond farewell to an old friend; looking back at the Empire Stadium, 1960s.

1993. Contemporary in design and traditional in scope, Momiji Garden will be a sanctuary of beauty and tranquility. Along with creeks and gentle waterfalls, Japanese maple (momiji) and flowering cherry trees, evergreens and azaleas will abound. Year-round colour changes will introduce each new season, as azaleas and Japanese cherry trees bloom in the spring and the leaves of the Japanese maple tree turn from green to a brilliant red in the fall.

Momiji Garden is a celebration of the rich combination of the many people who make up Canada's unique cultural mosaic and the remarkable history and contribution not only of our Japanese Canadians but of all Canadian citizens. Rocks and trees, flowers and waterfalls, all in perfect harmony. A magnificent reflection of cultures coming together and signifying what it means to be Canadian. Open on a year-round basis, Momiji Garden will be for the enjoyment of all residents of British Columbia and our visitors.

MOMIJI GARDENS IS A MAGNIFICENT TRIBUTE ... Located on three acres of park space at the corner of Hastings and Renfrew street ... creeks, rocks, gentle waterfalls, Japanese maple (Momiji), flowering cherry trees, evergreens and azaleas abound in harmony, creating a colourful all-season landmark. THE GARDEN IS OPEN TO THE PUBLIC ON A YEAR-ROUND BASIS FOR THE ENJOYMENT OF BRITISH COLUMBIANS AND OUR VISITORS ... Momiji Gardens was created with support from the Japanese Canadian Citizens Association, the Vancouver Japanese Gardeners' Association, the City of Vancouver and the PNE.

PNE Annual Report

ABOVE: An artist's rendering of the proposed Momiji Gardens, 1992. A Japanese priest and dancers at the blessing ceremony for the gardens in 1993.

BY 1998, THE full impact of plans to move the PNE to another site became evident. Supporters started lobbying to keep the PNE at Exhibition Park. A group calling itself Friends of the PNE brought public attention to the issue.

THIS IS MY heritage, a public asset that is my right to enjoy and I want to benefit from it. I want the whole site, all the buildings, declared a heritage site. Everyone said they love the PNE and they want their children to be able to attend it. I don't want to look back and think I didn't do anything about it.[7]

Mary Jewell, member of Friends of the PNE

THE QUESTION REMAINS: will the legacy that is Hastings Park be resolved with sober, far-reaching analysis, or will the sort of petty squabbling that occurs over family heirlooms prevail. (To the latter point, PNE general manager Annette Antoniak quipped, 'We're not dead yet!')[8]

The Vancouver Courier

TOP: Jim Kempling and Sandra Bannister speak with community members about the proposed changes to the PNE grounds, 1993.

THE GREENING OF THE PNE
Over the space of more than 50 years, the PNE has become an urban park with great facilities framed by lush green spaces. In 1957 (left) an aerial photo shows the original Playland in the lower left corner, where the Pacific Coliseum and Agrodome would later be located. The new Empire Stadium is at the top right. By 2009 (right), new gardens and green space, including Empire Fields at the top right, extend the park element throughout the site.

IN 1998, THE PNE welcomed its 60 millionth visitor to the Fair. It caused many to reflect on what the potential loss of the PNE would mean to Vancouver.

THE LANDMARK PATRON was Catherine Emes, a Langley woman, who arrived at the gate with her husband Lloyd Bennett and their three children. Emes, who received a number of gifts, said the PNE's unknown future was one reason she decided to attend this year's fair. 'We just thought: Oh, you never know how much longer it is going to be here. Now I'm more glad than ever that I came.' ... As Emes was feted ... a veteran concession operator said the fair's success this year proves that plans to return Hastings Park to green space should be reconsidered. Stephen Parson, owner of Jimmy's Lunch and seven other PNE food outlets said: 'The attendance this year is going to be close to record levels, well over 1.2 million. And I don't know how the city fathers and the powers-that-be can come in here with bulldozers and knock this down when over a million people are voting with their feet that they love this place.'[10]

The Vancouver Sun

BY THE END of the 1990s, the PNE was able to extend its stay at Exhibition Park. But it took until the next decade to secure its future. The ongoing insecurity caused confusion for employees and the Fair-going public. Yet visitors kept flooding through the Fair gates.

THE UNCERTAINTY ABOUT the future of the PNE dominated staff and the public's interest. During 1996, the PNE's Relocation Committee worked diligently towards finding a permanent home for British Columbia's number one tourist attraction ... Despite this over one million visitors to the PNE Fair entered The Party Zone! the Fair's theme. Packed full of entertainment, exhibits and attractions the 1996 Fair was highlighted by ... traditional favourites like SuperDogs, Demolition Derby and Timberthon, and a full contingent of new attractions such as the Extreme Pavilion and Star Spectacular.[9]

PNE Annual Report

BY THE END of the decade, the City of Vancouver began reconsidering the PNE's move.

1999 PROVED TO be a crucial year in the Pacific National Exhibition's long history. The ongoing debate over the Corporation's future was abated when the PNE reached a three-year operating agreement with the City of Vancouver ending December 31, 2002.[11]

Annette Antoniak,
PNE President and CEO, 1997-2003

ABOVE: Climbing to new heights; a big thumbs-up from The Wall, one of the feature attractions in the PNE Adventure Plaza, 1995.

THE GO-TO PEOPLE

AS A RESULT of the turmoil of the 1990s, the PNE began securing its future and launched a period of rebuilding and exploring new directions.

THE ORGANIZATION TURNED a huge corner in that decade. In a time of uncertainty, the PNE's goal was to emphasize its relevance through the offering of year-round events. Polls done then and later showed that nearly 87% of the people of Vancouver did not want the PNE to go somewhere else.

At one time the PNE had been the only game in town. All the main entertainment, sports and trade show facilities were here. But by the mid-1990s lots of events had left for downtown. The PNE had to determine what its future would be; if they were no longer the main spot for shows and sports, what were they?

It was clear that the PNE was a major gathering place, positioned at one of the Lower Mainland's major transportation hubs – roads, highways and transit linked up here. So they began to increase activity on the site by responding to the needs of people and organizations in the Lower Mainland and B.C. An array of niche events, concerts and cultural shows proliferated along with the PNE's mainstream events.

The Canucks were gaining momentum at GM Place, so the PNE repositioned sports on site to meet the needs of local families and communities. They also built relationships with the Vancouver Giants, which led to World Junior Hockey Championships and Memorial Cup wins in later years.

The PNE understood that they were living in times of global change. Asian communities in Vancouver were growing rapidly, and they saw this as a great opportunity to meet the evolving social and cultural needs of new Canadians. That's why they started doing events like Chinese New Year and Indo-Canadian shows. Vancouver was also becoming a very popular film destination — the PNE's facilities turned into a hive of film activity. Underground music raves were happening and soon became a big security and safety issue for the city. City Hall formed a Festival Committee to look into raves and the PNE positioned itself as the best place to safely host these all-night dance events.

Extreme sports grew in popularity and the PNE brought in wall climbing to the Forum, as well as in-line skating and skateboarding events such as Slam City Jam. They donated the Agrodome for space to clean birds injured in oil spills. They responded to a multitude of other community event needs. Before long they were the go-to people; they were plugged back into the city's energy. But, in retrospect, the PNE has always done this — re-visioning the future and responding to the needs of people.

The PNE has always done this, RE-VISIONING THE FUTURE and RESPONDING TO THE NEEDS OF PEOPLE.

CLOCKWISE FROM TOP RIGHT: New attractions like the Extreme Pavilion and a painting wall at the Vans' Extreme Tour meet traditional Fair favourites like SuperDogs and Demolition Derby.

BLOCK PARTIES

IN TUNE WITH the public impulse to reconnect, the PNE held a block party in 1992. Thousands of neighbours came out to see Exhibition Park sites like the Challenger Map, jump on Playland rides for free, find out about all the upcoming concerts and events, eat hot dogs and sip pop.

THE BEST WAY to get to know your neighbours is to invite them into your home for a casual and friendly get-together. And this is exactly what the PNE did ... we invited all neighbours within a six-block radius of Exhibition Park to be our guests and sample our food and entertainment.[12] *PNE Annual Report*

THE FOLLOWING YEAR, the PNE took the opportunity to party with the neighbours again — this time to celebrate Canada Day.

IN CELEBRATION OF Canada's 125th birthday, the PNE threw a party ... for the entire neighbourhood! This was the PNE's second annual neighbourhood bash ... Thousands of guests dropped in for an afternoon of entertainment, games, refreshments and free admission to Playland. A good time was had by all![13] *PNE Annual Report*

The PNE threw a party and the whole neighbourhood showed up! With dancers, live music, face painting and jugglers, it was no wonder everyone had so much fun, 1993.

Oh Man, Was I Ever Scared

MY FAVOURITE PNE memory was when I went on the wooden roller coaster for the first time, which was for a physics assignment. Oh man, was I ever scared, but at the end it was such a thrilling experience. Lovedeep Gidda, Vancouver

COASTER + CAROUSEL = WILD PHYSICS LESSON

LEARNING ABOUT FARM life is just one of the many exciting areas that kids (and adults) discover at the Fair. The PNE is also a great place to learn about science and physics during the PNE's Science of Fun days in May and October. Kids can find out why they don't fall out of a ride when it goes upside down. They can learn about acceleration and what the space shuttle and a fairground ride have in common. That's what a Surrey high school teacher discovered when he developed a science lesson based on a field trip to the PNE. The new curriculum had schoolchildren flocking to his physics classes. Eventually 30,000 students would visit the PNE each year to learn about physics. Who knew science could be so fun?

This Is Way Too Cool

IN 1977, I heard a woman speak at a science teachers' conference about a summer school program where she had taken students to an amusement park so they could experience what astronauts experience — acceleration, lift-off, free-fall and things like that. You could see all these light bulbs going off in other teachers' heads, including mine. This is way too cool, I thought. I could use amusement rides to help me teach my physics and science classes.

I did my first science lesson at an amusement park in San Francisco where I was living at the time. When I moved up here to teach at Princess Margaret High School in Surrey, I brought the program with me. Playland at the PNE was open to having me use their rides for one of my physics lessons in 1988. I doubled the number of students in my physics class after that. It was an authentic experience for them, and put education in their backyard. Learning became more real to them. It gave real-life meaning to what the teachers were doing in the classroom.

Eventually, I got a job with the Surrey School District to facilitate science teachers in other schools. I was able to offer my Playland lesson to all the schools in Surrey — at the time there were 14 secondary schools and 80 elementary schools.

On the 20th anniversary of the field trip in 2007, nearly 2,500 students attended with the teachers from their schools from all over the Lower Mainland. I asked at the beginning of the day, how many of the teachers had been at the first Playland science field trip. Quite a number of hands went up. That was so gratifying for me because it meant a generation of teachers who had learned physics and science with my Playland lessons were now teaching the same way.
Jim Wiese, Vancouver

LEFT TO RIGHT: Many good lessons were learned as science students headed to the PNE for Science of Fun days. Getting an authentic physics experience on the wooden rollercoaster, 2005.

THE STANLEY CUP BECKONS

THE CANUCKS GAVE Vancouverites one more night of revelry before losing the seventh and final game in the series. But for a brief moment at the PNE's Pacific Coliseum during the second to last game, Canucks fans dared to think big. Their mood was recorded in the papers the next day.

VANCOUVER HAS ALWAYS been a hockey city and its NHL hockey club, the Vancouver Canucks, is one of the darlings of the local sports scene. Passions reached a fever pitch when the Canucks made it to the final rounds of the Stanley Cup playoffs in 1982, against the New York Islanders. Emotions ran high again in 1994 when the Canucks vied with the New York Rangers for the coveted championship. During the '94 Stanley Cup the Pacific Coliseum was the place to be, even when the home team was away playing in its opponent's rink. It made the fans feel closer to their beloved hockey club. After this final exciting season at the Pacific Coliseum, the Canucks relocated to GM Place downtown.

Fandemonium erupts at rink

THERE WAS NO one on the ice and the rink was dark, but the seats were full of black, red and gold hope. More than 2,000 never-say-die Canucks fanatics filled the Pacific Coliseum with whoops, whistles, towel waves and air punches last night to cheer on their home-town heroes. The boys battling in the Big Apple may have been several thousand kilometres away but they got the message loud and clear and didn't let the fans down. The Canucks downed the New York Rangers 6–3, much to the delight of the mainly young fans who paid $5 each to watch the game on two giant-screen TVs and raise money for the food bank.[14]

The Province

OH YES! Vancouver erupts after Canucks win

THE CANUCKS ARE one win away from continuing the New York Rangers' 54-year Stanley Cup curse, thanks to a spellbinding 4–1 win last night before a delirious Pacific Coliseum crowd. The home-town towel-wavers gave great aural hex to help send the final series to seventh heaven, leaving hockey fans in the Big Apple crying: 'Curses! Foiled again!' ... 'That was the best game I've ever seen,' said Charles Currie Creelman between noisy blasts of his trombone. 'It was intense.' After a 3–1 series deficit knocked the wheels off the Canucks bandwagon, it carried a full load again last night with fans clamoring for a Stanley Cup to go with Stanley Park, also named after Lord Stanley of Preston.[15]

The Province

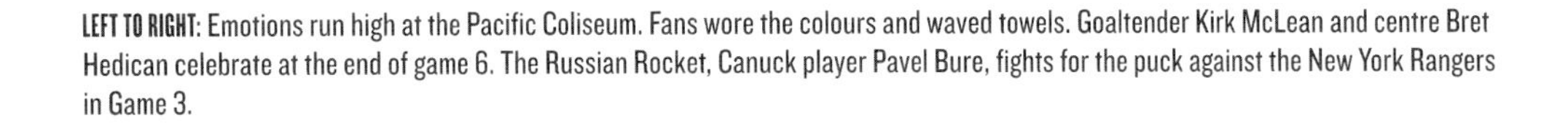

LEFT TO RIGHT: Emotions run high at the Pacific Coliseum. Fans wore the colours and waved towels. Goaltender Kirk McLean and centre Bret Hedican celebrate at the end of game 6. The Russian Rocket, Canuck player Pavel Bure, fights for the puck against the New York Rangers in Game 3.

KEVINKELLYPHOTOGRAPHY.COM

Highlights from the 1998 event calendar include the internationally observed **SUMO BASHO** wrestling event and the prestigious **NHL PINNACLE FANTASY HOCKEY** extravaganza.[16]

PNE Annual Report

SUMO AND FANTASY HOCKEY

TO APPEAL TO the diverse interests of British Columbians, the PNE hosted a wide variety of sports events. World-class tennis championship games, sumo wrestling and special NHL hockey events — it was all to be seen at Exhibition Park.

WORLD GROUP TENNIS COMES TO VANCOUVER AS THE PNE AGRODOME HOSTS THE DAVIS CUP ... **January 31st to February 2nd, 1992. Although Vancouver has hosted Davis Cup competitions three times in the past four years, the upcoming event will be the first ever World Group match to be held in Canada.**[17]

PNE Events

TOP: The Pacific Coliseum hosted Sumo Basho, providing a once-in-a-lifetime chance to see the legendary wrestling event outside of Japan, 1998.

LEFT: The PNE hosted the opening and closing festivities of the NHL Pinnacle Fantasy hockey extravaganza. Workers mount a giant Pavel Bure trading card on the side of the Pacific Coliseum in preparation for the event, 1998.

CONCERTS AND SHOWS

JUST ADD SKATEBOARDERS, BASKETBALL ...

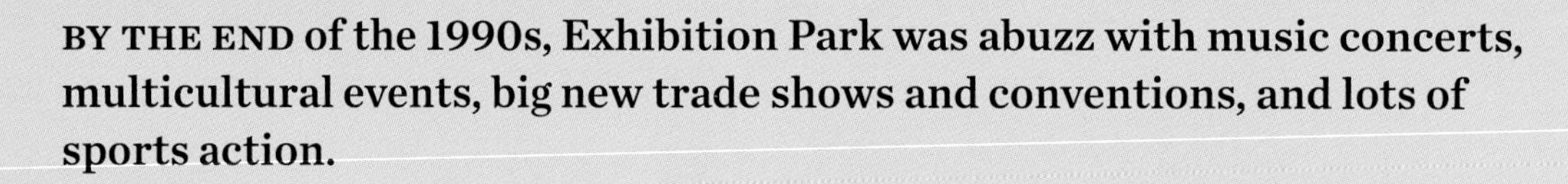

BY THE END of the 1990s, Exhibition Park was abuzz with music concerts, multicultural events, big new trade shows and conventions, and lots of sports action.

WE HOSTED A wide range of professional and amateur sporting events during the 1999 year. On-site facilities were utilized for over 200 sporting event dates, attracting more than 50,000 spectators. The PNE's versatile facilities saw sports action ranging from hockey and basketball to boxing, in-line skating, skateboarding and wrestling events.

Top draw events included: Slam City Jam — largest skateboarding championship in North America; CAT Tour — Canadian aggressive in-line skating tour; Monster Truck Madness; BC Boys Basketball Provincial Championships.[18] *PNE Annual Report*

OVER 18 TRADE and consumer shows were held on the PNE site in 1999 ... From the highly successful Sun Brite Lunar New Year Festival, which was attended by more than 55,000 guests, to the Hadassah Bazaar ... the PNE played host to many of the top shows and cultural events in the province. Cumulatively these shows generated tens of millions of dollars of economic impact throughout Vancouver and British Columbia.

Among the notables are: Lordco Autoparts Show; Sun Brite Lunar New Year Festival; Watchtower Assembly.[19] *PNE Annual Report*

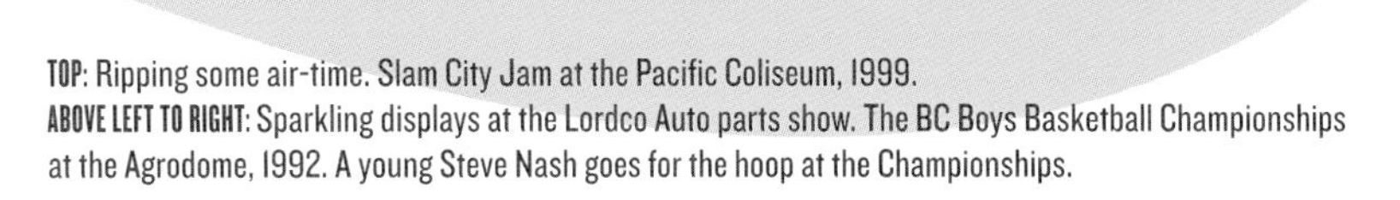

TOP: Ripping some air-time. Slam City Jam at the Pacific Coliseum, 1999.
ABOVE LEFT TO RIGHT: Sparkling displays at the Lordco Auto parts show. The BC Boys Basketball Championships at the Agrodome, 1992. A young Steve Nash goes for the hoop at the Championships.

... BRYAN ADAMS, AND A DASH OF BOLLYWOOD

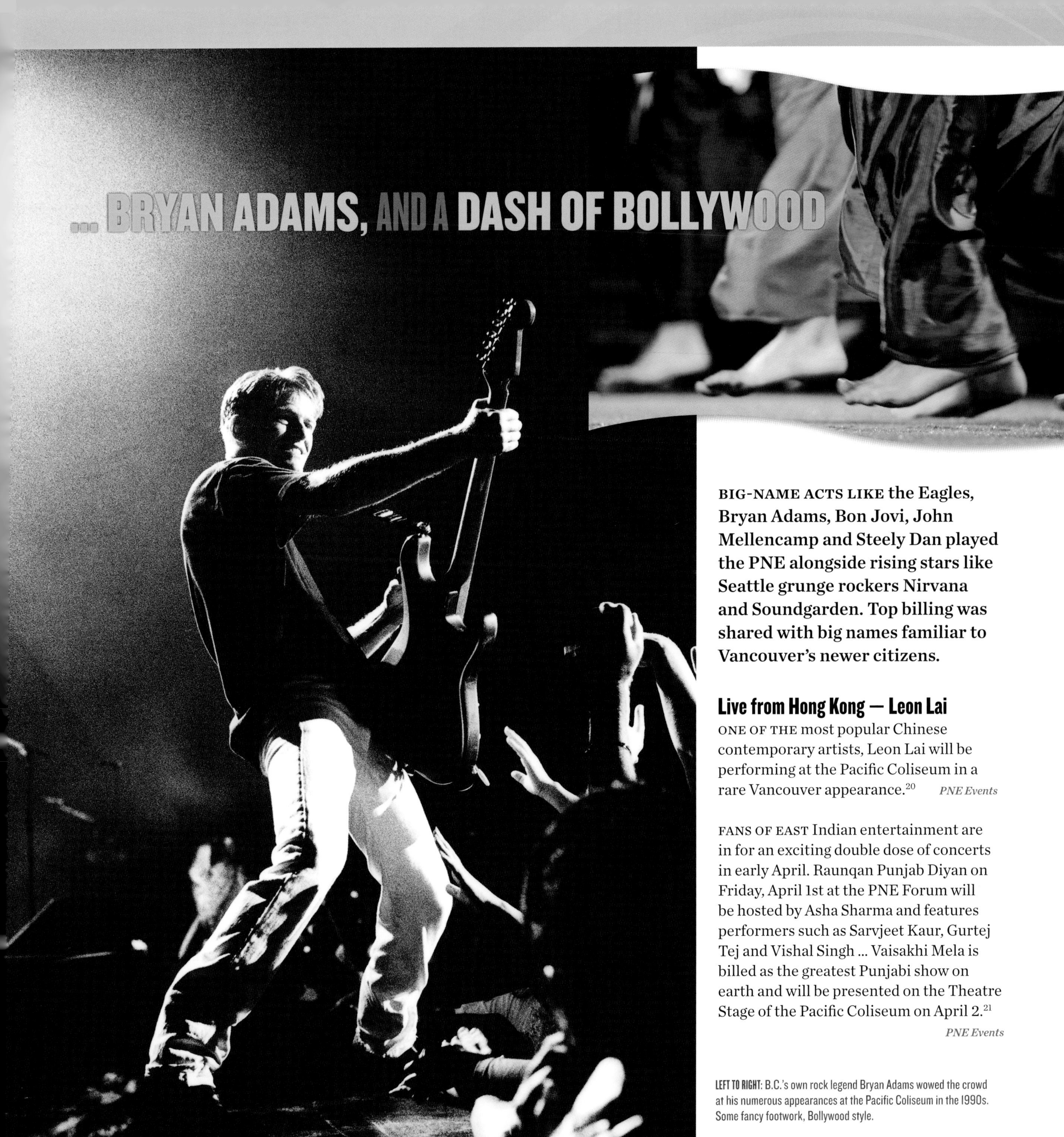

BIG-NAME ACTS LIKE the Eagles, Bryan Adams, Bon Jovi, John Mellencamp and Steely Dan played the PNE alongside rising stars like Seattle grunge rockers Nirvana and Soundgarden. Top billing was shared with big names familiar to Vancouver's newer citizens.

Live from Hong Kong — Leon Lai

ONE OF THE most popular Chinese contemporary artists, Leon Lai will be performing at the Pacific Coliseum in a rare Vancouver appearance.[20] *PNE Events*

FANS OF EAST Indian entertainment are in for an exciting double dose of concerts in early April. Raunqan Punjab Diyan on Friday, April 1st at the PNE Forum will be hosted by Asha Sharma and features performers such as Sarvjeet Kaur, Gurtej Tej and Vishal Singh ... Vaisakhi Mela is billed as the greatest Punjabi show on earth and will be presented on the Theatre Stage of the Pacific Coliseum on April 2.[21]

PNE Events

LEFT TO RIGHT: B.C.'s own rock legend Bryan Adams wowed the crowd at his numerous appearances at the Pacific Coliseum in the 1990s. Some fancy footwork, Bollywood style.

KING OF THE TRACK

HORSE RACING HAS been a big feature at Exhibition Park right from the beginning. No man did more for the racetrack at Exhibition Park than the late Jack Diamond. His passion led him to invest heavily in the park's racing facilities in partnership with Sam Randall, who owned the Ascot Club. Together, the Diamonds and the Randalls made Exhibition Park a destination on North America's west coast racing circuit. When Jack died in 1991, Vancouver lost its "King of the Track" and an important champion of horse racing.

ON A SATURDAY afternoon in the summer of 1933, Frank Lund, the manager of Diamond's branch of the Dominion Bank, across the street from British Pork Butchers [owned by Jack], walked into the shop and asked Jack if he would like to go with him to the races at Hastings Park (now called Exhibition). Jack said sure, and off they went. Later that day, when Jack's two-dollar bet won and paid 14 dollars, he was hooked. 'I wondered how long this sort of thing had been going on.' He had never gone to the horse races in his life, and now suddenly, as he says, 'I was bitten by the bug.'[22]

Running Tough: The Story of Vancouver's Jack Diamond

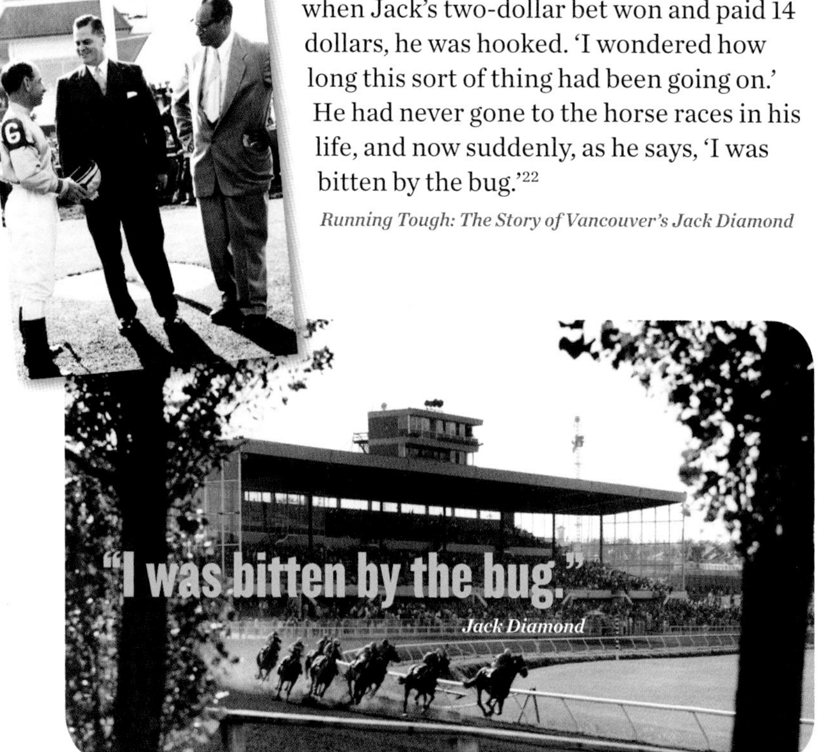

THE MAN WHO BUILT THE COASTER

THE PNE'S FAMED wooden roller coaster designed by Carl Phare in 1958 has delighted millions of riders. In 1998 the man who constructed Carl's vision came back to ride its tight curves and steep dips one more time to celebrate the iconic coaster's 40th birthday.

Nothing beats a wooden roller coaster ... IT WAS BUILT FOR CUDDLING.

Walker Leroy

IN 1958, WALKER LEROY built a new roller coaster for the Pacific National Exhibition. Wednesday, the 82-year-old Portland resident came up to Vancouver to help celebrate its 40th anniversary, and check on how it's running. Walking beside the coaster on the Playland site, he listens for every creak and rattle in the wooden frame as carloads of ride fans swoop around the coaster's dips and turns at speed of up to 100 kilometres per hour (62 m.p.h.). 'Sorry — I'm tuned into the ride, and I didn't hear you,' he apologizes after missing a question. 'Ninety percent of our maintenance is done through our ears ... We're looking for an odd noise that indicates it isn't normal.' This attention to detail made Walker Leroy a legend in roller coaster circles. Leroy is a living connection to the golden era of coasters in the '30s, '40s and '50s ... Over the years, he built coasters up and down the West Coast, Central America and the Philippines. But his most cherished creation is the PNE coaster, which has thrilled more than 10 million riders and is still the PNE's most popular ride.[23]

The Vancouver Sun

ABOVE LEFT: W.A.C. Bennett, racetrack owner Jack Diamond, and horse jockey. The racetrack after major improvements.
ABOVE RIGHT: The coaster, designed by Carl Phare, in 1995. Walker Leroy, who built the coaster, takes a ride with his wife during the coaster's 40th birthday celebrations, 1998.

A MULTITUDE OF NEW YEARS

THE PNE WAS the place to hold a party in the 1990s. January 1 marks the beginning of the New Year for many Canadians. But a growing number of Vancouverites consult their calendars and ring in a different kind of New Year.

Chinese New Year Fair

THIS YEAR'S CHINESE New Year Fair promises to be more exciting than ever as you welcome the Year of the Dog to a dazzling display of firecrackers, traditional Chinese dance, modern karaoke singing, mouthwatering food, auctions, prize draws and much more. Now with five days of fun and excitement, the Fair's nonstop activities will fascinate and delight you and your family. So join in on Vancouver's biggest and grandest Chinese New Year celebration at the PNE's Forum, Food and Showmart buildings.[24] *PNE Events*

Vietnamese New Year Festival

TAKES PLACE IN the Showmart Building of the PNE on Saturday, January 9th, 1993. This festival will feature Vietnamese traditional folk songs and dances, magic shows, plays, modern music performances as well as Vietnamese foods, an arts exhibition, and cultural displays ... All this and lotto draws with traditional Vietnamese games plus much, much more promise to make this an exciting and colourful event.[25] *PNE Events*

First Night

IT'S FIRST NIGHT — Pacific National Exhibition-style, that is. The annual non-alcoholic, family-oriented festival, which since 1987 was held in downtown Vancouver, was cancelled in 1992 ... The PNE revived the idea this year.[26]

The Vancouver Sun

IMAGINE, YOUNG KIDS on rides, laughing so hard they cry on the scrambler, families playing minigolf, a chance to see a rare ice show and then gathering as a family to ring in the new year in a fun, safe environment. The PNE was and is that social gathering place for all interests, all ages, all cultures.[27]

PNE media kit

THE MAGICAL EVENING WILL BEGIN AT 6:30 P.M. WHEN ALL FAMILY MEMBERS CAN JOIN A LANTERN PROCESSION ... visitors can experience everything from musical theatre and dance to a musical revue. PNE media kit

ABOVE: Traditional dancers, lanterns and food mark the Chinese and Vietnamese New Year celebrations in the late-1990s.
LEFT: First Night lantern procession, 1994.

THANKS FOR THE MEMORIES

ALMOST EVERYONE WHO has ever been to the PNE has a special memory — of a moment at a concert or a game, of the Fair, of a trade show. Here are some of those stories.

This Picture Is Extra Special

MY FAVOURITE MEMORY of the PNE is from a picture. In 1956, my parents attended the PNE. They had what appears to be a professional picture taken while walking down the Midway. We have very few pictures of my parents together. This picture is extra special to me, as my mother was eight months pregnant ... with me. Heather Jackson, Surrey

Here is a Second Generation

EVERY YEAR AT the PNE gives me great memories but my greatest of all time was taking my niece and nephew last year for the firsttime. It was great because I had started going as a kid and now here is a second generation. They loved it. The rides, the candy and toys. Now, every time we drive by Exhibition Park they point their little fingers and say P-N-E! Maria B., Vancouver

CLOCKWISE FROM TOP: Making treasured memories is a legacy of the PNE. Picking the perfect prize. A smile and a scream from a roller-coaster ride to remember. On Dad's shoulders, a popular ride at the Fair.

Something Far More Precious

OUR FAVOURITE FAMILY memory was of a phone call we received while standing by one of the PNE cars in the summer of 2006, the last day of the PNE. My cell phone was off because I was a finalist in the $10,000 golf putting challenge. I lost the challenge but gained something far more precious than any prize. I turned my phone on and there were about 20 messages. Just then my sister called to say our adoption agency was frantically trying to reach me and my husband. We called them right away and stood crying in the middle of the PNE while we found out that we had been chosen by a young girl who had just given birth to a beautiful baby girl on Vancouver Island. We were told to catch the first ferry in the morning to come pick up our baby girl. Now, every year we go to the spot where we received the call and celebrate receiving the good news of adopting our baby girl Sophia. The long weekend at the PNE has a special place and meaning for our family. We gained a daughter and our son Maxwell gained the sister he had always wished for.

Shelley Routley, Port Coquitlam

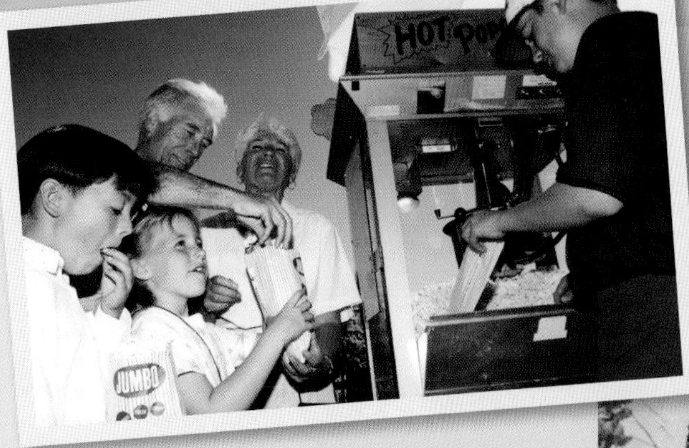

A Circle Completed

WHEN I WAS a kid, I bought a glo-stick at the PNE when they were still a relatively new invention. I was mesmerized by this tube glowing in the dark. I spent almost half of my allowance for that glo-stick, which cost $2. They are cheap and common today ... but back then $2 was a lot of money. I played with that glo-stick until its energy source died, probably after just a few short days. Many years later, when I was at the fair with my daughter, she fell in love with a T-shirt that had a design that glowed in the dark. She begged me to buy her one — at a cost of $25. She laughed all night running into darkened rooms to look at the design glowing in the dark. It was like a circle completed.

Raymond Louie, Vancouver City Councillor and Chairman of the PNE board

My Other Favourite Memory

WE USED TO live on Pandora Street, close to Nanaimo Street. During the fair, I remember always walking up the street to watch the amazing fireworks display EVERY NIGHT. I loved it! My other favourite memory is the lion drinking fountain. I am so glad that you still have it. Since my daughter was born, we have gone every year, and every year we take a picture of her and the lion — so that's 10 years!! The lion was also my sister's favourite spot; she passed away 11 years ago. That is why it's important we go to the PNE and have a drink from the fountain. We love going to the PNE!!!

Louella Charlston, Vancouver

CLOCKWISE FROM TOP: They just keep coming back for more! A popcorn vendor at the PNE scoops up a hot, buttery treat. Don't be afraid, he won't bite; the Lion Fountain, 1995. Playland at dusk.

RACIN' FOR THE BACON
Pig racing has been a fixture at the Fair at the PNE since the 1980s. Seeing the wee porkers fly down the track to the finish line is a must for Fairgoers of every age.

vancouver 2010

CHAPTER 10

2000 – 2010

GOING FOR GOLD

'00-'10

Men's short track speed skating at the Pacific Coliseum during the 2010 Vancouver Winter Olympics.

GOLDEN DREAMS AND "HIGH BOHEMIANS"

On February 12, 2010, Vancouver opened its arms to the world again when it hosted the 21st Olympic Winter Games. As the world watched, Canadian athletes won Olympic gold on Canadian soil for the first time in history.

THE CITY HAD spent much of the decade preparing for the big event, after winning the honour to host the games in 2003. Vancouver hummed with anticipation and work projects. Bright new sports facilities sprang up and existing spaces were buffed and polished. Construction was started on the Canada Line, a spiffy new transit route linking downtown Vancouver to Richmond and the international airport. Granville Street was given new life, becoming the entertainment zone for downtown as well as a home for new clubs and restaurants. Later in the decade, an Olympian facelift elevated the once-shabby strip to a whole new level.

Visitors were offered more than dazzling games and sportsmanship. A Cultural Olympiad ignited people's imaginations with a dazzling array of entertainment, dance and theatre, art shows and street performances. Public art graced city streets, and parks and buildings were wrapped in giant banners that celebrated Canada and its athletes.

Early on, the PNE's facilities were tagged as a perfect fit for an Olympic-sized dream. Nowhere else could organizers find so many ready-made venues in one spot. With a $21-million retrofit, the Pacific Coliseum took centre stage as the location for short track speed skating and figure skating, two of the Games' most-watched events. The Agrodome revved up as the operations hub for the PNE Olympic site. Rollerland became the press centre for Pacific Coliseum events. The Forum turned into an accreditation venue. And the east Livestock Barns were used as a mammoth storage centre.

In the midst of all the golden dreams leading up to 2010, Vancouver experienced another one of its notorious real estate booms. Housing prices skyrocketed, making the city one of the most

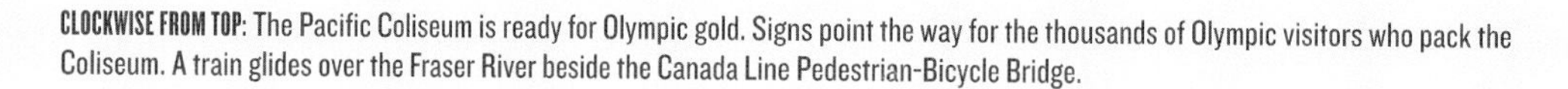

CLOCKWISE FROM TOP: The Pacific Coliseum is ready for Olympic gold. Signs point the way for the thousands of Olympic visitors who pack the Coliseum. A train glides over the Fraser River beside the Canada Line Pedestrian-Bicycle Bridge.

expensive places in the country to call home. Still, people wanted to live here, and not just for the view. Vancouver was getting a reputation for having a "creative class," a new term coined to describe concentrations of high-tech workers, artists, musicians and an amorphous sub-group called "high bohemians," people living more unconventional lives closely connected with the arts. Recognizing a good thing, in 2008, Vancouver City Council unveiled its new culture plan — a strategy to support the city's burgeoning new business sector centred on environmental companies, the film industry, new media, high-tech and other knowledge-based initiatives.

Cell phones and text messaging, combined with new Internet-based social media like Facebook and YouTube, changed the way Vancouverites thought about their public and private spaces. It was common to see people walking down the street talking on their cell phones. Text messaging gave rise to the "thumb generation" as the opposable digit became the primary mode of communication. Words morphed to accommodate reduced time and space for communication; abbreviations like LOL (laughing out loud), BTW (by the way) and the ubiquitous happy/sad/winking faces symbol gave rise to a new etiquette rooted in virtual encounters.

DAVID NIDDRIE PHOTOGRAPHY

While the 2000s saw the global village becoming smaller and more connected for some, those same connections also made people feel more vulnerable. The World Trade Center attacks in New York City in 2001 changed everyday life in Vancouver as people became aware of the need for more security. Nor were Vancouverites safe from the 2008 recession that spread around the world. Economic activity slowed, workers lost jobs, and people tightened their belts.

Throughout these difficult times, the PNE continued to thrive as an economical social gathering place for families. It remained a place to escape from worry. Playland was a haven for traditional fun, and the introduction of Fright Nights provided a new and safe way to celebrate the creepiest of holidays. The new WHL franchise, the Vancouver Giants, became an overnight sensation as crowds flocked to the Pacific Coliseum to catch their new hockey team. A hundred years after it had started, the PNE is still the place to take the family for affordable fun.

CLOCKWISE FROM TOP LEFT: PNE President and CEO Michael McDaniel lighting his torch as he starts his leg of the Olympic Torch relay in Vancouver, 2010. Don't forget the view — Hellevator riders seem a bit preoccupied, 2005. A bubble-blowing performance artist is part of Vancouver's emerging "creative class." A renewed Granville Street opens in time for the downtown Olympic bash.

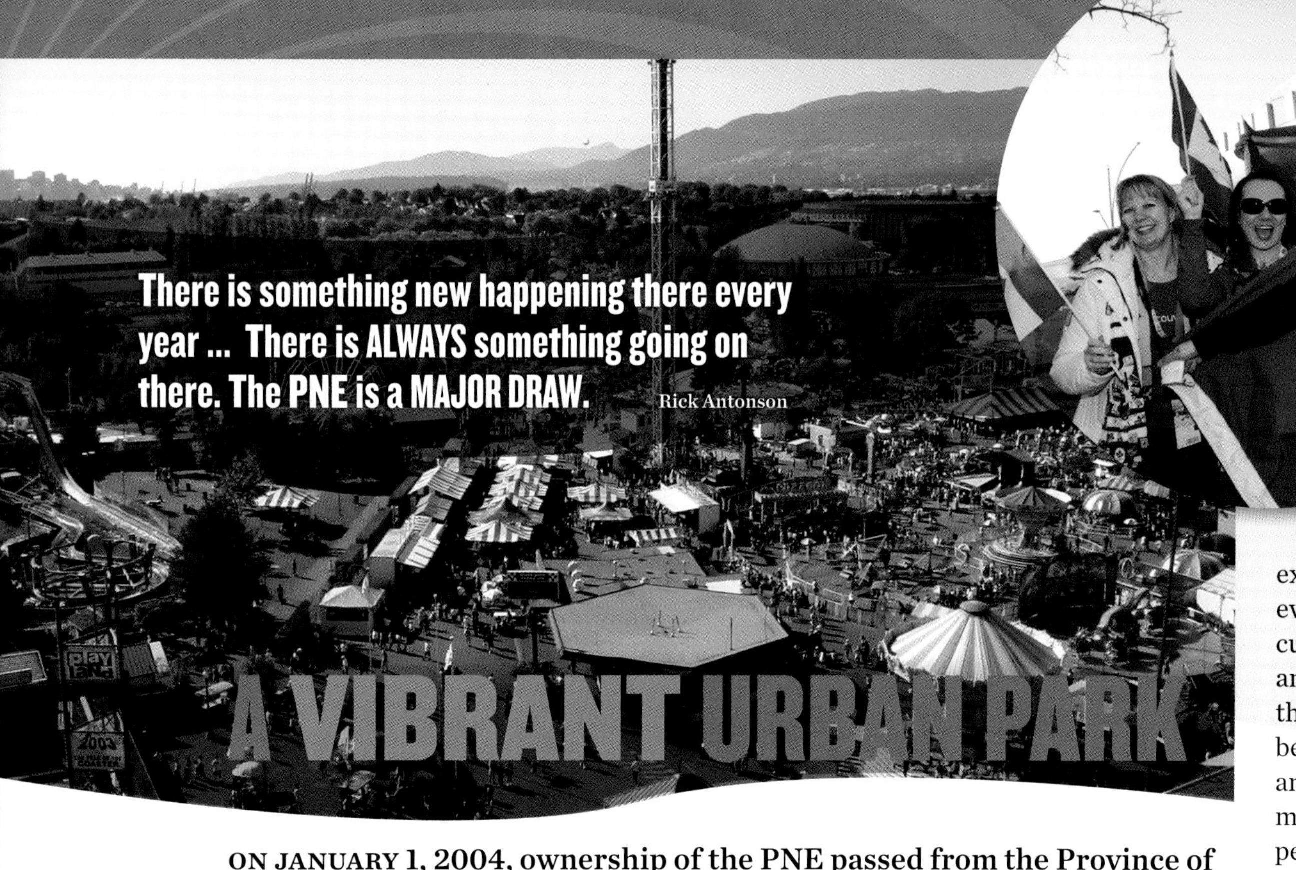

There is something new happening there every year ... There is ALWAYS something going on there. The PNE is a MAJOR DRAW. Rick Antonson

A VIBRANT URBAN PARK

NO SINGLE LOCATION in Vancouver has captured the spirit and history of this City, its people and its many achievements as well as the PNE. For more than nine decades, millions of guests have enjoyed shows, exhibits, sporting events, community events, amusement rides, concerts, cultural activities and of course, the annual summer Fair at the PNE. Today, the PNE ... is also the longest running and best attended event in British Columbia and the site of hundreds of famous milestone events — from early live performances by Elvis and the Beatles to the historic Miracle Mile. Over the decades, the PNE has showcased the best of Vancouver to the rest of Canada and to the world.[1] *PNE Annual Report*

ON JANUARY 1, 2004, ownership of the PNE passed from the Province of British Columbia to the City of Vancouver. After more than a decade of uncertainty about its future, a commitment was made to keep the PNE at Hastings Park. Its strengths as a key part of the city became clear when surveys and polls from local East Vancouver neighbourhoods and across the Lower Mainland showed overwhelming support from a large majority of Vancouverites who wanted the PNE to stay where it had entertained and educated people for nearly a century. This was a huge turning point for the PNE, allowing the organization to think long-term and to redefine what the future would hold.

THE PNE IS a cornerstone of the Vancouver experience. As a tourism and destination marketing organization, Tourism Vancouver identifies what our strengths are and promotes them. The PNE is a huge part of that and it has been that way since the beginning of the Fair. The PNE grew from modest beginnings to one of the largest fairs in Canada and in North America. There is something new happening there every year. We know that there are people visiting Vancouver in part because of the Fair at the PNE but also people who stay here longer once they find out about the calibre of the Fair. Another aspect is that the PNE is a site open 12 months of the year for various activities. There is always something going on there. The PNE is a major draw.

Rick Antonson, Tourism Vancouver President and CEO, 2009

CLOCKWISE FROM TOP LEFT: Playland is a key part of the PNE's bright future, 2003. Fans busting with pride at the Olympic short track speed skating event held at the Pacific Coliseum, 2010. Tons of people, the Fair at the PNE and the greening of Hastings Park make for an outstanding urban experience, 2009. Project Dynamite wows the crowds at the 2009 Fair.

CIRCUS KIDS

FOUNDED IN 1984 at an East Vancouver community centre by a mother-daughter duo, Jacqua and Zoe Pratt, CircusWest provides classes, camps and workshops on circus arts to thousands of children and adults in Vancouver each year. CircusWest is a great source of local programming, and students have the opportunity to explore their creativity and build self-esteem, confidence, team skills and fitness. Alumni have been accepted to the National Circus School, Cirque du Soleil and professional circuses around the world. In 2003, CircusWest found a new home at the PNE's Garden Auditorium.

IT WAS LIFE CHANGING FOR THE YOUTH TO COME HERE. Being at the PNE is wonderful because it's such a central location. Plus THE PNE'S ROOTS ARE IN EAST VANCOUVER, LIKE CIRCUSWEST, AND IT HAS STRONG CONNECTIONS TO THE LOCAL COMMUNITY. It has been a great fit for us.

Robyn McGuinness,
CircusWest executive director

Circus means laughter in any language.

THE MAGIC OF circus is at the heart of CircusWest. Very real and powerful magic, it goes by many names: laughter, fun, silliness, joy, delight. But it boils down to the way you feel when circus gets inside you ... lighter, brighter, like you can fly. We recommend it for all that ails you and we believe in its powers because we've seen it work, again and again. Whether you watch or play a more active role, the many pleasures and life-affirming benefits of circus come from the simple combination of physical feats, comedy and possibility with the absolute need for precise and highly-integrated teamwork. Everyone plays a meaningful role, one that fits them and their skill or talent. And none can do their part without the others. Bring joy. This is our mandate, the underlying principle in everything we do.[2]

circuswest.com

CLOCKWISE FROM TOP LEFT: CircusWest gives kids the chance to be a part of an age-old dream. CircusWest at the 2009 Kaboom! show. Happy circus students learn how to hang out, 2004.

MICKEY DOES A DOUBLE AXEL

SINCE 1981, A touring ice show with famous Disney characters has delighted children and their parents around the world. The name changed in 1998 to Disney On Ice, but the show continued to feature dazzling skating performances by professional figure skaters and much-loved Disney characters including Mickey Mouse, Donald Duck, Snow White and Tinker Bell. The popular ice show was brought to the PNE in 2005 and has smashed North American attendance records every year since.

JOIN IN THE non-stop fun when Disney On Ice presents Worlds of Fantasy bringing four magical Disney stories right to Vancouver. This brand new ice spectacular showcases beloved characters from Disney/Pixar's *Cars* and Disney's *Tinker Bell*, *The Lion King* and *The Little Mermaid* ... Audiences will journey to the mystical world of Pixie Hollow to meet Tinker Bell and her fairy friends; race through Radiator Springs with Lightning McQueen; trek across the African Pride Lands with Simba; and dive under the sea with Ariel and Sebastian. World-class skating, breathtaking set design and amazing animatronics make this an unforgettable experience for the whole family! Prior to each performance, families will be treated to the Disney Princess Pre-Show, an exclusive collection of enchanting ball gowns and mementos from the Disney Princess stories.[3]

asianpacificpost.com

The Disney On Ice production "Worlds of Fantasy" played at the Pacific Coliseum November 25 to 29, 2009, and brought to life characters from Disney movies like *The Little Mermaid, The Lion King, Tinker Bell* and *Cars*. Ten-year-old Cheyenne Fleming was one of the thousands of children and their parents laughing and cheering in the stands. She was thrilled to see her favourite characters come alive on ice and soaked up the stories. It was a dream to last a lifetime.

"I SAW THE *Little Mermaid* and *The Lion King* on a DVD at home. Today, I got to see them skating around on the ice. I almost can't believe I'm here. It's a dream. Tinker Bell is my favourite — she wrecked spring, it was an accident but then she made it better. I bought a slushy in a cup with Tinker Bell on it. I'm taking that home. I also got a journal with Tinker Bell on the front and it comes with a purple flower pen. I can hardly wait to write in it. This is so fantastic."

Cheyenne Fleming, Coquitlam

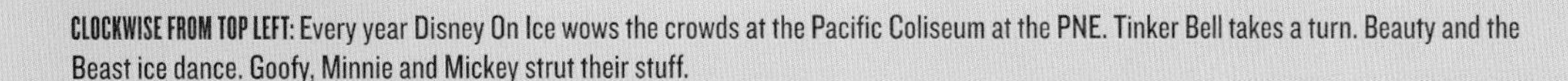

CLOCKWISE FROM TOP LEFT: Every year Disney On Ice wows the crowds at the Pacific Coliseum at the PNE. Tinker Bell takes a turn. Beauty and the Beast ice dance. Goofy, Minnie and Mickey strut their stuff.

THE PNE HAS a knack for knowing what the public wants. In 2003, it launched its now famous Halloween spectacular — Fright Nights. Playland stayed open at night during the last two weeks of October and dished up a scary buffet for Halloween lovers. Several new haunted houses and a ton of chill-inducing attractions were added to the usual Playland rides, midway games and food concessions. Mechanical ghouls and werewolves were supplemented by performers who added to the eerie mood with their zombie walks. The first year was a huge success and by the second year devoted fans were gathering at the gates. More than 43,000 people came in 2003 to be spooked, horrified and otherwise entranced. By 2008, attendance had grown to more than 82,000.

THE NEW HAUNTED houses are, in fact, pretty scary. Hollywood Horrors [one of the haunted houses] takes its cue from silver screen epics such as *Dracula*, *Texas Chainsaw Massacre*, *The Exorcist* and *Halloween*. Jason [a haunted house character] lunges at you with a knife, you walk through a ring of dead people hanging from the ceiling, and there are all sorts of vampires, mummies and werewolves. Darkness [another haunted house] is even scarier. It's so dimly lit you really can't see where you're going, which enhances the horror of walking through a waterfall of human skulls, seeing a werewolf feast on a dead body, and having unseen hands grab you as you walk by. Naturally all the attractions come with blood-curdling screams, spooky noises and appropriately dissonant music.[4] *The Vancouver Sun*

Crazy Time Screaming

THE DAY BEFORE Halloween a group of my friends and I got together for Fright Nights at Playland. It's great catching up with familiar faces but combine that with haunted houses, rides, curly fries, mini donuts, and games with stuffed toy prizes, what more can you ask for? The Best, right?!

It was an extremely fun night. Just the hype and energy there is exciting. Well worth the trip for sure, even if the weather gets moody.

That didn't stop everyone from flashing their cameras ... as they would take pictures of themselves ... or have us huddle for group shots to remember the evening's events.

We had such a crazy time screaming endlessly at anything that either jumped at us or had fake blood. We laughingly made our way from one haunted house to the next, excited to top each attraction off with the next scary thing. All good things had to come to an end and it came to that point when it was soon closing time. We had managed to make it through most of the houses, which was more than enough, and after a couple more games and some hugs to call it a night, we soon broke off and said our goodbyes. Carlos Perfecto, Surrey

THIS PAGE: Fright Nights at Playland draws huge crowds keen to get scared silly and laugh out loud.

AND THE AWARD GOES TO ...

WITH A MORE certain future at Hastings Park, the first decade of the 21st century allowed the PNE to reposition itself and spread its wings. Groundbreaking industry concepts were introduced, along with an expansion and redesign of the Fair's footprint. The PNE became a leading player in the attractions and entertainment industry by developing new event models and focusing on up-and-coming artists. Chances are, if you had a favourite new artist or loved a new song on the radio, that singer or group had performed at the PNE on their way to the top of the charts.

The PNE bounded into the 2000s with creativity, energy and a passion for being the best. This was evidenced by the hundreds of awards the PNE has won since its re-emergence this century — recognition bestowed by the industries and audience the PNE represents.

THE WESTERN FAIRS Association (WFA) awarded the PNE first place in the Community Outreach Program category of its Annual Achievement Awards. The PNE has a strong history of giving back to the community. One of the oldest and best-loved traditions of the Fair at the PNE is the Report Card Fair Ticket Program. Through this program, the PNE gives complimentary admission tickets to all students in kindergarten through grade seven across B.C. Other highlights of the PNE's award-winning community outreach program included the PNE bike patrol, a security patrol protecting a two-kilometre radius of surrounding neighbourhoods during all major events, as well as the PNE neighbourhood clean-up crew, which picks up garbage two to three times a day in neighbourhoods surrounding the PNE during the Fair.

PNE Community Relations

In 2006, the PNE was named BEST FAMILY ENTERTAINMENT IN CANADA by *Today's Family*, an American television program. The PNE was chosen as the best place for parents to bring their families over many other major Canadian attractions, fairs and amusement parks. The award was based on the PNE's many successes and the entertainment value of the Fair, Playland and year-round events as THE BEST PLACE FOR FUN, AFFORDABLE FAMILY ENTERTAINMENT. PNE Press Release

TOP ROW: KC the PNE's mascot with PNE CEO, Mike McDaniel, and a student in the ticket program. The Raise a Reader booth catches the eye of a small Fairgoer, 2006. The neighbourhood clean-up crew keeping things tidy, 2006. Mike McDaniel, Red Robinson and KC with Jessica Cox at the PNE's 2009 Red Robinson Talent Showdown. The Container Art show at the Fair, 2009. KC and kids explore the Fair, 2005.

One of Those Rare Things We Did Every Summer

THE PNE WAS a fun, free place of my childhood. I had strict parents but for some reason if it was on the PNE grounds, it was okay by Mom and Dad. Whether it was a summer job (scooping ice-cream), a concert (Duran Duran) or getting my ears pierced (again), somehow they approved. I think it was because they loved the PNE too. It was one of those rare things we did every summer as a family.

Marijana Palmieri, Coquitlam

THE PNE TAKES great pride in working to be the best it can be, and the hundreds of awards it has received this decade highlight the organization's collective achievements in many areas. Our efforts and successes have been recognized by the International Fairs and Exhibitions Association (IAFE), Western Fairs Association (WFA), Canadian Association of Fairs and Exhibitions (CAFE), Digital Marketing Awards, London International Awards, Lotus Advertising Awards (AAABC), The Extra Awards for Entertainment and Media, Canadian Event Industry Awards, Canadian Marketing Awards, Clio Awards and The Advertising and Design Club of Canada. For example, Playland was named Advertiser of the Year in both 2007 and 2008 by *Strategy Magazine* and our new Fair exhibits such as Container Art, which premiered at the 2009 Fair, won international acclaim and a national industry award for Best Innovative New Concept. Many of the new and original shows that have helped to redefine the Fair entertainment experience, such as Bring on the Night and Kaboom!, have been recognized through awards from the Canadian Event Industry (CEIA) and the BC Event Industry Association.

Chair of the PNE Awards Committee

A NEW MASCOT

IN 2004, THE PNE introduced its new mascot, a lovable fluffy bear called KC, to replace Hammy the Pig. Dressed as a conductor for the Kettle Creek Railway, one of the new kiddie rides, the character required someone special to play the role.

The gentle man in the mascot suit.

HE'S BEEN DOING the job for three years, even though he never applied. And even after all that time, few people know his real face. He's the man inside the mascot at the PNE. For the past two summers, 19-year-old Oliver Podwysocki has bounced around the PNE dressed as a train-conductor bear named K.C. The name stands for Kettle Creek, the roller coaster he supposedly conducts. But most of the time, K.C. entertains kids. Carefully. 'I'm super gentle with young kids because I know their interaction with me could make it or break it,' Podwysocki said. 'If it goes badly, they could easily end up with mascot-phobia.'[5]

The Vancouver Sun

MIDDLE ROW: The PNE Neighbourhood Patrol does the rounds, 2006. At the 2002 SuperDogs show. Party Patrol, 2009. Busker Kim Potter is a big crowd-pleaser. The 2009 Kaboom! show explodes to the Jailhouse Rock.
BOTTOM ROW: A friendly dinosaur at the Family Adventure Parade thrills the kids, 2005. Award-winning ad campaigns in the 2000s drew thousands of new Playland fans.

A NIGHT OUT WITHOUT BREAKING THE BANK

IN 2001, THE PNE and Vancouver businessman Ron Toigo started discussions about leasing the Pacific Coliseum, a venue active with concerts and trade shows and where the PNE hoped to bring back sporting events. Toigo, who once owned a junior hockey team in Washington State and whose family owns the White Spot restaurants, dreamed of bringing junior hockey to Vancouver. Little did he know that his vision to introduce junior hockey and family entertainment at the Pacific Coliseum would bring a whole new tradition to the city.

The Dream

I OWNED THE Tri-Cities Americans who played down in the southeast corner of Washington State. I wanted to bring them to Vancouver. I knew it wasn't an easy thing to do. Vancouver was looked upon as a difficult market. You're up against the Vancouver Canucks.

I continued watching the Vancouver market though. As pro sports got more expensive and moved up to the $100 ticket price point, a lot of people were left out because of the cost. I thought there was an opening — the opportunity to provide a hockey experience to any family. I convinced the PNE I could deliver a junior hockey franchise team.

We convinced the Western Hockey League board of governors to grant an expansion franchise for Vancouver, provided I sell the Tri-Cities Americans. We told them we believed there was a niche for our level of hockey, in particular the family market. For less than $100, you could bring a family of four to a hockey game, park the car, eat and have a good night. It doesn't take as much out of your pocketbook and you could have a similar experience as going to professional hockey games.

Ron Toigo

FROM TOP: The Vancouver Giants score their first Western Hockey League goal in a game against the Kamloops Blazers, 2001. The team celebrates their Memorial Cup victory, 2007. Giants' owner Ron Toigo hoists the Memorial Cup in 2007.

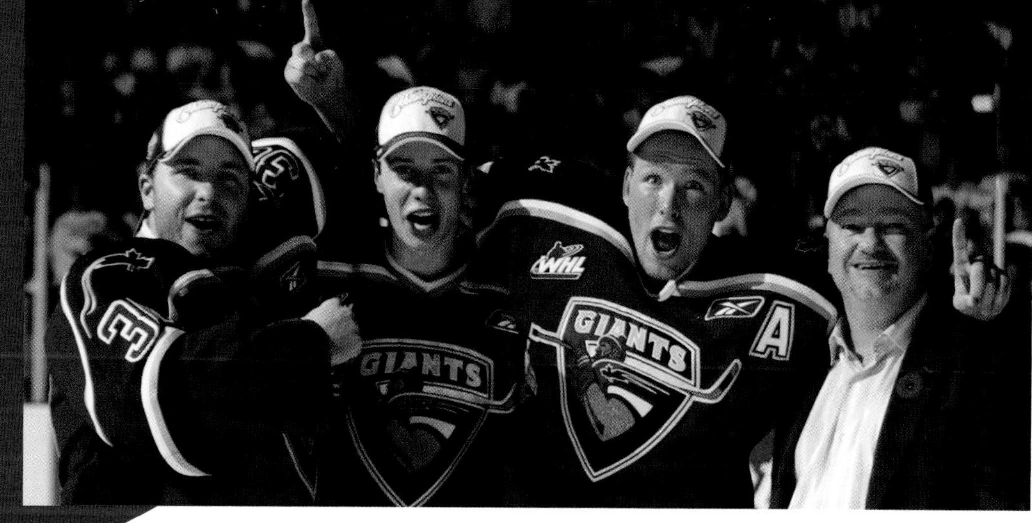

Selling Out Opening Night

ON SEPTEMBER 21, 2001, the whole PNE team was amazed. This was opening Night for the Vancouver Giants and we had the Coliseum ready for a crowd of 7000. It sold out! The audience for this franchise had been underestimated and no one expected how many people would want to come. We squeezed 8000 guests in using standing room only spots. That's when we all realized the demand to see this team would be high as we could have easily filled the Coliseum. It was the first game and people wanted to be there. PNE Operations Team

A Vision Realized: Families Having the Time of Their Life

ONE THING WE also got, which I didn't see at the time, was the number of seniors that enjoyed the game. There are a lot of season's ticket holders who are seniors. They might not be able to afford the Canucks. We've developed a real solid support base with families and seniors.

The biggest event for us so far was the 89th Memorial Cup in May 2007. We won it against the Medicine Hat Tigers. Boy, was that exciting! Again, the Coliseum was jammed. There were 16,000 guests every night. In the last game, the Giants dominated the game but going into the third period it was a 1–1 tie. It could have gone either way until Michael Repik scored to make it 2–1 and we never looked back. After we won, I went to the middle of the ice. Standing there looking around at all the people having the time of their life, it was incredible. Ron Toigo

THE MEMORIAL CUP run was a big highlight for the PNE organizers, who noted the large crowds it attracted.

WELCOMING THE GIANTS to the Pacific Coliseum was an important part of the PNE plan to reposition the event mix and provide a wide range of affordable family fun. Management agreed with Ron [Toigo] that there was a market for bringing hockey to families, young kids, seniors and anyone else who felt a $150 Canuck ticket might be unattainable. The best part was to see the calibre of play in the building. The WHL juniors play heartfelt, great hockey. And they do it for the love of the game. The fans can feel that energy.

The Giants were a successful franchise and provided Ron Toigo with the leverage to work with the league to bring some very high profile events to the Pacific Coliseum. His first venture was the Canadian Hockey All-Star game, which brought over 14,000 fans out. And then, it was on to Top Prospects, a game bringing together all the top Junior players from across the country and league. The success of both these games led to a successful bid to bring the World Junior Championships to the Pacific Coliseum in 2006 and then the Memorial Cup in 2007. Both tournaments were a huge success with sold-out arenas, passionate fans and great hockey. The highlight, of course, was having the Giants win the 2007 Memorial Cup at home, with over 92,000 fans having come out to watch their run for the cup. Management Interviews

CLOCKWISE FROM TOP LEFT: Giants' Gilbert Brule, 2005. Ron Toigo (right) with team members at the Memorial Cup. Giants' player proudly displays the Memorial Cup, 2007.

THE BEAT GOES ON

THE PNE HAS continued to shine as a hub for cultural activity year-round. Whether it's the Peking Acrobats or Indo-Canadian musical theatre, the beat goes on.

THE 2007 FAIR features the newest entertainment programming in the history of the PNE. A highlight of the Fair's new live shows is The Peking Acrobats. For the first time at the PNE the acrobats will perform treacherous wire walking, trick cycling, precision tumbling and amazing displays of contortion, flexibility and control.[6] *The Pinwheel Pages*

Bollywood Wedding brings a lavish musical to the great outdoors

THE ITALIAN GARDENS at the PNE ... where the lavish dance musical *Bollywood Wedding* will unfold nightly ... The audience will be limited to 200, but there will be 13 actors, 25 dancers, three roving musicians, and the hot five-piece bhangra band En Karma. Collectively, these artists will tell the story of the groom, Hanuman Singh, and the bride, Sunava Patel, whose families have brought them together for a potentially ill-conceived arranged marriage.[7] *The Georgia Straight*

PREVIOUS PAGE: The Peking Acrobats wow Fair audiences, 2007.
ABOVE AND INSET: The PNE Italian Gardens was the perfect backdrop for a 2009 outdoor staging of *Bollywood Wedding.*

CLOCKWISE FROM TOP LEFT: Oh Canada! The Pacific Coliseum rang to cheers for our Olympic athletes: Women's short track skater, Marianne St-Gelais is in second place. Charles Hamelin (205) and USA's Apolo Anton Ohno (256) in action during the men's 1000 metre final. Happy fans share the warmth. Canada's Olivier Jean (207) at the men's 1500 metre. The Pacific Coliseum was packed for every Olympic event.

GOING FOR GOLD

THE 2010 OLYMPIC Winter Games brought Vancouver to billions of television viewers all over the world. Scenes from the Pacific Coliseum, decorated in the blue and green of the Vancouver Winter Games colours, broadcast the thrill of competing against the very best in the world and the glory of winning gold. There was also the poignant image of a skater who, facing personal loss, chose to compete before a standing-room-only crowd at the Pacific Coliseum.

IT WAS THE final night of the Olympic Winter Games short track speed skating at the Pacific Coliseum and the air was electric. You could tell everyone in the building just wanted so badly for Charles Hamelin to win this race. He was Canada's short track 'rock star' and fate had curtly interfered with his medal hopes during his last two race attempts. US skater Apollo Anton Ohno had scraped by him in a previous race so tonight was it — his last opportunity to win a medal in 2010 and to share his success and joy with a hopeful Canadian audience. It was so cute; his girlfriend Marianne St-Gelais, also a Canadian Olympic short track speed skater, was pacing anxiously by the boards. She was so recognizable because several days earlier, she had won two silver medals and overnight had become the sweetheart of Canadian short track. Everyone talked about her giggles on the podium and her unedited excitement as she skated around the rink wearing the Canadian flag as her cape. And the TV cameras had captured her tears for Charles as she watched from the stands during his last two unsuccessful races. But tonight, as the gun sounded and the skaters jockeyed for position, it looked like Charles was staying out in front — and as the crowd screamed and cheered, he stretched his blade across the finish line and rightfully won his gold. No victory lap, just a race to the boards where Marianne jumped up into his arms and they cried and screamed, and hugged and kissed, and the crowd roared! This was no ordinary medal, this was the introduction of Canada's new golden couple of Canadian short track, and we couldn't have been prouder to have it happen at the Pacific Coliseum.

PNE Management

ABOVE, FROM LEFT: Canada's Marianne St-Gelais celebrates winning the silver medal on day six of the 2010 Olympic Winter Games. Gold medalist Charles Hamelin embraces girlfriend Marianne after winning the men's 500 metre short track speed skating final on day 15.

I was lucky to be in the Pacific Coliseum when Joannie Rochette won her bronze medal during the Olympics and lit up the arena. It was so emotional and an incredibly powerful moment. I grew up watching the Canucks in that building, including their 1994 Stanley Cup play-off run, so I've seen my share of exciting moments there. But I've never seen the building as electric as it was the night Joannie skated. A number of international officials and dignitaries remarked to me afterwards how intense and lively the Coliseum is. It has so much history and an intimacy that infuses the building and takes it to a whole other level of experience.

Mayor Gregor Robertson, 2010 Interview

THERE WAS NO road map for the lonely territory Joannie Rochette had to cross Tuesday night. No sports psychologist, among the many who worked with Canadian Olympians in the lead-up to the Games, could have prepared her for having the moment she's waited for all her life arrive amid the terrible grief of her mother's death two days earlier. The capacity crowd at Pacific Coliseum would have gladly rushed onto the ice and carried the 24-year-old from Ile-Dupas, Que. through the two minutes of her short program, but a figure skater must literally face the music alone, in the middle of a vast white surface, and try to carve something memorable out of the ice in the time allotted. So Joannie Rochette stood there, letting the fans' warmth wash over her, knowing that when it grew quiet, she would have to do this thing, all by herself. And she did it all, every jump, every spin, every flourish to the Uruguayan tango *La Cumparsita*, whose lyrics begin: 'The little parade of endless miseries.'[8] *The Vancouver Sun*

FROM LEFT: Bronze medalist in women's figure skating, Canada's Joannie Rochette, performs at the Exhibition Gala. After an emotional performance in the ladies short program figure skating on day 12, Rochette takes a moment to reflect.

Canadian figure skating duo Tessa Virtue and Scott Moir flawlessly danced into history Monday night, capturing hearts and a gold medal. A CAPACITY CROWD AT THE PACIFIC COLISEUM EXPLODED IN A DEAFENING OVATION AS THE PAIR FINISHED THEIR FINAL SKATE, a lyrical and passionate performance to Gustav Mahler's *Symphony No. 5*. It was the first ice-dancing victory for North America.

The Vancouver Sun

CLOCKWISE FROM TOP LEFT: The Olympic Exhibition Gala at the Coliseum. Ice dance gold medalists, Tessa Virtue and Scott Moir of Canada, perform at the Exhibition Gala. Virtue and Moir show the ecstatic audience their haul of gold. More song and ice dance at the Olympic Exhibition Gala.

MY GRANDMOTHER, MY MOTHER AND ME

MILLIONS OF PEOPLE have gone through the PNE gates creating millions of memories. This giant gathering place is so many things to so many people. Generations of Vancouverites and British Columbians talk about how their grandparents, parents and now their children and grandchildren know what it means to share a PNE moment. That is the real power of the PNE. The family stories are endless.

When My Son Turned Four, I Took Him There

I HAVE BEEN going to Playland since I was four (I am now 27) ... My best friend Chris and I would get season passes every year and we would go there at least three times a week. We made a game plan every day about which rides we would go on, and what and when we would eat. His grandmother would follow us around with a book, wait for us to get off the rides, and give us money to play the games. When my son turned four, I took him there. Now he has the same love for Playland that I have had my whole life.

Ashley Schoffenburg, Vancouver

People Walking About and Having Fun

MY FIRST VISIT to the PNE fair was in September 1998 and I was nine months pregnant. I was very excited to see so many people walking about and having fun. My husband was very kind and bought me everything I wanted. I remember having fish and chips, those delicious mini donuts and a whale tail. My son is 11 years old now and he still remembers what he ate when he was in my tummy because he always asks for those things every year when we go to the fair.

Sophia Liu, Vancouver

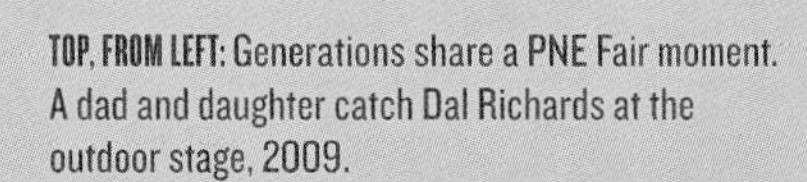

TOP, FROM LEFT: Generations share a PNE Fair moment. A dad and daughter catch Dal Richards at the outdoor stage, 2009.

BOTTOM, FROM LEFT: Fair time is family time, 2009. The Family Adventure Parade, 2005. Kids can't resist the big critters they meet at the Fair.

The Car Ride Home Was Full of Stories

GROWING UP, MY three sisters and I, and Mom and Dad went to the PNE every year. We had tickets from school and when I was 12, my sisters and I got permission from our parents for a designated amount of time. FREEDOM! We all had our ride bands and took off to the log chute first. Our favourite rides were the Gravitron, Rainbow and Wild Mouse. While our parents went to the Home Show we would gorge on cotton candy, play the games and ride on roller coasters. Our final stop was at the demolition derby ... We would slowly make our way back to the log chute where the whole family would go on the ride together and come off soaking wet from splashing each other (whoops, was that allowed?!). The car ride home was full of stories of our day and the anticipation of going again next year.

Jaswant Kaur Bains, New Westminster

FREEDOM!!

The Most Intrepid Art Event in Vancouver

LAST SUMMER, I saw the Container Art exhibit going on down at the PNE. This art exhibit was by far the most intrepid art event I have ever seen in Vancouver. There were ten metal containers, the ones normally used for shipping things on ships and trains, but in this case each one was used as a mini art gallery with a show dedicated to each of the artists. Architects have started using containers in new innovative ways for housing, and the PNE found a new way to use them too. It astounded me to see this serious, cutting-edge art at a fair.

Kate Jensen, Vancouver

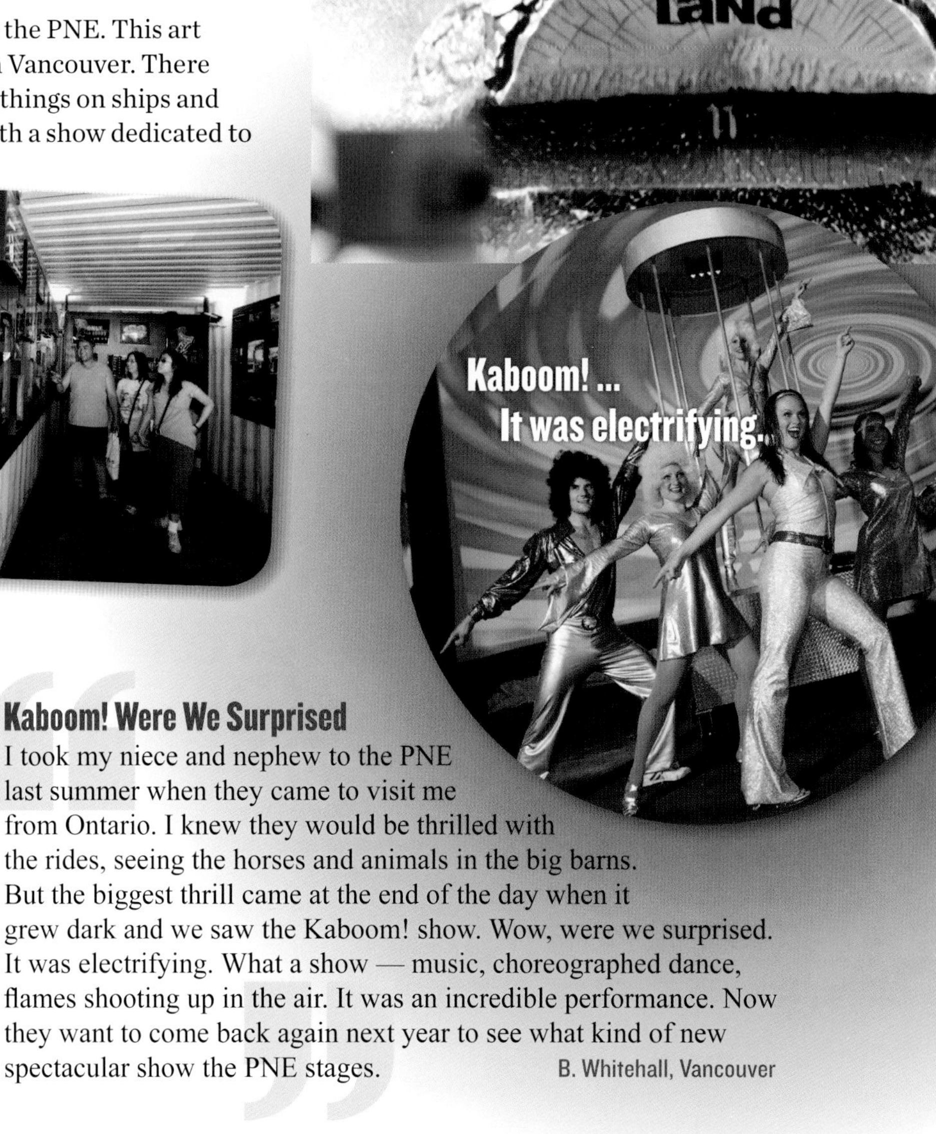

Kaboom! Were We Surprised

I took my niece and nephew to the PNE last summer when they came to visit me from Ontario. I knew they would be thrilled with the rides, seeing the horses and animals in the big barns. But the biggest thrill came at the end of the day when it grew dark and we saw the Kaboom! show. Wow, were we surprised. It was electrifying. What a show — music, choreographed dance, flames shooting up in the air. It was an incredible performance. Now they want to come back again next year to see what kind of new spectacular show the PNE stages.

B. Whitehall, Vancouver

CLOCKWISE FROM TOP RIGHT: Riding the Flume, 2006. The 2009 Kaboom! show gets into 1970s disco. Christian Dahlberg's display at the Container Art display at the Fair, 2009. Fireworks light up the sky above the Container Art complex.

It Brings Out the Fearless Person in Me

I WAS FIVE years old when I went on the roller coaster with my older brother and my dad. My dad and I sat together and I remember feeling so scared and so small next to him. I remember the feeling of going up the first hill and the fear and the joy I felt going down the first hill. It was so fast and intense and like nothing I have ever felt before. I felt so free and so alive. I go to the PNE every year and the wooden roller coaster is always the first ride I go on. Every time I go down that hill, I remember the feeling of being free and I think back to the simpler, less complicated days. I love the PNE — it brings out the fearless person in me.

Jennifer McFarlane, Port Moody

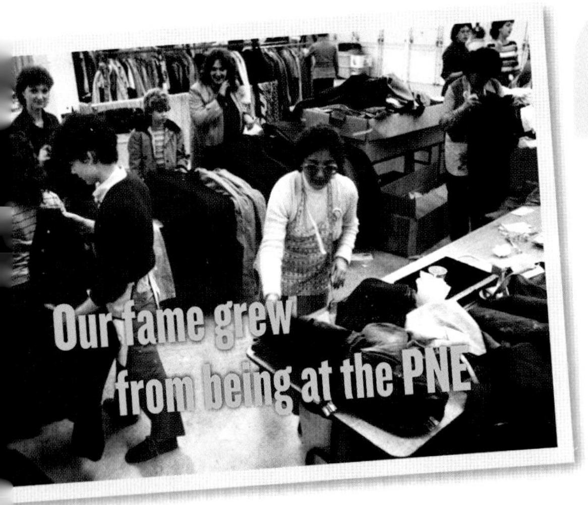

The Most Exciting Time of My Life

I STARTED THE first Hadassah Bazaar in 1952 and we moved to the PNE in 1958. Best decision we ever made because we became big league then. Our fame grew from being at the PNE. So many people from our community came and lots of other people from Vancouver showed up too. It became a huge event. At its height, we had three buildings. I used to almost sleep there for the two days the event was on. We celebrated our 50th anniversary there in 2002. It was the most exciting time of my life.

Marjorie Groberman, Vancouver

I Loved the Mini Donuts

I GREW UP in Prince George, so it was always a long wait until the PNE opened in the summer, just so that my sister and I could win some stuffed animal to take back to PG and show it off. I was afraid to ride the roller coaster, but after a lot of convincing between us sisters, we decided to give it a shot. We loved it. I'm too scared to go on it now though. I used to love going on the sky ride that took us from one end of the PNE to the other end, swinging our feet on top of the world. I remember losing my slippers one year and walking back barefoot to our car. I loved the mini donuts and cotton candy and always had to fight my sister for them. My mother sat on a bench and just smiled watching us have lots and lots of fun. I miss those times more than anything.

Aurbjeet Sandhu, Surrey

Those Were the Good Old Days

BEING JEWISH AND a member of the Jewish community of Vancouver, I vividly remember a few years ago the opening ceremony of the Maccabi Games, which was held at the Coliseum. I also remember the Hadassah Bazaar at the PNE. In the early 1970s and '80s the bazaar was held in a string of attached buildings and to get from one building to another you had to walk in freezing cold walkways because the doors were always open. Those were the good days because the world is crazy now.

Jori Fisher, Vancouver

CLOCKWISE FROM TOP LEFT: Another happy crew take off on the wooden roller coaster, 2006. Tempting, sweet mini donuts are an essential Fair-time experience. Savvy shoppers pack the Hadassah Bazaar.

Now the Tradition Is Passed to My Kids

LIFE IS SO simple when you're a kid and it was tradition for my grandparents to take us every year to the PNE. I looked forward to it — the cotton candy, rides and watching my grandpa filling out what seemed like hundreds of prize home tickets. That was our tradition and my favourite memory. Now the tradition is passed to my kids. Tessa Sucloy, Coquitlam

FROM LEFT: Climbing the wall at the Fair. Sharing a laugh on the Scrambler, 2006. What's a Fair without a painted face and a stuffed animal, 2009.

AND THE EVENTS — THEY JUST KEEP COMING

In the past decade, the PNE has become a hub for national and international events. In 2006, it was the World Junior Hockey Tournament; in 2008, the Memorial Cup and the World Cup of Short Track Speed Skating; in 2009, the Four Continents Figure Skating Competition. From wrestling to community hockey, the Maccabi Games to the Olympic Winter Games, when the Coliseum wasn't ablaze with sport competition it was alive with all genres of music: heavy metal, electronica, country, new rock and old rock.

And with all the memories and emotion that the Fair evokes, from the kiddie rides to the thrill of the historic wooden roller coaster, the PNE has firmly secured its position as the place for everyone: providing affordable family entertainment and a social gathering place for the diverse interests of our community.

As a great entertainer once said,

"IF IT'S NOT FUN, YOU'RE NOT DOING IT RIGHT."

CLOCKWISE FROM TOP LEFT: Great moments at the Pacific Coliseum. At her 2003 Up! concert, Shania Twain sported a Giants' jersey and brought down the house. The Dalai Lama and Archbishop Desmond Tutu talk about "Universal Responsibility." Canadian pairs figure skaters Anabelle Langlois and Cody Hay at the 2008 Canadian Figure Skating Championships. Frontman Scott Weiland of Velvet Revolver, 2003.

CLOCKWISE FROM TOP LEFT: 2003 was another hot year at the Pacific Coliseum. Brad May and Friends Hockey Challenge. Black Eyed Peas sold-out concert. A spectacular RV show. Some serious contenders taking to the ring. Rocker John Mayer.

WISH YOU WERE HERE! PLAYLAND

WHAT A SCREAM!

LAUGHS AND SMILES GUARANTEED ... Scenes from Playland's craziest rides.

Wet 'n' wild — The Flume, circa 2000.

Hang on to your coconuts — Crazy Beach Party, 2000s.

Double Your Pleasure, Double Your Fun — the Drop Zone, 1990s.

Big enough to go alone on the Tilt-O-Whirl, 1976.

What some people won't do for a picture! Photographer Doug Shanks taped his hands to his camera to provide this remarkable self-portrait during a bungee jump, 1992.

The best air conditioning in town — the Wave Swinger, 1986.

Up, down and around at 100 kph — the Revelation, 1995.

So that's a double helix inversion — the Corkscrew, 1990s.

It's 100 feet down? The Drop Zone, 1990s.

INTO THE FUTURE

THE NEXT 100 YEARS OF FUN

The PNE is not just 100 years old ... we're 100 years strong. And today we sit on the threshold of our next 100 years, poised for a bright future, a future that we welcome and embrace.

The greatest strength of the PNE has always been our people and their ability to respond to changing times and reflect the emerging needs of our guests, our city and our province. This strength, coupled with our deep connection to Vancouver, has enabled us to work with stakeholders to help shape a new plan for Hastings Park that will create a celebration site and a unique urban park — allowing for great events, experiences and memories for generations to come.

So, what can you expect for the PNE's next 100 years? First and foremost, the PNE will remain a social and cultural gathering place for Vancouver. The breadth of events will continue to echo the diversity of our communities. This is the heart of the PNE story: providing moments of celebration, sport, music and play; a place to spend time with family and friends in a fast-paced and changing world. As we look to the future, imagine expanded green space with links to the city's green corridors; quiet blooming gardens; and pathways to and from every corner of the site. Softer landscapes and broader activities will allow Playland to expand for families and kids of every age. Facilities will be redeveloped to provide increased access to celebrations, festivals, sports, music and family entertainment. And imagine a site that allows for the evolution and growth of the largest event in B.C., that beloved summer tradition — the Fair at the PNE.

As we turn the next page in our storied history, we thank you for being part of the past 100 years and we invite you to share in the excitement of our next 100.

Come along for the ride!

Michael McDaniel
PRESIDENT AND CEO, PACIFIC NATIONAL EXHIBITION

COME TOGETHER

- Imagine a great gathering place, inviting people to come together in a unique urban park setting
- A central location accommodates social and cultural gatherings of every type
- Facilities and park area will be designed to serve all types of groups, from family or community get-togethers to grand-scale events that welcome thousands
- Year-round festivals and events will make the PNE the place to have fun and celebrate together

EASY TO GET TO

- Walk or bike to the PNE. Access will be easy with Hastings Park's integration into Vancouver's greenway system
- The PNE will be a major destination for Vancouver's transit system, with routes making a trip to the park simple and fast
- Expanded and redesigned parking facilities will make the PNE an efficient, convenient, appealing destination for people throughout the Lower Mainland

MORE FUN AT PLAYLAND

- Softer landscaping and green space will provide inviting places to relax and refresh
- Redesigned space will allow for the evolution of activities at Playland that will appeal to families and kids of all ages, making it one of North America's best amusement parks

EXHIBITION FORUM
BIGGER BETTER SPACES
Restored and new facilities will provide for expanded community and entertainment events
New spaces will link with restored and upgraded amenities, offering flexible, easy-to-use community, exhibition and entertainment venues
The PNE will be presenting even more sporting events, concerts, festivals and family programs to meet the needs of guests
DAVID NIDDRIE PHOTOGRAPHY
ONE GREAT PLACE
Catch a Vancouver Giants' game
Take in a show at the Amphitheatre
Scare yourself silly at Fright Nights
Experience Indo-Canadian music festivals and a range of other cultural events
Take the family out to the Fair
Spend the day enjoying a redesigned Playland
Play pick-up games on the sports fields

1910 I CAN APPRECIATE THE IMMENSE VALUE WHICH THIS EXHIBITION ASSOCIATION WILL BE TO BRITISH COLUMBIA, AND I WILL SAY FURTHER, TO THE WHOLE OF CANADA ... **I understand that you intend to make this beautiful park the meeting place of the people. I wish you every success in your efforts and assure that I think you have a place which the people may well be proud of.**

Sir Wilfrid Laurier

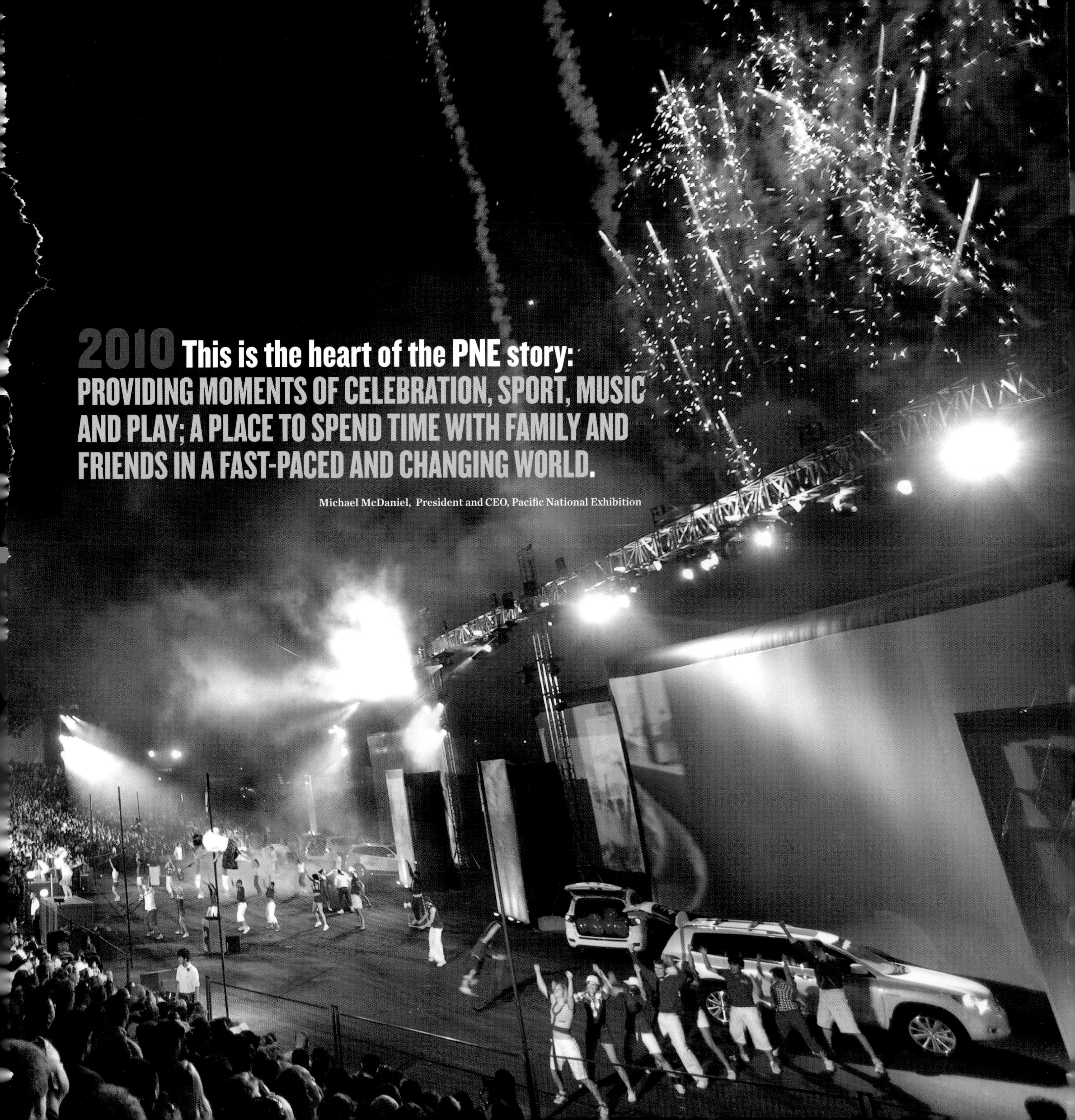

2010 **This is the heart of the PNE story:**
PROVIDING MOMENTS OF CELEBRATION, SPORT, MUSIC AND PLAY; A PLACE TO SPEND TIME WITH FAMILY AND FRIENDS IN A FAST-PACED AND CHANGING WORLD.

Michael McDaniel, President and CEO, Pacific National Exhibition

OPEN & GREEN
Hastings Park will be redeveloped to include increased green space
Inviting new spaces will welcome the public to explore the park, run with the dog, have a family picnic or come together for a sizzling summer concert
New bike and pedestrian paths will make getting around the PNE easy and fun
SUSTAINING OUR FUTURE
The PNE is a multi-functional urban park and the events held on site sustain the beautiful park setting and gardens. Experience the best that Vancouver has to offer.
NO FAIR LIKE IT
The expanded Fair at the PNE will be better than ever in its new park setting
B.C.'s biggest event has all the fun, food, entertainment and exhibitions that make it the province's summer place to be
The PNE: all your summer favourites, with room to build for the future
PART OF THE NEIGHBOURHOOD
Cheer on local amateur sports at Empire playing fields and the Agrodome's community ice rink
Explore parkland and amenities that make the PNE the heart of a lively neighbourhood
Celebrate seasonal festivals
Bring the family for a picnic or enjoy the peaceful new gardens

For 100 years, more than 160,000 people have worked on these grounds, given their best and made the PNE the organization it is today.

SALUTE TO STAFF

When you think of the PNE, so many great things come to mind. Its rich history, its tenacity and flexibility, its creativity and scope, the memories it has created and the impact it has had on generations. But what brews behind the scenes to make this a truly great institution ... is its staff. For 100 years, more than 160,000 people have worked on these grounds, given their best and made the PNE the organization it is today.

The PNE story is as much about its staff as it is about its events and guests. There are so many stories we will never hear about publicly. For many people who worked here, the PNE was their first job. Some have spent more than 30 years here, some can claim 40 years or more. These are people who are passionate about the PNE; who work endless hours so that things are perfect for Fair opening; who stay late into the night to make sure concerts and other public events are safe and fun.

Families were shaped here. In some cases, three generations in a family have worked at the PNE. In other cases, staff met, fell in love and went on to share their lives with the PNE. People come here each day, contribute ideas and make things happen. This is what makes the PNE a winner, its people and their passion. They have all been touched in some way by what happens here, and the PNE has been touched by them.

NOTES

INTRODUCTION: GETTING UNDERWAY (pp. 15–23)

1. Minutes of the first meeting of the Vancouver Exhibition Association, held on May 31, 1907, in realtor Thomas Duke's office.
2. Major James Skitt Matthews' pamphlet *Early History of the Vancouver Exhibition Association*, Vancouver: City Archives, 1953, pp. 8–9. J.S. Matthews was also an early historian and city chronicler.
3. *Vancouver's Fair: An Administrative & Political History of the Pacific National Exhibition*, David Breen and Kenneth Coates, University of British Columbia, 1982, p. 9.
4. ibid., p. 10.
5. Editorial in the *Vancouver Daily Province* newspaper exhorting Vancouverites to go to the Vancouver Exhibition, August 11, 1910, p. 6.
6. *Vancouver's Fair*, Breen and Coates, pp. 7–8.
7. *Early History*, Matthews, p. 3.
8. Minutes of the Executive Council, V.E.A., July 3, 1908.
9. *Vancouver's Fair*, Breen and Coates, p. 20.
10. B.C. Agricultural Fairs Association, Report on First Annual Convention, B.C. Sessional Papers, 1910, p. N17.
11. *Vancouver's Fair*, Breen and Coates, p. 12.
12. ibid., p. 13.
13. ibid., pp. 15–16.
14. ibid., p. 12.
15. Speech by V.E.A. president J.J. Miller reported in the *Vancouver Daily Province*, August 13, 1910, p. 17.

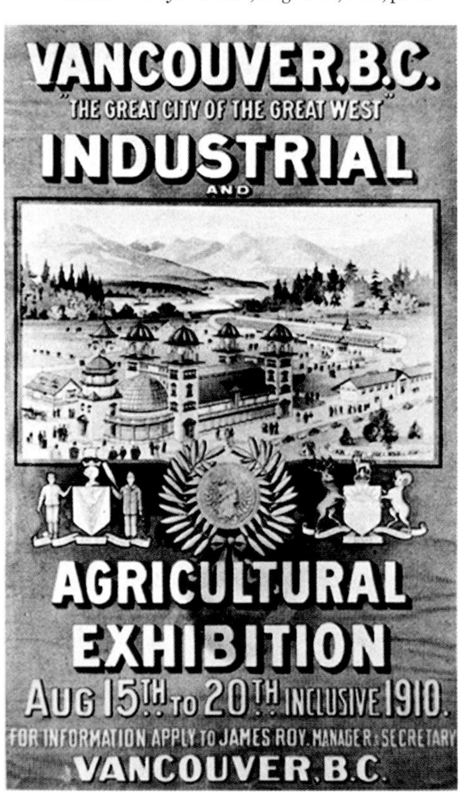

CHAPTER 1: STARTING A TRADITION (pp. 25–41)

1. *Vancouver Daily World*, August 15, 1910, p. 2.
2. *Early History*, Matthews, p. 41.
3. *Vancouver Daily World*, August 15, 1910, p. 1.
4. ibid., August 15, 1910, p. 2.
5. ibid., August 16, 1910, p. 17.
6. ibid., August 15, 1910, p. 2.
7. V.E.A. Manager-Secretary Henry Rolston quoted in Matthews' *Early History*.
8. *Vancouver Daily World*, August 15, 1910, p. 2.
9. *Early History*, Matthews, pp. 20–22.
10. J.J. Miller, president of the V.E.A., addressing a fair crowd, as quoted in the *Vancouver Daily News-Advertiser*, August 16, 1910.
11. *Vancouver Daily News-Advertiser*, August 16, 1910.
12. ibid., August 17, 1910, p. 1.
13. ibid.
14. *Vancouver Daily News-Advertiser*, August 17, 1910, p. 6.
15. ibid.
16. ibid.
17. ibid.
18. *Early History*, Matthews, p. 17.
19. *Vancouver Daily World*, Thursday, August 18, 1910, p. 1.
20. ibid.
21. *Vancouver's Fair,* Breen and Coates, p. 28.
22. *Vancouver Daily World*, Thursday, August 18, 1910, p. 1.
23. *Vancouver Daily News-Advertiser*, August 21, 1910, p. 1.
24. Letter sent to the V.E.A. from the Vancouver Kennel Club, as entered in the Council meeting minutes September 17, 1910.
25. *Vancouver Daily World*'s report of a remark made by Rev. G.F. Dawson of Chatham, New Brunswick. Rev. Dawson was passing through Vancouver on his way to the Methodist General Conference in Victoria that year and decided to enjoy the Vancouver exhibition. Monday, August 15, 1910, p. 2.
26. V.E.A. president J.J. Miller quoted in the *Vancouver Daily Province*, August 22, 1910, p. 3.
27. *Vancouver's Fair*, Breen and Coates, p. 52.
28. ibid. p. 32.
29. J.J. Miller, quoted in Matthews' *Early History*, p. 32.
30. *Vancouver's Fair*, Breen and Coates, p. 34.
31. J.J. Miller, quoted in Matthews' *Early History*, p. 32.
32. J.J. Miller, V.E.A. Bulletin No. 3, 1912, p. 15.
33. *Early History*, Matthews, pp. 28–29.
34. Excerpt from "The Green and Gold" in Matthews' *Early History*, p. 29.
35. *The Sun*, August 5, 1914, p. 2.
36. *Early History*, Matthews, pp. 24–25.
37. V.E.A. Bulletin No. 9, 1918.

CHAPTER 2: THE BEST IN THE WEST (pp. 43–65)

1. *Vancouver's Fair.* Breen and Coates, p. 77.
2. ibid., p. 73.
3. Hon. S.F. Tolmie, minister of Agriculture in the Dominion Cabinet (later premier of B.C.), as reported in the *Vancouver Daily World*, September 11, 1920, p. 1.
4. *Vancouver Daily World*, September 10, 1920, p. 17.
5. W.C. Nichol, lieutenant-governor of B.C., in a speech formally opening the 12th annual Vancouver Exhibition, August 15, 1921.
6. Vancouver Exhibition ad in *The Vancouver Sun*, August 3, 1926, p. 4.
7. ibid.
8. *The Vancouver Sun*, September 11, 1920, p. 1.
9. ibid., August 3, 1926, p. 10.
10. Vancouver Exhibition ad in *The Vancouver Sun*, August 3, 1926, p. 4.
11. ibid., September 11, 1920, p. 1.
12. ibid., August 3, 1926, p. 10.
13. *Vancouver's Fair*, Breen and Coates, p. 73.
14. *Vancouver Daily World*, September 4, 1920, p. 13.
15. ibid., August 16, 1922, p. 3.
16. *The Vancouver Sun*, August 3, 1926, p. 10.
17. ibid., August 12, 1926, p. 4.
18. *Vancouver Daily World*, September 13, 1920, p. 15.
19. ibid., August 22, 1922, p. 2.
20. ibid., August 19, 1922, p. 3.
21. ibid., August 23, 1922, p. 11.
22. ibid., August 24, 1922, p. 2.
23. ibid.
24. ibid., August 19, 1922, p. 3.
25. ibid.
26. ibid., September 11, 1920, p. 7.
27. ibid.
28. Lewis Piano House Ltd. ad in *The Vancouver Sun*, August 3, 1926, p. 11.
29. *The Vancouver Sun*, September 11, 1920, p. 1.
30. ibid., 1920, p. 12.
31. *Vancouver Daily World*, August 22, 1922, p. 2.
32. *The Vancouver Sun*, August 21, 1921, p. 17.
33. Poster ad in *The Vancouver Sun*, August 13, 1927, p. 16.
34. *Vancouver's Fair*, Breen and Coates, pp. 77, 176.
35. *The Evening Sun*, August 18, 1927, p. 1.
36. *Vancouver's Fair*, Breen and Coates, p. 57.
37. E.H. Parker, sales manager of Begg Motor Car Co., quoted in *The Vancouver Sun*, August 21, 1921.
38. *Vancouver Daily World*, September 11, 1920, p. 1.
39. *Vancouver's Fair*, Breen and Coates, p. 73.
40. ibid., p. 73.
41. The Vancouver Exhibition Association in a letter to the federal government asking for financial aid for the Winter Fair, January 1927. Vancouver City Archives.
42. *Vancouver's Fair*, Breen and Coates, p. 74.
43. ibid., p. 72.
44. ibid., p. 59.
45. *The Vancouver Sun*, August 12, 1924, p. 1.
46. *Vancouver's Fair*, Breen and Coates, p. 73
47. ibid., p. 64
48. ibid., p. 64.
49. Draft letter re: Proposed Amalgamation of New Westminster and Vancouver Exhibitions, February 1926, RG 17, vol. 3207, file 150-23(1), Public Archives of Canada.
50. E.S. Archibald, the federal minister of Agriculture, letter dated April 4, 1929, RG 17, vol. 3208, file 150-23(2), Public Archives of Canada.
51. *Vancouver's Fair*, Breen and Coates, p. 66.

CHAPTER 3: WHEN TIMES GET TOUGH (pp. 67–87)

1. *The Vancouver Sun*, August 8, 1930, p. 1.
2. ibid., August 30, 1933, p. 1.

3. *One More Time: The Dal Richards Story* by Dal Richards with Jim Taylor, Harbour Publishing, 2009, p. 158.
4. *The Vancouver Sun*, August 31, 1933, p. 16.
5. ibid., August 28, 1935, p. 17.
6. ibid., August 30, 1938, p. 20.
7. *The Vancouver Sun*, August 4, 1930, p. 1.
8. ibid., August 8, 1930, p. 1.
9. ibid., September 4, 1934, p. 2.
10. ibid., August 18, 1930, p. 4.
11. ibid., August 31, 1932, p. 1.
12. ibid., August 11, 1930, p. 2.
13. ibid., June 30, 1930, p. 2.
14. ibid.
15. ibid., August 8, 1930, p. 1.
16. ibid., August 9, 1930, p. 1.
17. ibid., August 11, 1930, p. 2.
18. V.E.A. souvenir booklet, 1936.
19. The Pacific Coast Amateur Hockey Association, pcaha.bc.ca/rules/ruleshistory.html.
20. *The Vancouver Sun*, August 7, 1930, p. 2.
21. ibid., August 4, 1930, p. 9.
22. ibid., August 7, 1930, p. 2.
23. ibid.
24. B.C. Electric Stores ad in *The Vancouver Sun*, August 28, 1935, p. 17.
25. *Vancouver's Fair*, Breen and Coates, p. 80.
26. ibid., pp. 79–80.
27. ibid., p. 79.
28. *The Vancouver Sun*, August 28, 1935, p. 1
29. ibid., August 28, 1935, pp. 1, 4.
30. ibid., August 29, 1935, p. 2.
31. ibid., August 26, 1936, p. 1.
32. ibid.

CHAPTER 4: WAR, VICTORY AND SOMETHING NEW (pp. 89–117)

1. *Vancouver's Fair*, Breen and Coates, p. 94.
2. *The Vancouver Sun*, August 27, 1940, p. 13.
3. *Vancouver's Fair*, Breen and Coates, p. 95.
4. *The Vancouver Sun*, August 26, 1940, p. 1.
5. ibid., August 23, 1941, p. 19.
6. ibid., August 25, 1941, p. 13.
7. Closed Canadian Parks: Coaster Enthusiasts of Canada: Happyland Park (1890s – 1910 – 1957), http://cec.chebucto.org/ClosPark/HappLand.html.
8. *The Vancouver Sun*, August 27, 1940, p. 12.
9. ibid., August 27, 1940, p. 12.
10. Poster ad in *The Vancouver Sun*, August 25, 1941, p. 8.
11. *The Vancouver Sun*, August 25, 1941, p. 13
12. ibid., August 26, 1941, p. 3.
13. Poster ad in *The Vancouver Sun*, August 25, 1941, p. 8.
14. *The Pacific National Exhibition: An Illustrated History*, David Breen and Kenneth Coates, University of British Columbia, 1982, p. 70.
15. *The Vancouver Sun*, August 27, 1940, p. 12.
16. ibid., August 27, 1940, p. 12.
17. *Pacific National Exhibition*, Breen and Coates, p. 61
18. *Vancouver's Fair*, Breen and Coates, p. 96.
19. *The Vancouver Daily Province*, December 8, 1941, p. 1.
20. ibid.
21. *Vancouver's Fair*, Breen and Coates, p. 97.
22. ibid.
23. ibid., pp. 98–99.
24. *Pacific National Exhibition*, Breen and Coates, p. 70.
25. *Vancouver's Fair*, Breen and Coates, p. 106.
26. Introduction to PNE editorial by the Honourable Senator G.G. McGeer, Mayor of Vancouver, quoted in *British Columbia Digest* magazine, Vol. 2, No. 7, July 1947, pp. 80–85.
27. PNE editorial in *British Columbia Digest* magazine, Vol. 2, No. 7, July 1947, pp. 80–85.
28. ibid.
29. *The Vancouver Daily Province*, January 28, 1947, p. 28.
30. ibid., p. 18.
31. ibid., p. 16
32. *Backstage Vancouver*, Greg Potter and Red Robinson, Harbour Publishing, 2004, p. 61.
33. *The Vancouver Sun*, August 25, 1949, p. 1.
34. *Pacific National Exhibition*, Breen and Coates, p.75.
35. *PNE Bulletin*, No. 40, 1949.
36. *The Vancouver Daily Province*, December 18, 1948, p. 19.
37. "Fair Just Keeps Getting Better and Better," John Mackie, *The Vancouver Sun*, August 22, 2009.
38. *The Vancouver Sun*, August 26, 1948, p. 1.
39. *Steaming Through Northern Waters*, Phylis Bowman, 1987, p. 41.
40. *PNE Bulletin*, No. 40, 1949.

CHAPTER 5: LET US ENTERTAIN YOU (pp. 119–141)

1. *The Vancouver Sun*, August 21, 1950.
2. ibid., August 24, 1950, p. 15.
3. ibid., August 25, 1950, p. 1.
4. ibid., August 19, 1958, p. 3.
5. ibid., August 21, 1958, p. 23.
6. *The Vancouver Daily Province*, August 20, 1951, p. 15.
7. *PNE Bulletin*, No. 41, 1950, p. 6.
8. Poster ad in *The Vancouver Sun*, August 24, 1955, p. 10.
9. *The Vancouver Sun*, August 19, 1959, p. 23.
10. ibid., August 26, 1950, p. 19.
11. *PNE Bulletin*, No. 44, 1953, p. 8.
12. *PNE Bulletin*, No. 43, 1952, p. 8.
13. *Vancouver's Fair*, Breen and Coates, p. 127.
14. *The Vancouver Sun*, September 3, 1957, p. 2.
15. *Vancouver's Fair*, Breen and Coates, p. 116.
16. *Pacific National Exhibition*, Breen and Coates, p. 95.
17. *The Vancouver Province*, August 12, 1955.
18. *The Vancouver Daily Province*, March 3, 1950, p. 13.
19. *Vancouver's Fair*, Breen and Coates, p. 127.
20. *The Vancouver Daily Province*, March 7, 1950.
21. *PNE Bulletin*, No. 45, 1954, p. 10.
22. President's Report, *PNE Bulletin*, No. 50, 1959.
23. Letter sent to the PNE, *PNE Bulletin*, No. 45, 1954, p. 10.
24. *The Vancouver Daily Province*, April 29, 1950, p. 13.
25. ibid., March 3, 1950.
26. *PNE Bulletin*, No. 42, 1951, p. 5.
27. *The Vancouver Province*, June 10, 1954.
28. *Vancouver's Fair*, Breen and Coates, p. 130.
29. *The Vancouver Sun*, August 18, 1958.
30. *PNE Bulletin*, No. 50, 1959.
31. *The Vancouver Sun*, August 24, 1959.
32. ibid., July 31, 1958, p. 42.

CHAPTER 6: A WHOLE NEW GENERATION (pp. 143–173)

1. *The Vancouver Sun* headline, August 13, 1960.
2. *The Vancouver Sun*, August 13, 1960.
3. *PNE Bulletin*, No. 51, 1961.
4. ibid.
5. *PNE Annual Report*, 1966.
6. ibid.
7. ibid.
8. *The Vancouver Sun*, August 17, 1963.
9. *PNE Annual Report*, 1962.
10. ibid.
11. ibid., 1960.
12. ibid., 1964.
13. *The Vancouver Sun*, August 21, 1968.
14. ibid., August 22, 1960.
15. ibid., August 20, 1966.
16. ibid., August 18, 1969.
17. *PNE Annual Report*, 1966.
18. *Vancouver's Fair*, Breen and Coates, Page 136.
19. *PNE Program Guide*, 1963.
20. *PNE Annual Report*, 1968.
21. *The Vancouver Sun*, August 23, 1967, p. 29.
22. *Vancouver's Fair*, Breen and Coates, Page 143.
23. *PNE Annual Report*, 1968.
24. ibid., 1963.
25. ibid., 1968.
26. ibid., 1966.
27. *The Vancouver Sun*, August 22, 1964, p. 1.
28. ibid., August 24, 1964.
29. *Pacific National Exhibition*, Breen and Coates, p. 112.
30. *Vancouver's Fair*, Breen and Coates, p. 141.
31. *PNE Annual Report*, 1968.
32. *The Vancouver Sun*, August 16, 1969.
33. *PNE Annual Report*, 1962.
34. ibid.
35. ibid., 1963.
36. ibid., 1969.
37. *Vancouver's Fair*, Breen and Coates, p. 144.
38. *PNE Fairtalk Newsletter*, Vol. 3, No. 24, October 1962.
39. *Pacific National Exhibition*, Breen and Coates, p. 109.
40. ibid., p. 110.

CHAPTER 7: AN EMERGING GEM (pp.175–199)

1. *Vancouver's Fair*, Breen and Coates, p. 147.
2. *The Province*, October 10, 1970, p. 19.
3. ibid.
4. whitecapsfc.com/club/history/
5. *The Province*, August 4, 1978.
6. ibid., September 10, 1979.
7. ibid., November 25, 1974.
8. ibid., May 2, 1972.
9. ibid.
10. *Pacific National Exhibition*, Breen and Coates, p. 114.
11. *PNE Annual Report*, 1972.
12. ibid.
13. *The Vancouver Sun*, September 2, 1970.
14. *PNE Annual Report*, 1970.
15. *The Vancouver Sun*, August 21, 1974.
16. ibid., p. A3.
17. ibid.
18. ibid., August 24, 1979, p. A10.
19. ibid., August 24, 1978, p. B4.
20. ibid., August 22, 1977.
21. ibid., August 18, 1975.
22. ibid., August 27, 1979, p. A3.
23. Poster ad in *The Vancouver Sun*, August 16, 1974.
24. *The Vancouver Sun*, August 16, 1974.
25. *PNE Program*, 1973.
26. *Vancouver's Fair*, Breen and Coates, p. 136.
27. *PNE Annual Report*, 1971.
28. *The Vancouver Sun*, August 15, 1975.
29. ibid., August 27, 1971.
30. *The Province*, June 5, 1972.
31. ibid., March 20, 1975.

CHAPTER 8: BIGGER AND BETTER (pp. 201–223)

1. *PNE Events*, March 1987, PNE archives.
2. ibid., June 1987.
3. *The Vancouver Sun*, August 31, 1984, p. A17.
4. *PNE Media Notebook*, 1989, PNE archives.
5. *PNE Events Newsletter*, January 1988.
6. ibid., September 1988.
7. ibid., September 1986.
8. ibid., October 1988.

continued

9. ibid., May 1989.
10. ibid., June 1989.
11. ibid., December 1984.
12. ibid.
13. *The Vancouver Sun*, August 25, 1984.
14. *PNE Events Newsletter*, April 1989.
15. ibid. March, 1988
16. ibid., October 1989.
17. ibid., April 1989.
18. ibid., September 1988.
19. ibid., October 1989.
20. ibid., November 1988.
21. ibid.
22. ibid., June 1988.
23. ibid., April 1988.
24. ibid., November 1983.
25. ibid.
26. *PNE Media Notebook*, 1989.
27. *FANFAIR '88: PNE Fair Facts*, PNE archives.

CHAPTER 9: A NEW LEASE ON LIFE (pp. 225–247)

1. *PNE Annual Report*, 1992.
2. *The Vancouver Sun*, August 22, 1997, p. B3.
3. ibid.
4. *Round Table* newsletter, 1993, PNE archives.
5. Donald Luxton, heritage consultant, quoted in *The Vancouver Courier*, November 2, 1997.
6. *PNE Annual Report*, 1993.
7. Mary Jewell, member of Friends of the PNE, quoted in *The Vancouver Courier*, November 2, 1997.
8. *The Vancouver Courier*, November 2, 1997.
9. *PNE Annual Report*, 1996.
10. *The Vancouver Sun*, September 1, 1998.
11. *PNE Annual Report*, 1999.
12. ibid.
13. *PNE Annual Report*, 1993.
14. *The Province*, June 10, 1994.
15. ibid., June 12, 1994.
16. *PNE Annual Report*, 1998.
17. *PNE Events Newsletter*, January 1992.
18. *PNE Annual Report*, October 1999.
19. *PNE Annual Report*, 1999.
20. *PNE Events Newsletter*, June 1994, PNE archives.
21. ibid., April 1994.
22. *Running Tough: The Story of Vancouver's Jack Diamond*, Gareth Sirotnik, published by the Diamond family, 1988, p. 68.
23. *The Vancouver Sun*, July 2, 1998.
24. *PNE Events Newsletter*, February 1994, PNE archives.
25. ibid., January 1993.
26. *The Vancouver Sun*, December 30, 1993.
27. PNE media kit, 1994, PNE archives.

CHAPTER 10: GOING FOR GOLD (pp. 249–273)

1. *PNE Annual Report*, 2004–2005.
2. circuswest.com/about
3. asianpacificpost.com/news/localnews/article/disneyicepresentsworldsfantasy
4. *The Vancouver Sun*, October 16, 2009.
5. ibid., August 24, 2006.
6. *The Pinwheel Pages* newsletter, August 2007.
7. *The Georgia Straight*, straight.com/article241558
8. *The Vancouver Sun*, February 24, 2010.
9. ibid., February 23, 2010.

PHOTO CREDITS

Unless otherwise specified all images are part of the PNE Collection. Images are listed in clockwise order, starting at the top left corner of the page.

SOURCE IDENTIFIERS

CVA: City of Vancouver Archives
RBCM: Royal BC Museum, BC Archives
VPL: Vancouver Public Library

INTRODUCTION: GETTING UNDERWAY (pp. 6–23)

6: Introduction, CVA, Harry T. Devine, LG 454 / Chapter 3, VPL, Dominion Photo Co., 25129 / Chapter 4, CVA, Artray Photographers Ltd., CVA 180-1533 / Chapter 5, CVA, CVA 180-1759. 7: Chapter 7, © The Province / Conclusion, iStock. 9: Courtesy of Reprise Records, Andrew MacNaughtan photographer. 10: Band, CVA, CVA 180-2249 / Kettle, CVA, Artray Photographers Ltd. Art Jones & Company, CVA 180-1562 / Pro Rec, CVA, Artray Photographers Ltd. Art Jones & Company, CVA 180-1534. 11: Majorette, CVA, CVA 180-2248 / Eaton's, CVA, Patton's Studio, CVA 180-1556 / Clowns, CVA, CVA 180-2223. 12: BC Tel, CVA, Artray Photographers Ltd. Art Jones & Company, CVA 180-1552 / BSA, CVA, Steffens-Colmer Ltd., CVA 180-1348 / Georgia Street, CVA, CVA 180-2251 / Float, CVA, R. A. Ramme, CVA 180-1548. 14: CVA, Harry T. Devine, LG 454. 16: Panorama, CVA, P88 / Map, CVA, Map 547 / Building, CVA, Philip T. Timms, CVA 677-627. 17: Parade, CVA, Str P316 / Family, RBCM, A-02063/ Automobile, RBCM, B-05707. 18: Group, CVA, Philip T. Timms, CVA 677-739 / Crowd, CVA, Port P 878. 19: CVA, Park P7. 20: CVA, CVA 677-92. 21: VPL, Philip T. Timms, 6760. 22: CVA, CVA 677-1024. 23: Grounds, CVA, CVA 677-1012 / Caboose, VPL, Philip T. Timms, 7482.

CHAPTER 1: STARTING A TRADITION (pp. 24–41)

26: CVA, Trans P38. 27: Soldiers, CVA, Stuart Thomson, CVA 99-703. 28: Crowd, CVA, James L. Quiney, CVA 7-108 / Building, CVA, Stuart Thomson, CVA 99-738. 29: CVA, W.J. Cairns, MIL P320.2. 30: CVA, James L. Quiney, CVA 7-106. 31: CVA, James L. Quiney, CVA 7-105. 32: CVA, Port P878. 33: CVA, W.J. Cairns, CVA 371-629. 35: CVA, Stuart Thomson, CVA 99-738. 36: CVA, Stuart Thomson, CVA 99-1297 / Birth certificate, Courtesy of the family of Wilemina Isabel Wilson. 37: Automobiles, CVA, BC Electric Railway Company photographer, LGN 933 / Cows, CVA, Stuart Thomson, CVA 99-719 / Milking, CVA, CVA 180-9 / Car show, CVA, Stuart Thomson, CVA 99-5130 / Horses, CVA, Stuart Thomson, CVA 99-803 / Group, CVA, CVA 180-3 / Lacrosse, CVA, W.J. Cairns, CVA 371-578. 38: Team, CVA, Stuart Thomson, CVA 99-1215 / Buggies, CVA, Stuart Thomson, CVA 99-715 / Tent, CVA, Bu P475. 39: Elephants, VPL, 18406 / Women, VPL, Stuart Thomson, 17817. 40: CVA, Stuart Thomson, CVA 99-558. 41: Women, VPL, 2024 / Pipeband, CVA, Stuart Thomson, CVA 99-558 / Buggy, CVA, Stuart Thomson, CVA 99-558.

CHAPTER 2: THE BEST IN THE WEST (pp. 42–65)

44: CVA, Stuart Thomson, CVA 99-2582. 45: Crowd, CVA, Stuart Thomson, CVA 99-1687 / Float, VPL, Stuart Thomson, 17965 / Orpheum, VPL, Stuart Thomson, 11035. 48: Cow, CVA, Dominion Photo Co., CVA 180-180 / Royal, CVA, Dominion Photo Co., CVA 180-224 / Chicken, CVA, CVA 180-74 / Butter, CVA, Dominion Photo Co., CVA 180-109 / Sheep, CVA, Dominion Photo Co., CVA 180-164 / Delicatessen, CVA, Dominion Photo Co., CVA 180-229. 49: Pig, CVA, Dominion Photo Co., CVA 180-150 / Dates, CVA, Dominion Photo Co., CVA 180-271. 50: Crowd, CVA, CVA 180-6. 51: Rides, VPL, Stuart Thomson, 11691 / Grounds, VPL, Leonard Frank, 7926 / Dance Hall, VPL, Frank Leonard, 12264. 52: VPL, 12266. 54: Building, VPL, Dominion Photo Co., 20876 / Man, VPL, 78345 / CVA, CVA 1477-677. 55: Men, CVA, Dominion Photo Co., CVA 180-334 / Mountains, CVA, Dominion Photo Co., CVA 180-302 / Rocks, CVA, Dominion Photo Co., CVA 180-339 / Typewriters, CVA, Dominion Photo Co., CVA 180-59. 56: Steer, VPL, Dominion Photo Co., 20980. 57: Women, CVA, Stuart Thomson, CVA 99-1766 / Hall, VPL, Dominion Photo Co., 20976 / Cakes, CVA, Dominion Photo Co., CVA 180-238. 58: VPL, 70725. 59: CVA, Dominion Photo Co., CVA 180-202. 60: Stage, CVA, Dominion Photo Co., CVA 180-293 / Inset, CVA, Dominion Photo Co., CVA 180-291 / Men, CVA, Port N840.2. 61: Background, VPL, Leonard Frank, 12263. 62: Golf, CVA, Stuart Thomson, CVA 99-1616 / Camp, VPL, Stuart Thomson, 18320. 63: Hastings Park, CVA, CVA 371-2830 / Exhibition, VPL, Philip T. Timms, 6417. 64: © Vancouver Sun. 65: All, © Vancouver Sun.

CHAPTER 3: WHEN TIMES GET TOUGH (pp. 66–87)

66: VPL, Dominion Photo Co., 25129. 68: CVA, Stuart Thomson, CVA 99-5062. 69: Bicycle, CVA, Stuart Thomson, CVA 99-2735 / Boys, CVA, Stuart Thomson, CVA 99-2993, Spectators, CVA, M.H.H. Waddington, CVA 180-602. 70: © Vancouver Sun. 71: Crowd, CVA, Dominion Photo Co., CVA 180-617 / Gazebo, CVA, Stuart Thomson, CVA 180-596 / Girls, © Vancouver Sun / Kids, © Vancouver Sun / Spectators, CVA, M.H.H. Waddington, CVA 180-602 / Stage, VPL, Stuart Thomson, 11704. 72: Kids, CVA, Stuart Thomson, CVA 180-363. 73: Wagons, CVA, Stuart Thomson, CVA 99-2599 / Automobile, VPL, 11656 / Bronco, CVA, Stuart Thomson, CVA 99-2600. 74: All, © Vancouver Sun. 75: Olympiad, © Vancouver Sun / Crowd, CVA, Stuart Thomson, CVA 99-2730. 76: Girls, VPL, Stuart Thomson, 11662 / Pipers, CVA, Stuart Thomson, CVA 99-2098. 77: Shot put, CVA, Stuart Thomson, CVA 99-3188 / Girl, CVA, CVA Stuart Thomson, CVA 99-2096 / Log, CVA, Stuart Thomson, CVA 180-1704 / Shorts, CVA, Stuart Thomson, CVA 99-2095. 78: Rink, CVA, W.J. Moore, Bu N521.3 / Players, CVA, Stuart Thomson, CVA 99-4536. 79: Garden, CVA, Dominion Photo Co., CVA 180-667 / Foliage, VPL, 12271 / Seeds, CVA, Dominion Photo Co., CVA 180-530 / Lumber, CVA, Dominion Photo Co., CVA 180-449. 80: Fridges, CVA, Dominion Photo Co., CVA 180-773. 81: Building, CVA, W.J. Moore, Bu N508 / Bridge, VPL, Leonard Frank, 9631 / Construction, CVA, Stuart Thomson, CVA 99-3864. 82: Home, CVA, Stuart Thomson, CVA 180-597 / Queue, VPL, Province Newspaper, 41011. 83: CVA, Dominion Photo Co., CVA 180-660. 84: Telephone, CVA, Dominion Photo Co., CVA 180-657 / Tourist, VPL, Leonard Frank, 11628. 85: Dairy, CVA, Stuart Thomson, CVA 99-3158 / Record, © Vancouver Sun / Boat, CVA, Stuart Thomson, CVA 99-3164 / Parade, VPL, Philip T. Timms, 19341 / Float, CVA, Stuart Thomson, 99-2961 / Imperial, VPL, Leonard Frank, 11629 / McGavin's, VPL, Leonard Frank, 11630 / Parade, © Vancouver Sun. 87: CVA, CVA 180-1063.

CHAPTER 4: WAR, VICTORY AND SOMETHING NEW (pp. 88–117)
88: CVA, Artray Photographers Ltd. Art Jones & Company, CVA 180-1533. 90: Women, CVA, Artray Photographers Ltd. Art Jones, CVA 180-1515 / Boy, VPL, Claude P. Dettloff, 8516. 91: CVA, CVA 180-1219. 92: Army, CVA, CVA 180-933 / Aircraftsmen, VPL, 25675 / Women, CVA, CVA 180-856 / © Vancouver Sun. 93: Tools, CVA, CVA 180-1129 / Battleships, CVA, CVA 180-1140 / Swan, CVA, CVA 180-1121 / Water / CVA, CVA 180-1119. 94: CVA, CVA 180-797. 95: Baby Dipper, CVA, CVA 180-792 / Four-legged Woman, CVA, CVA 180-1033 / Men, CVA, CVA 180-794 / Women, CVA, Steffens-Comer, CVA 180-1401 / Plane, CVA, CVA 180-798 / Woman, CVA, CVA 180-886. 96: Ferris Wheel, CVA, CVA 180-1183 / © Vancouver Province / Planes, CVA, CVA 180-1166. 97: Len Norris. 98: Totems, CVA, CVA 180-1151 / Baskets, CVA, CVA 180-1165. 99: Honey, CVA, CVA 180-1015 / Bulbs, CVA, CVA 180-1011 / Dairy, CVA, CVA 180-875. 100: Bunks, VPL, Frank Leonard, 14918 / Kids, VPL, Frank Leonard, 14925. 101: VPL, Frank Leonard, 14931. 102: Girls, CVA, Steffens-Comer, CVA 180-1352 / Float, CVA, Steffens-Comer, CVA 180-1359 / Street, CVA, Steffens-Comer, CVA 180-1328 / Building, CVA, Steffens-Comer, CVA 180-1399. 103: CVA, Steffens-Comer, CVA 180-1384. 104: CVA, Steffens-Comer, CVA 180-1398. 105: Night, CVA, Steffens-Comer, CVA 180-1410 / Fence, CVA, Steffens-Comer, CVA 180-1427. 106: CVA, Artray Photographers Ltd. Art Jones & Company, CVA 180-1520. 107: CVA, CVA 180-892. 108: Hockey, VPL, Ray Munro, 84088 / Program, Courtesy of the B.C. Sports Hall of Fame / Bing, Courtesy of the Red Robinson collection / Canucks, Courtesy of the B.C. Sports Hall of Fame / Lacrosse, VPL, Artray Photographers Ltd., 84106. 109: Stage, CVA, CVA 180-789. 111: Shrine, VPL, Artray Photographers Ltd., 81413. 112: Beauties, © Vancouver Sun / Waving, © Vancouver Sun / Car, CVA, Artray Photographers Ltd., CVA 180-1554. 113: CVA, CVA 180-2013. 116: VPL, 25435. 117: VPL, 25672.

CHAPTER 5: LET US ENTERTAIN YOU (pp. 118–141)
118: CVA, CVA 180-1759. 120: Boat, CVA, CVA 180-2397 / Majorettes, CVA, CVA 180-2238. 121: © Vancouver Sun / Round-up, VPL, 44445. 122: CVA, CVA 180-2385. 123: CVA, CVA 180-2329. 124: CVA, CVA 180-2234 / VPL, Artray Photographers Ltd., 81413C. 126: Courtesy of the Red Robinson collection. 127: VPL, Province Newspaper, 61267 / Courtesy of the Red Robinson collection. 128: © Vancouver Sun. 129: © Charles Warner. 130: VPL, 47699. 131: Ski jump, VPL, Province Newspaper, 47088 / Tents, CVA, CVA 180-1761 / Jitney, VPL, Artray Photographers Ltd., 81402. 134: Brian Kent, © Vancouver Sun / Number 88, VPL, Art Jones, 84780Q / Boxers, VPL, Artray Photographers Ltd., 84066. 135: Cheerleaders, Deni Eagland, © Vancouver Sun / CKNW, CVA, Patton's Studio, CVA 180-1574 / Soccer, VPL, Ray Munro, 84103E. 136: Elizabeth, CVA, Q E P16 / Car, CVA, Q E P17.18. 137: Map, VPL, 44408. 138: VPL, 60223. 140: 1923, VPL, 12261 / 1932, VPL, 12276 / 1950s, VPL, 44439A / 1950, VPL, 44439.

CHAPTER 6: A WHOLE NEW GENERATION (pp. 142–173)
145: Pacifists, © Vancouver Sun, Bob Dibble photographer. 147: Bennett, © Vancouver Sun, Tony Cousins photographer. 148: VPL, 44416. 152: Calves, CVA, CVA 180-2081 / Reader, CVA, CVA 180-2095 / Chickens, CVA, CVA 180-2097. 154: Youngsters, CVA, Artray Photograpers Ltd. Art Jones & Company, CVA 180-1491 / Jump up, © Vancouver Sun. 155: CVA, Artray Photographers Ltd. Art Jones & Company, CVA 180-1493. 156: Food, © Vancouver Sun, George Diack photographer. 157: Hot dogs, CVA, CVA 180-2219 / Shriner Kids, © Vancouver Sun / Pink Candy Floss, CVA, Artray Photographers Ltd. Art Jones, CVA 180-1519. 165: Spirotower, © Vancouver Sun, Ralph Bower photographer / Courtesy of Debie Leyshon. 166: Miss Yokohama, © Vancouver Sun, Ray Allen photographer. 167: Beatles, © Vancouver Sun, George Diack photographer / John and Paul, Courtesy of the Red Robinson collection / Fans, © Vancouver Sun, George Diack photographer. 168: Rink, CVA, Bill Cunningham, CVA 180-3625 / Construction, CVA, Graphic Industries, CVA 180-5838 / Steps, CVA, Graphic Industries Ltd., CVA 180-5854. 148: Elephant, The Jewish Museum and Archives of British Columbia/Nemetz Jewish Community Archives, L.10545.

CHAPTER 7: AN EMERGING GEM (pp.174–199)
174: © The Province. 176: Crowd, © Vancouver Sun, Ian Lindsay photographer/ © The Province. 177: Soccer, © Vancouver Sun. 178: BC Sports Hall of Fame. 179: Possee, © Vancouver Sun, Kent Kallberf photographer / Lenarduzzi, © Vancouver Sun, Deni Eagland photographer / Whymark, © Vancouver Sun. 180: 13, © Vancouver Sun / Football, © Vancouver Sun / Program, BC Sports Hall of Fame. 181: Punch, © Vancouver Sun, Ralph Bower photographer. 182: Flood, Courtesy of the Canadian National Sportsmen's Shows. 183: Races, CVA, CVA 180-4206 / Basketball, Courtesy of the Harlem Globetrotters / Jump, Courtesy of Gaitpost Magazine, Rick Maynard photographer. 184: Stand, Courtesy of Bill McMichael / Yakatori, iStock / Hot dog, © Vancouver Sun, Peter Battistoni photographer. 185: Tikidog, © Vancouver Sun / Mona Brun, © Vancouver Sun, George Diack photographer. 186: Helicopter, © Vancouver Sun. 187: Rodriguez, © The Province, Wayne Leidenfrost photographer. 192: Wonderland, © Vancouver Sun, George Diack photographer. 193: Peterson, © Vancouver Sun / Fitzgerald, Corbis. 194: Petty, © Vancouver Sun, Glenn Baglo photographer / Drawing, © Vancouver Sun. 195: Mitchell, © Vancouver Sun / Cash, Courtesy of the Red Robinson collection / Pointers etc., © Vancouver Sun / Jones, Courtesy of the Red Robinson collection. 196: Crowd, VPL, Fred Rosenberg, 86279 / Queen, Dee Lippingwell Photography; Metallica, Dee Lippingwell Photography / Stones, Carter Tomassi, Messyoptics.com. 197: Heart, Dee Lippingwell Photography / Stewart, Dee Lippingwell Photography. 199: Dee Lippingwell Photography.

CHAPTER 8: BIGGER AND BETTER (pp. 200–223)
202: Expo, CVA, CVA 780-505. 205: Hansen, Courtesy of the Rick Hansen Foundation / Eggs, iStock. 206: Reducing Machine, VPL, 81403 / Pitchman, © Vancouver Sun, Jon Murray photographer. 214: Rocky, Courtesy of the BC Film Commission / Tyler, Dee Lippingwell Photography. 215: Kiss, Dee Lippingwell Photography / Clapton, Dee Lippingwell Photography / Plant, Dee Lippingwell Photography / Michael, Dee Lippingwell Photography. 217: Horse show, Courtesy of White Stallion Productions, Rick Maynard photographer. 220: High jumper, © Vancouver Sun, Glenn Baglo photographer. 221: Consul-General, © Vancouver Sun, Dan Scott photographer / Fashion, © Vancouver Sun, Mark van Manen photographer.

CHAPTER 9: A NEW LEASE ON LIFE (pp. 224–247)
227: Summit, © Vancouver Sun, Nick Didlick photographer / Singh, Courtesy of Chandra Bodalia. 228: Chicks, iStock. 229: Big Bob, © Vancouver Sun, Craig Hodge photographer. 230: VPL, Province Newspaper, 42620. 231: VANCOUVER PROVINCE, 42620. 232: VPL, Province Newspaper, 47699. 238: Hedican and MacLean, © Vancouver Sun, Ralph Bower photographer / Bure, © Vancouver Sun, Ralph Bower photographer. 239: Sumo, Kevin Kelly Photography / Hockey, © Vancouver Sun, Ian Lindsay photographer. 240: Skateboarders, Courtesy of Slam City Jam / Nash, Courtesy of British Columbia High School Boys Basketball Association. 241: Adams, Courtesy of Bruce Allen Talent, Andrew Catlin photographer / Feet, Courtesy of David Niddrie Photography. 242: Track, Courtesy of the Diamond family / Leroy, © Vancouver Sun, Jon Murray photographer. 243: Lanterns, Pho and Dolls, iStock. 244: Couple, Courtesy of Heather Jackson.

CHAPTER 10: GOING FOR GOLD (pp. 248–273)
250: Skytrain, Courtesy of Translink. 251: Stilts, Courtesy of David Niddrie Photography. 253: Acrobat, Courtesy of CircusWest. 254: Mickey, Disney On Ice Celebrates 100 Years of Magic, © Disney / Beauty, Disney On Ice Celebrates 100 Years of Magic, © Disney. 258: All, Courtesy of the Vancouver Giants. 259: 1 and Cup, Courtesy of the Vancouver Giants. 263: St-Gelais and Hug, Getty Images. 264: Reflection, Getty Images. 265: Gold, Getty Images. 268: Bazaar, Jewish Western Bulletin fonds, L.10488.

CONCLUSION: INTO THE FUTURE
276: Cyclists, City of Vancouver. 278: Forum, VPL, 36518 / Banghra, Courtesy of David Niddrie Photography.

Type set in Chronicle Text and Knockout. Both typefaces designed by Hoefler & Frere Jones.

Thank You

- Bruce Allen Talent
- Jason Beck at the BC Sports Hall of Fame
- Richard Bonner at The Coaster Enthusiasts of Canada
- Sandra Boutilier, Kate Bird and the staff at the Pacific Newspaper Group Library
- Michele Greig and the staff of the Vancouver Public Library Photography Archives
- Jeannie Hounslow, Leslie Robinson and the staff at the City of Vancouver Archives
- Gordon Kennedy
- Dee Lippingwell
- Bill McMichael
- Red Robinson
- Ken Winslade and the B.C. High School Boys' Basketball Association photography collection

Thanks to Craig Hodge Photography and Peter Male for their generous assistance with image sourcing and for photographing thousands of magical PNE moments, many of which are included in this book ... and thanks to Patrick Roberge Productions for providing years of entertainment worth photographing.

PNE
PNE
hot barbecued chicken
CHIPS BURGERS CORN on COB

THIS BOOK WAS WRITTEN, DESIGNED AND PRODUCED BY

Echo Memoirs Ltd.
70 East 2nd Avenue, Suite 302
Vancouver, BC
Canada V5T 1B1

WWW.ECHOMEMOIRS.COM
1 877 777 ECHO

Creating distinctive company history and personal biography books since 1999.